CONTEMPORARY
AMERICAN THEOLOGY

Contemporary
American Theology

THEOLOGICAL AUTOBIOGRAPHIES

Edited by

VERGILIUS FERM

SECOND SERIES

Essay Index Reprint Series

BOOKS FOR LIBRARIES PRESS
FREEPORT, NEW YORK

First Published 1933
Reprinted 1969

STANDARD BOOK NUMBER:
8369-1181-4

LIBRARY OF CONGRESS CATALOG CARD NUMBER:
78-86749

PRINTED IN THE UNITED STATES OF AMERICA

CONTENTS

INTRODUCTION

I N THE companion volume which was published a
year ago, the editorial preface set forth the general
plan for the series of theological autobiographies to
which the present volume also belongs. Twenty-three
of America's leading theologians and religious thinkers
were asked to set down in an intimate manner the
stories of their religious and theological pilgrimage;
twelve of these appeared in the earlier volume and the
remaining eleven are here presented. Contemporary
American theology is thus for the first time being given
its long overdue exposition and interpretation by means
of the autobiographical method leading up to the *con-
fessio fidei* of those who are among its acknowledged
leaders.

It becomes plain that the men who have been
brought together here have not only lived through one
of the most significant periods in the development of
Christian religious thought, but also have been actively
engaged in sowing germinal ideas with which the coming generation of theologians will have to reckon. The
disclosure of their intellectual development, particularly as it has affected their religious beliefs, furnishes a
commentary on some of the significant intellectual and
religious changes that have taken place during their
life span, changes that have come with remarkable
rapidity in one generation, reaching as they do across
the border of two centuries and touching what would
appear, at close perspective, to be two eras.

In the preface to the first volume some of the main
features in the contemporary religious and theological
landscape were outlined. A few further comments are

offered upon the cross-section of religious thought indicated in the essays that appear in this volume. One can hardly escape asking oneself some such questions as these: What recurrent emphases do these autobiographical confessions reveal? What are some of the issues that have come to focus in contemporary theological debate? What features are stressed which would indicate the particular theological topics bequeathed to those who follow? Without assuming to take the place of the reader, who will be answering some such questions for himself, one may venture to set down some of the major trends which appear to be underlined in these essays and some of the topics that are now being stressed and will undoubtedly continue to hold the center of theological interest.

We are coming to realize more and more that words have a peculiar way of playing tricks upon us. In many instances a word which our fathers used and which we continue to use does not carry the same meaning for us as it did for them; we are often deceived in thinking that the sameness of form guarantees the same content. One generation feels related to a given heritage by the continued use of a word, though as a matter of fact the changed meaning of that word has broken that relationship. Many a stand-patter in politics and traditionalist in religion would find himself embarrassed were this realized even to a small degree. The five-foot-shelf commentaries on the Bible written by homiletic exegetes [and sold to seminary students at bargain prices and decorating many a ministerial library] furnish examples enough of the elusive and mischievous character of words. For such a realization we do not need to point to the work of critical historians, but only to turn to any commonplace dictionary and to the language of the street.

For example, we often hear it proclaimed from pulpit and platform that what the world needs is religion.

But it is not at all clear what is meant, unless we know
the peculiar bias of him who proclaims. Religions
range from atheism to pantheism, from positivism to
supernaturalism, from a system of beliefs to mere
forms of behavior, from individual asceticism to social
reforms, from devilish practices to high, practical idealism. It is no longer self-evident without further definitions and distinctions what the relation is between
religion and art, religion and culture, religion and
ethics, or religion and the sciences. What a given
group has meant by the term religion in one age is not
necessarily what is meant in another; the term continues
but the meaning has changed. Historical, comparative
and psychological studies of religion have shown the
term sometimes to mean something grossly narrow, at
other times something hopelessly vague. The framing
of a definition which will stand all proper descriptive
and normative tests continues to be one of the chief
objects of concern for religious thinking in the future.

Again, we are asked to become Christians. But we
are no longer sure of that term, standing alone and
undefined. We are told that we should become members of the church and thus continue in an illustrious
heritage. But we are not certain, unless it is made
clearer, whether it is corporate fellowship, kinship in
spirit, or identification with institutionalism that is
meant to bind us to that heritage. To be called out,
as the root meaning of *ecclesia* implies, may well mean
for some to travel alone, or at least without visible fellowship. The church may well mean, as it appears to
mean for mystical souls, a companionship with things
invisible but fearfully real.

We are supposed to be respectful of science. But
this term is equally vague and misleading. True, there
is a scientific spirit as a methodology and there are special sciences—but what and where is this all-inclusive
"science" which is to command our reverence and with

which there is to be no longer any warfare on the part of theology? We are asked to become "spiritual" or "spiritually-minded." But what is meant? Is this a commitment to a kind of neo-Platonic way of life and an abrogation of the Aristotelian world of flesh and blood? It is hard to imagine a word more often employed with the vaguest kind of meaning. Many of us are still called Protestant. But what does such a term now mean?

Finally, we still employ the terms "theology" and "theologian." These terms used to connote certain definite characteristics, not to say idiosyncrasies. But with the older distinction between revealed and natural theology in process of being gradually wiped out, with theology becoming historical, psychological, philosophical, and inspired by scientific methodology, with more modest designations of its branches (systematic theology and philosophy of religion taking the place of dogmatics and the older apologetics), and with the term "God" now somewhat commonly employed for concepts less definitely theistic, it is becoming increasingly difficult to locate theology as a special discipline and to single out the theologians. A wide correspondence underlying the editing of these volumes has made this painfully real.

Of course, the ambiguity of words, their ceaselessly changing meanings, is no modern discovery. There has been, however, in modern theology, a growing conviction of the importance of definitions. Indeed, one of the conspicuous characteristics of modern religious and theological thought among those who are its leaders is this sensitiveness to definitions, and it is an entry upon the credit side of the ledger.

It is becoming almost commonplace now to expect theologians to distinguish sharply between the religious spirit and theology. And it is this disjunction between the two that has made for considerable debate as to their relation. Which of the two looms as more important? Shall we understand that a way of life, a temper of mind, is more significant than a system of beliefs about the Universe or about the more-than-human to which intellectual assent is to be given? Is it psychologically justifiable to split apart activity and patterns of belief and theory? Is there a peculiar kind of truth given in the religious feeling, a logic which the "religious experience" rightfully claims as its own, which is lacking in theoretical speculation; or, is the category of truth confined to purely metaphysical interests? Answers to such live questions in contemporary religious and theological thinking wait upon light from psychology. If the theologians find themselves in quite sharp disagreement at these points they are not to be too severely censured. For when they turn for light to those specialists whose business it is to diagnose human nature they find no united chorus of expert testimony. There are psychologists and—"psychologists."

With the breakdown of earlier norms and following a period of restless uncertainty and relativity in religious thought, there is now going on an eager quest for certainty. There are those who proclaim their satisfaction with a pragmatic and relative theology and who are quite certain that this affords the only certainty. For the most part, however, contemporary theology is seeking something stable. Even humanism is no exception. Many of the contributors—not only those who have made their transitions in easy stages but those whose wanderings have been colorful—reveal in the account of their pilgrimage that they would remain loyal to a great heritage, if only they could find in it elements of the persistent, of the time-and-place-transcending.

This search for foundation-stones upon which to build a theological superstructure continues to be a marked characteristic of our time. There is general agreement among so-called liberals that external authorities and the literalism of those *credos* which are confined to a specific time and place and culture can no longer hold them. And when one knows their reasons, and more particularly when one has had something akin to the experiences they relate, one is assured that there is here no taint of that intellectualism which spells lack of "spiritual" vision; nor are there instances of the religious spirit become apathetic. Rather, one senses the same sincere and high-minded interest in the larger concerns of the human spirit at its best as has characterized those wrestlers with truth who are now for us glorified in the greater literatures of the past.

When it comes to giving testimony to that "something stable"—from the human point of view—the reader will easily discern wide disagreements. There are some who claim for the religious feeling a peculiar insight which can neither be approved nor discounted by the pronouncements of scientific discoveries or metaphysics; there are others who claim that such a divorcement is too costly if not too artificial psychologically, to be of permanent significance to theology. There are, similarly, those who stress values as inherently more akin to the typically religious spirit than are facts. These would thus free theology as an intellectual expression of religion from the cares and woes of changing speculations. In opposition to this the counter-claim is that unless there is due respect for the findings of a scientific cosmology and other scientific deliverances, the theologian is building upon ground which for critical minds, trained to respect brutal facts, will always seem detached and unreal. There are those who would wed religion and theology with the scientific cosmologies and metaphysics, values with facts, in a kind of mutual interplay and reinforcement of the varieties of human experience. In opposition to both camps there are those who are unconcerned with any special claims of the religious spirit so far as knowledge about the universe is concerned. The nature of the world and the meaning of life would appear to be investigations proper to the sciences and to philosophy. It is enough if the religious spirit can do something to knock off the rough corners of human character and behavior, to which end it ought to be encouraged to turn from speculation to the more difficult and significant task of social well-being.

Underneath these various emphases one finds, however, certain agreements and convergences in these testimonies. Many of them appear only between the lines, but they are nonetheless there, at least as haunting convictions. These agreements constitute what are for this generation of theologians the foundation-stones of theology and it is more than likely that they will remain such for those who follow. Some of them are basic inheritances from generations long buried and some of them are fresh convictions. An opinion is here ventured as to what these may be; space allows mention of but a few of them.

There appears the recognition that, however stately the theological structure to be built, however imposing and ornamental it is to become, it must rest upon certain humanly unassailable and unimpeachable fundamentals. There has been going on a Cartesian search for the indubitable, for that something which if doubted makes further progress impossible. What these minimal features are may be stated in different ways by theist and extreme humanist, by liberal and fundamentalist; to deny them no respectable religion or theology would dare. There may be a dispute as to the essential nature of the religious response from a descriptive point of view—one may for example affirm or dispute Rudolph Otto's insistence that first-hand religious experience is the sense of eeriness, a non-moral *numinous* feeling—but as to what religion ought to be, what it must be from a normative point of view there is hardly any disagreement. Whatever else goes into the foundation and however different the method and terminology the agreement is that religion—and particularly Christianity—ought to be morally significant. We are hardly right in saying that this is merely a reflection of the Kantian influence by way of a standard set up in defiance of the antinomies of reason; rather, it is something that goes far back in the history of social living and deep in human experience. This is the thread of continuity persisting throughout contemporary theology, particularly in evidence in these essays, and it is a thread carried over from past generations of Christianity, though not easily discernible in some of them.

Interpreting moral experience, theologians find now this phase and now that upon which they like to dwell. For all, this means social implications; for some almost nothing else; for others there is here found an open gateway where the more-than-human makes its vital contact and presence felt. For some, moral experience needs nothing more than a positivistic metaphysics —if, indeed, there be such; for others, moral experience is revelatory of the fundamental nature of the world and the divine significance of human life and destiny. The validity of the moral experience is more and more coming to be sustained on the proving ground of individual and social history and less and less on external and authoritarian settings; not even so sacred a place as Mt. Sinai is sufficient ground for the validity of the claims of this experience. Not that Mt. Sinai is without meaning; there is a certain authoritarian claim of the moral consciousness which will seem external only to those who have become strangers to themselves.

Another common characteristic of these essays is the

testimony of loyalty to the institutional expression of religion. How much this is due to personal conditionings and to professional circumstances is not easy to say. Whether or not the reasons given are rationalizations, they at least seem reasonable. The defence of institutionalism here is hardly different from the defence of institutionalism in politics, formal education or other group practices. Certain values are preserved in the organized social life that are lost if the individual is left wholly to himself. The pressure of social suggestion comes whether we will or not; that such suggestion ought to have in it elements of inspiration for things of worth, both seen and unseen, goes almost without saying. Though organized religion tends to carry over from one generation to another much baggage that is not only unessential but even harmful—and in this it is not unlike other institutional forms—it does not follow that it should have no baggage at all. The conservative character of institutions not only acts as a balance to the radicalism of individualism but offers accumulated insights essential to every new generation. Organized religion to save its soul, however, will have to make necessary adjustments, as every institution has had to do, and in some cases these adjustments will mean radical changes in method, in ritual, in leadership and in relationships with like-minded institutions.

The thesis that theological dogmas and ecclesiastical practices reflect social cultures will have a purging effect upon institutions which have long claimed immunity from criticism and reformation on the ground of their alleged supernatural origin and character. Elements in this thesis are unquestionably sound. There is an appeal to indisputable facts of social psychology. It is no accident that such a thesis has come to definite formulation in our day. The generation represented in this volume has seen the world literally transformed before its eyes, a world grown smaller and with social contacts so multiplied in the onward march of achievement as to make many a political, economic, educational and other social theory and practice crumble almost over night. The social category—so conspicuous in modern theological and philosophical thought and so emphasized in the pages of this book—finds a singular means of justification: it is itself a product of social forces.

What historical criticism has done to the sacred writings is now an open book. It has seemed that the Bible would have to take its place alongside of other great literature with no special privileges granted. True, the Bible still lies somewhere near the altar; it is still being quoted at the beginning of sermons; it is still relied upon to lend prestige and sacred sanction to individual opinions. Little technique and no great degree of imagination have been required to find passages which would give discourses on any faddish topic the benefit of a halo. Even conservatives who have anathematized liberals for practicing deceit in this regard are themselves, as a class, not without guile. For many liberals, however, there has been no attempt to disguise the fact that sermons represent the opinion of the preacher at the moment of his utterance; there has been no attempt to play the rôle of the anointed. To them frankly, the Bible is sacred literature and so is other great literature. What this changed conception—coming to be widely diffused among the masses—from a time honored Word of God has meant to Protestantism, to the church, its program of worship, its mission, its influence in the community, its missionary enterprise, no one can fully appreciate, for our generation is still in the midst of it and is limited by a short perspective. But that higher criticism has been of enormous significance in changing the total complexion of Protestant Christianity can hardly be denied.

It is, then, of special interest to hear the testimony of those whose life work has been spent in the exacting field of criticism. It is of prophetic interest when from those grown mature in the field the testimony comes not only applauding the evident virtues but reflecting concern over the faults inherent in the historico-critical approach. The conservative reader is likely to be surprised when he reads some of the conservative utterances coming from those whom he has indiscriminately labeled "destructive critics." We are now being told that we have expected too much of higher criticism; the method is sound as far as it goes; but it is a method which when pressed to the extreme tends to defeat its very purpose. To understand is more than to dissect and analyze; one must have imagination and poetic insight. There are situations and truths grasped only by sympathetic intuition, truths that elude the categories and methods so dear to the heart of coldly analytical criticism. With apologies to Kant for a free paraphrase of his classical formula we may say: the higher critic is now telling us that criticism applied to the study of the sacred writings without poetic imagination tends to blindness; and poetic imagination without criticism tends to emptiness. If this be true, it would appear possible that in the coming generation the Bible may once again come into a place of unique prestige, but one which will no longer need the sustaining power of a special theory of inspiration, since it will be supported by an appeal to that kind of insight which is known to musicians, artists, and poets, and which all along has been evading the vision of the mere critic with his microtome and scalpel. Thus, there may well again be a discernment in Scriptures of something like the *norma normans* of which the older Protestant theologians spoke.

Contemporary theology in its liberal expression is, in general, marked also by its unconcern about absolutes. Norms are sought but these are taken to be certainties so far as human experience goes and not necessarily non-relational absolutes. This attitude of mind is the direct outgrowth of the scientific temper. The scientist is content to have convictions but these convictions are tempered with the possibility of revisions with further data, light and insight. He is always ready and expects to make revisions when these are required; he well knows that further light is to be expected from future experience and that it is unreasonable to expect to make the final pronouncements. In theology there is now, similarly, the spirit of openmindedness, a place for possibilities as yet unrealized, for convictions open to corrections. No longer is there any feeling of discomfort in the admission that it is not to be expected of finite creatures that they shall comprehend the Infinite, nor of a necessarily limited perspective that it shall encompass the all-comprehending whole. This is a spirit that underlies these essays, and it is the typically contemporary spirit as asserted in philosophy and the special fields of scientific investigation.

A preceding generation undoubtedly would have chafed under the thought that possibly convictions were not absolutes; its ministers would have felt that there was nothing that could be preached with prophetic ardor, that there was then no word of God with which to reprove, admonish, instruct and inspire the sons of men. The modern spirit no longer expects to deliver *ex cathedra* utterances; it is enough if one quietly testifies to what seem to him abiding and consecrated convictions. There is, then, a lack of that note of finality which overpowered the critical thought of generations preceding, but at the same time there is possibly an increase in humility and in poise in the realization that so-called solutions of the problems of life and of the world are far from being so simple and undebatable as they were long supposed to be. If the loss is great in dogmatic authority, the gain is great in the realm of faith and credibility.

A word more about this change of temper. In the nineteenth century much was said about impossibilities. The physical sciences had become judgment-seats; philosophical disputes were referred to the men trained in the exacter sciences for solution and final verdict. These sciences in the intoxication of their success had become disrespectful even of their own scientific temper in making possibilities impossible and judgments final. It appeared that the theologian had forever lost his place of leadership; there was nothing further for him to do but fall back in line and follow the commands of those in charge. Orders were to be taken; it was clear from what source these were issued. All this has now changed. Natural scientists of the first rank no longer speak of impossibilities but of degrees of probability; no longer pronouncing judgments as final, they assert their present inductions and conclusions as opinions and beliefs; though having moved forward they no longer feel that they have caught up with the horizon of knowledge, but see it still where it seemed to be before—namely, just ahead. As though born again, they are now catching once more the truly scientific spirit and temper.

All this is of immeasurable consequence to modern thought in general and of no less importance to religious and theological thinking. It is now a nineteenth-century mode of speaking to declare certain age-old doctrines impossible. We would venture to be specific: to speak, for example, of the Virgin Birth, the resurrection, the miracles as impossibilities smacks of the accent of yesterday; today we speak of them rather as doctrines high or low in the scale of probabilities and as significant or unessential in the scale of religious values. By this admission, however, the conservative theologian has by no means been vindicated; rather, the liberal theologian has been chastened from a liberalism that had run headlong into dogmatism.

Perhaps no single general factor has been of greater value to the general progress of theology and religious philosophy than the application of the scientific temper to these wider areas of thought. For some, as already indicated, this means nothing to religion itself since it is held to occupy a wholly autonomous field; but to many it means a *rapprochement* between two bitterly contested fields of enquiry—the natural sciences and scientifically grounded metaphysics on the one hand and religion and religiously grounded theology on the other —and of great consequence to both. That this spirit will be increasingly applied in matters religious and theological is the opinion which would be endorsed in this introduction. Its effect upon the reconstruction of theology will be to mark the beginning of a new era—and there are signs of this new beginning already taking place. Theology will have fewer doctrines, perhaps, in its list of fundamentals, but what it will have to say will be more deeply founded and will cover wider and, for this age, more significant areas. There is in this trend a genuine hope that theology may regain its lost place of leadership among the disciplines. We are learning that in the pursuit of truth there is no method of greater consequence than the application of the truly scientific spirit. And this spirit is not to be identified wholly with laboratory technique; it consists of a passion for facts, being truthful with truth, being courageous with discovery, being cautious, alert, honest, testing subjectivities with objectivities, neither one excluding the other. So defined, the scientific temper of mind is not far removed from the religious spirit at its best.

The College of Wooster   VERGILIUS FERM
Wooster, Ohio

THEORY IN PRACTICE

By EDWARD SCRIBNER AMES

(b. April 21, 1870, Eau Claire, Wisconsin)

Professor of Philosophy and Chairman of the Department of Philosophy in The University of Chicago; Minister of the University Church of Disciples of Christ; Dean of the Disciples Divinity House of The University of Chicago

Chicago, Illinois

THEORY IN PRACTICE

By EDWARD SCRIBNER AMES

M Y FATHER was a minister. He was reared in a suburb of Boston where the family line had descended through several generations. He became pastor of a church in West Rupert, Vermont. In that town was a church which belonged to the new movement led by Alexander Campbell whose members called themselves Disciples of Christ. He united with them and became their pastor. In making the change he felt that he attained great freedom—freedom from creeds, from Old Testament authority, and from sectarianism. His new associates were fired by a passion for union and peace among all Christians; they held that the Bible should be studied and interpreted in a common sense way; and they denied the necessity of emotional conversion. My memory vividly recalls from childhood years his sense of release from old doctrines and his enthusiasm for the new found simple, reasonable faith. He moved west at the close of the Civil War.

My dawning consciousness found me the youngest of four children encircled in the warmth and happiness of a pious, earnest household. Morning prayers, grace at table, hymns around the parlor organ, Sunday the high day of the week, and an encompassing group of friendly souls were characteristics of a minister's home. Gripping poverty, church troubles, and other parental anxieties scarcely penetrated the serenity and lively dream world of childhood. School years and the long summer days of play flowed on into adolescence until the fourteenth autumn when I got a job in a general store. Then for the first time the meaning of real work appeared. There were four vigorous young men in the firm and I was the one clerk. They were methodical, energetic, courteous, and all but one members of a church. He was secretly an object of curiosity to me as I tried to imagine why such a good man should be an outsider and how he dared to take the risks involved. I learned more of practical life in that year than in any other. Many of the tasks were menial enough—packing butter and candling eggs in the cellar, stoking the furnace, sweeping out every morning, scrubbing the floors twice a week, washing the windows, and delivering goods. But there were also the finer duties of selling plug tobacco to farmers and calico to their wives and daughters. The traveling salesmen brought the breath of a wider world, and the unpacking of new shipments was like opening prize boxes at a party. From six o'clock until nine was a long day but not without excitement and plenty of village gossip.

Then came college. It was a new school founded only a few years before by a gift of $20,000 from General Francis Drake and by a gift of land from the citizens of Des Moines. The land was to be a source of income when the city developed under the stimulus of the growing college community. It was a denominational college established to educate youth, to train ministers, and to fulfil whatever other motives animate the founders of such institutions. We all went to chapel every day and to church on Sunday. Naturally there was suggestion enough for the son of a minister to go into the ministry and even to become a missionary. But I withheld any such decision until after graduation and then took studies which might serve either for preaching or teaching. As editor of the college paper I looked over the exchanges. From them and from other casual discoveries I became interested in further study at Yale. Finally, though ,without much encouragement from the denominational leaders, I entered the Yale Divinity School.

During that year I began to realize that many problems raised in theology are dealt with more fully and freely in philosophy. I borrowed money from my sister and plunged into courses with George T. Ladd. We read Pfleiderer's *Philosophy of Religion* and I was asked to write a paper on the Hebrews. In that task it dawned upon me, like a great light, that the religion of the Hebrews had evolved, and that its evolution moved with the changing fortunes of the tribes and nation. I also read Schopenhauer's *World as Will and Idea*. He shook me out of my complacent optimism and showed me the abysmal craving, cruelty and cunning in the human heart. More important, he set forth the deeper nature of the will as impulse, desire, habit, and partly conscious action. Being forced thus to look at all life from a new and contrasted point of view, and to gain some conception of the complex, tangled, and desire-driven human world, I was thrust out upon deep and wide seas of inquiry and reflection.

Then I came upon William James. His *Principles of Psychology* had just been published and we went through it in a seminar. His range of scholarship, penetrating analyses, lively and intensely human rewriting of psychology without a soul, opened the field of the new science just then entering upon an epoch of the profoundest significance in all fields, including religion. There were many enriching experiences for a western boy at Yale, in addition to classroom experiences. Timothy Dwight was President. Sumner and Hadley were in their prime. Munger and Smythe were pastors of local churches. William T. Harris, James, Royce, John Watson were occasional lecturers in philosophy.

An appointment to a special fellowship in philosophy at the new University of Chicago brought me to Chicago for the last year of graduate study. With Professor Tufts I made a special study of English philosophy and discovered the intimate relation between Locke's *Essay on the Human Understanding* and the religious thought of Alexander Campbell. Here were revealed the sources of my own religious inheritance and new insight into its empirical character. For two years, as instructor in the Disciples Divinity House and as privat-docent in philosophy I had opportunity to carry research further in that field and establish a point of view of permanent fruitfulness. Professor John Dewey had become the head of the department of philosophy who, with Professors Tufts, Mead and Addison Moore, developed what William James called the "Chicago School of Philosophy." It was a stimulating atmosphere for one who had been introduced to philosophy through the idealistic philosophy of George T. Ladd.

After three years as professor of philosophy and pedagogy at Butler College I returned to Chicago in 1900 to accept the pastorate of the Church of Disciples, near the University. I was soon invited to assist again in the department of philosophy, and later became a regular, part-time instructor. My interests naturally led to specialization in the psychology and philosophy of religion while also giving courses in psychology, ethics, logic, and the history of philosophy.

The Psychology of Religious Experience was the outcome of several years' work influenced by the new studies of Hall, Starbuck and Coe, dealing with conversion, and the illuminating studies in social psychology by Mead and Thomas among my associates and by such social psychologists as Durkheim, Levy-Bruhl, and their followers. Rich materials were becoming available from anthropological studies by men like Spencer and Gillen, Howitt, and Rivers, and from investigations of primitive religion by Frazer, Robertson Smith, Marett, Crawley, Cornford, Jane Harrison, and others.

All the time I was pastor of the church. There were perhaps fifty members when I began and it was six years old. While the leadership was from university circles, the congregation was then, and has always been, constituted of just the kind of people found in any church of the neighborhood. Fortunately the church belongs to a denomination in which each congregation is independent in the conduct of its affairs. I was a charter member and the members well knew the kind of a minister they were engaging. There was from the first complete understanding as to the general spirit and attitude which would characterize the conduct of the church.

My experience as a student and as a teacher of philosophy had brought me to regard religion as a natural growth in human life, and as subject generally to slow and unconscious changes in the prevailing culture. The success of the physical sciences through the use of experiment and the consequent modification of their ideas and procedure was being duplicated in the biological sciences, and the suggestion naturally followed that the social sciences might also utilize the method of experiment in various institutions. Experiments were being made in education, such as Dewey's Laboratory School in our neighborhood; in social settlements, as at Hull House under Jane Addams; in politics and industry and in the arts. Why not in religion?

Looking back upon those scenes of thirty years ago, it is apparent that the first manifestations of radical change were in the sermons. Weekly church bulletins were printed from the first which give a complete record of sermon subjects and organizational activities. There are also files of a monthly paper which contain

many sermons in full. These show that the verbaliza-
tion of changing ideas was the first expression of con-
scious difference.   They reflect the rejection of author-
ity and offer reinterpretations of traditional doctrines.
The subjects of some of those printed sermons are:
The Conception of God; Salvation; The Right to
Make Mistakes; The Authority of Experience; The
Perplexities of Faith; Prayer; Social Ideals; The
Divinity of Christ; The Religious Nature of Man.

One of the first experiments of a practical character
was with reference to the conditions of membership.
The Disciples had emphasized union from the beginning, but they had uniformly practiced immersion. New
Testament criticism, the surrender of the conception
of Biblical authority, and recognition of the divisive
effect of the maintenance of a primitive custom as a
divine command, tended to relax adherence to the custom. The final result was formal action by the congregation establishing the practice of receiving persons by
letter from any denomination, and on confession of
faith with or without baptism according to their preference. The observance of this ordinance has practically
ceased with no noticeable detriment to the religious
life. Upon the basis of this experience a new plan of
union is suggested for all churches. It might be called
union by declaration! That is, if all congregations of
whatever name would exchange members and receive
converts without insistence upon creed or form, the
traditional differences would no longer operate as
divisive but would undergo a desirable vestigial decline. That which makes serious divisions in Christendom is the claim of various bodies to the possession and
administration of certain beliefs or rites by which alone
salvation is possible.

Another line of experimentation related to the
organization of the congregation. The assumption
among all churches has been that there is some valid

Biblical constitution for congregations. Elders, deacons, presbyters, bishops and other officers are alleged to be required by the New Testament. Yet scholars have not been able to agree upon the precise form. Rather their studies have made it clear that such organization as existed was of a practical nature and took form as varying needs dictated. The result of an assumed type of church authorization by divine revelation has been the claim of prerogatives by elders and deacons out of all relation to the demands of the situation and to the abilities of men holding these offices. No such difficulties were encountered in our local church, but in the interest of a more flexible and realistic policy the congregation was organized upon a genuinely democratic plan such as is common in voluntary associations in our social order. Therefore an annual election of officers is held providing for a president or chairman of the congregation, an official board or directorate, with special appointees, committees, and delegates to care for the various functions and interests of the group.

The business conduct of churches is notoriously unbusinesslike. A multiplicity of organizations, such as church school, missionary societies, clubs, age groups, and the rest, often results in constant appeals to the whole congregation in the interest of special causes. The result is a confusion of cross-purposes which distracts attention from the main concerns and dries up the springs of generosity by feeble and inconsequential efforts for special organizations. Bazaars, parties, dinners for profit, entertainments to raise funds, and repeated collections in church services put too much emphasis upon financial solicitation and give churches the appearance of always begging for support. We therefore unified the entire budget, asking each member for but one subscription to current expenses and one for benevolences.

No other funds are solicited for any purpose. No

collections are taken in public services.   Individuals
and organizations are discouraged from raising money
for any cause.   The expenses of the church school,
woman's club, young people's groups, and all the rest
are paid from the church treasury.   Through many
years this plan has minimized talk about money and
also secured larger returns.   While it is often said that
a church must be rich to operate on such a plan, the
fact is that it was developed under straitened circumstances as a method of strictest economy.   Churches
can never be so "spiritual" as to make it possible to
ignore financial matters, and it is a matter of common
observation that their spirituality is often destroyed by
fiscal troubles.   So long as these institutions are involved in the affairs of this world their practical needs
are integral with the religious life.

Another experiment which does not belong to the
high domain of theology but comes close to the human
foundations of religion concerns the social and recrea-
tional life.   When a new building, with a parish house
adjoining, had been built, facilities were available for
these interests.   Dinners—not for profit—were served
on Sundays at one o'clock and on Friday evenings.
Doubts were expressed about Sundays.   Naturally it
was thought that people would wish to be in their
homes.   But experience has shown that in the city
many single persons, childless couples, and others are
glad to meet with friends at such dinners.   Through
eight years this Sunday dinner has justified itself, paid
for itself, and contributed very vitally to happy fellowship.   The Friday evening dinner is followed by a
short address, or music, or a play, or pictures, and regularly by games and dancing.

None of these features is merely allowed or apolo-
getically provided "for the young people."   Everyone
participates, old and young together, ministers and laymen, spinsters, matrons, and maids.   It is a church-

family affair and conducted on principle. The distinction between the Church and the world is not allowed to be made by identifying the world, or the works of the devil, with card playing, theatre-going and dancing. That always seemed to me a very feeble conception of wickedness. It does not do justice to the devil especially in an age of so much social injustice, violence, ignorance and poverty. Protestantism has been too puritanical, too prudish. A religion vital enough for its great task must be virile, realistic, sane and gay.

Other illustrations of this experimenting laboratory of religion might be cited. For example, the social service council is an important attempt to leaven the church by more adequate attitudes and information concerning the theories and the processes of modern social work. The council consists of the professional social workers and any others interested to participate. In times of depression, race riots, labor troubles, and crime waves, attention centers upon these social problems, the Church is ready to listen to experts in these matters, and often to engage in practical efforts.

There have also been new curricula for the church school, the latest of which is more fully described in a chapter on religious education in my book, *Religion*. The guiding purpose has been to help children and adults discover and develop significant values in actual experience. There have been open forums following the Sunday morning services for the discussion of the sermon. This helps to make of the church what Professor Coe calls a "deliberative assembly." It gives laymen opportunity to participate in thinking about religion and to bring to bear their practical common sense in interpreting the suggestions of the day to one another in their own terms. Often it is an illuminating and not infrequently a chastening experience for the minister. Other experiments have resulted in the unification of all the women's organizations into a woman's club which has been for years a member of the general federation of woman's clubs in the city and state and nation; there is a church library of carefully selected books on religious, scientific, social, and cultural subjects; novel programs for church services have been organized, and there has been some publication of sermons, books, and programs of activities.

There never were any formal theological tests to which prospective members were subjected. No church has ever been able to achieve doctrinal uniformity among its own members, and at last it is realized that such a state is not desirable. Therefore anyone is welcome to membership who is in sympathy with the spirit and work of the congregation. Differences of social background, of religious tradition, of individual temperament, of vocation and ambition are inevitable. They are valuable if frankly acknowledged and allowed to interplay in friendly discussion and mutual understanding. "Utilizing Our Differences" was the topic of a sermon directed toward the fuller use of these resources.

My pastorate is now in the thirty-third year. For several years the weekly calendar has carried the following formulation of the ideals of the church: This church practices union; has no creed; seeks to make religion as intelligent as science; as appealing as art; as vital as the day's work; as intimate as the home; as inspiring as love. The last two phrases were recently added to express what have always been marked characteristics. I have found that series of sermons are much more interesting to all concerned than isolated discourses. They sustain interest from week to week and afford hearers a means of anticipating more clearly the line of thought. A few months ago when planning such a series at the beginning of the new year it occurred to me that sermons dealing with the phrases just mentioned might serve to clarify our own loyalties, and might afford opportunity to declare more definitely my own changing and enlarging convictions about religion in relation to the times in which we live.

This church practices union. The Disciples of Christ began a great religious movement a little over a hundred years ago with the idea of union central in their thought. But it was a union of churches, or rather of church people, which they sought. The union they contemplated was to be based upon biblical authority or upon the authority of Jesus and His Apostles; it looked to the past for its form; and it conceived the development of religion as a life over against the world. All progressive Protestant churches have accomplished this kind of union to some degree. They receive members freely from other bodies and most large city churches of any denomination have individuals from a dozen or twenty different communions. But this achievement does not greatly fire the imagination of most persons. They take it for granted that a respectable church will hold the old differences lightly, and will be hospitable to all other Christians.

What is now needed is an interpretation and practice of religion that will unify all religious people—those that are in and those that are outside existing churches. Such a union should not merely tolerate differences, but should seek to utilize them as resources for enlarging and vitalizing the religious life. This can be done only by training individuals of diverse views to learn from one another in the cooperative quest for truer ideas and finer attitudes. No doubt there are many religious persons outside organized religion who are less religious and less effective than they would be in a congenial and vital fellowship. Something is needed that is more thoroughgoing, more radical and appealing than the conventional churches. It must be something beyond Protestantism. Christianity has always been an "unworldly" religion. Reasons for this in the early

Church are evident. The world that stood over against the Church was the Roman world of material power, of luxury, of antisemitic hatred, a world decadent and disintegrating. In organizing and fortifying itself to meet that situation the Church developed a system of ideas and of administration that continued to grow in power into the middle ages. The Protestant Reformation was the beginning of the end of that system, and now Protestantism is feeling its own dissolution under the influence of modernism. Historical criticism of its Scriptures, scientific demolition of its cosmology, and the secularization of all values through the industrial revolution and its effects leave the traditional forms of religion archaic and exhausted.

Christianity now faces the alternative of becoming a religion of this world or of having no appeal to this age. For a generation we have heard of the social gospel, but that has usually meant a gospel touched by the magic of a supernatural religion, rather than a religion arising in the social process and seeking to fulfil inherent, natural social values. A religion is needed which discovers these values in experience, not one that endeavors to import and impose them from without. If religion does not have its proper field in clarifying and furthering the values of the economic, political and social life, then its inner attitudes and sentiments lose substance and significance.

In other times and lands religion has had this natural function. It has been concrete and practical, dealing with all the important crises of life, from birth to death, in seedtime and harvest, in war and cataclysms of nature. It should still deal with the whole of life, and not as mere contemplation but as active participation and idealizing reconstruction. What kind of union would we get in this way? The union of purpose and spirit in devotion to an all-comprehending cause, the cause of human welfare and the common good. It

would be a union not on the ground of external authority, or beliefs, but of appreciable goals and concrete
tasks.   Such a union would require freedom of inquiry
and of discussion.   There would be recognition of experimental method, liberating change, and enlightened
renovation of ideologies and institutions.   Whoever
could be brought to see and feel the value of cooperation in such undertakings would thereby become members of societies working for their realization, just as
now men participate in political parties and leagues for
mutual benefit and social advancement.

A free church can have no creed.   A creed is a statement of belief, "setting forth with authority certain
articles which are regarded by the framers as necessary
for salvation."   The so-called Apostles' Creed is the
one most generally accepted by Protestant churches.   It
does not, of course, go back to the Apostles but dates
from the fourth century.   The only parts of this creed
that I would care to subscribe to are the statements of
fact and of experience.   These are contained in the
declarations that Jesus Christ suffered under Pontius
Pilate, was crucified, dead, and buried.   One may also
believe in the communion of saints and in the forgiveness of sins, though even here one must reserve his
own interpretation.   All the rest are assertions beyond
the realm of verifiable fact.

It is well known that there has never been uniformity
of belief in all the points of any creed, and it should
be evident that such agreement is psychologically impossible.   The attempts to enforce belief in creeds leads
to divisions and throws doubt upon more important
features of the faith.   Creeds, like miracles, once held
to be supports of religious faith, have now come to be
burdens upon it.   The profession of any traditional
creed in our day weakens religion, and weakens the
character of religious people.   It tends to make them
insincere and inconsistent.   There is a tendency for

honest men to have a kind of contempt for ministers and institutions which profess them. Jesus set up no such creed nor did the early Church.

If creeds could be regarded as functioning ideologies, summarizing the general attitudes and working beliefs of groups, they would serve a purpose, but they have always tended to become tests of fellowship, rigidly held and often ruthlessly administered. What we do need, and in some form must always have, are general statements of the religious view of life, set in the frame of verified knowledge and of the great objectives of associated human hope and endeavor. Such statements are necessarily subject to change with enlarging horizons and consequent new tasks and problems.

One of the modern notes to be included in any formulation of religious outlook is just this of change itself. Familiar religious beliefs face the past and stress the need for a return to some previous standard, to the New Testament, to Jesus, to some lost age of faith, or unity, or inspiration. Interesting studies have lately been made of the meaning of the past both psychologically and philosophically. They aid in dispelling the illusion that it is ever possible to recover events or forms of behavior and exactitude. We live forward. Change is of the very nature of things and of ourselves.

While the study of history is important as showing the way we have come and perhaps indicating the direction of events, it is itself subject to restatement and to new perspectives and interpretations. Moreover, the future into which we go is uncharted. We cannot completely forecast it. We must make of it an adventure and deal with the days as they come and with the situations they bring. Accepting this attitude we need not be anxious about the morrow but may look forward to its novelty and surprise with as much interest as men formerly had fear of it. "The world is young," I heard a chapel speaker say years ago, and the word precipitated into clearness many impressions until that moment vague, and induced a mood of acceptance and expectancy which has remained.

The modern mind is also attaining freedom from the old doctrine of original sin and human depravity. Although the doctrine has long been repudiated in intention, its effects have remained. Religious people continue to be suspicious of the natural man. The notion survives that there are inherently evil impulses that must be guarded against. A strong hand of the law, or public opinion, or the counsels of religion, may be needed to check passions and evil designs. A more adequate psychology shows that human nature is indeed plastic, and that the direction of development depends upon conditions and upon conditioning.

Along with this change in the conception of human nature from that of its sinfulness to progressive growth in morality and social idealism there comes a change of mood. The old faith was depressing and gloomy. Religion was antagonistic to the natural joys of life and could only sanction the "solemn joy" of religious worship, or of the fellowship of the saints. Their satisfaction consisted largely in the inner assurance they cherished of superiority to the world about them, and in the hope of heavenly reward and blessedness. Churches constantly rebuked any kind of worldliness, were suspicious of youthful gaiety, and extolled the cross. Ministers dressed in long black coats and felt the duty of being serious. If their human nature demanded compensations in hearty social dinners and stories in lighter vein, these might be allowed but always seemed a little inconsistent and incongruous.

The newer idea of religion as a natural growth unifies life, legitimatizes the moral values and ideals of ordinary experience, and makes a direct relation between the natural outreachings of the heart in sympathy and love and the highest aspirations of religion. New and appreciable meaning appears in the idea that God is love, and that Jesus proclaimed His own strenuous mission as a joyous one. He seemed to know that serious, arduous tasks, intelligently pursued, yield the greater happiness. The Greeks knew that, and modern moralists know it, and Christians are beginning to discover it. It is helping to vitalize religion for modern men.

Having become accustomed to the use of scientific method in psychology, and to the conception of natural evolution in religion, I was not troubled by controversies over the conflict of science and religion. This conflict was resolved for me by seeing how it arose. Why has Christianity had so much difficulty in utilizing science? Because its creeds did not provide for their own revision. Another reason is that Christianity is Hebrew in its temper and outlook, while science is Greek. Our religious tradition has taught that the wisdom of this world is foolishness with God, and that knowledge puffeth up. Besides, the findings of science have been completely subversive of Biblical cosmology, and of traditional views of the authorship and inspiration of the Bible. The earth is no longer flat; the Garden of Eden, with its drama of the creation and fall of man, has disappeared; no early end of the world is probable.

There would be less opposition to science in religious circles if it were kept in mind that science means just a sensible way of getting knowledge about anything, and the results that such careful inquiries attain. Science solves problems. It is a problem for man to increase speed of travel, and science has invented various devices in reply. Men have long been curious about the distance, composition, weight and motion of the stars. Science has found interesting answers. The methodical, careful studies of religion have shown that it is universal in all tribes and races of men, with variations consistent with different cultures. The science of the psychology of religion, in the last thirty years, has answered many important questions about conversion, ceremonials, deities, mysticism and missionary enterprises. Science takes all sorts of questions about religious matters, such as the soul, immortality, prayer, and faith, shows how to study them, gives the record of any success or failure, and suggests ways and means for further research.

Science is friendly to all questioning, including religious questioning. All genuine science is religious in its spirit of wonder and awe, in its reverence for facts, in its patient and courageous persistence, in its unselfish and whole-hearted search for truth, and in its readiness to use its resources for the service of mankind. Science is in accord with the sayings of Jesus: Wisdom is justified of her children; and, Ye shall know the truth and the truth shall make you free. Science is an instrument, and like every other instrument it may have various uses.

A knife may be used to carve a beautiful figure from wood, or it may be used to destroy such a work of art. It is no just condemnation of the knife to show that it has been an instrument of destruction. The knife is not responsible for its uses; neither is science. We continue to prize knives for their value as instruments to fulfil good ends, in spite of their occasional misuse. Science is not the whole of life. Besides knowledge there are also appreciation, love, and the quest for beauty. Religion is a living experience of the great values found in the rich and growing life of the world, and in the realization of what philosophers have called the kingdom of ends. Science may be made a means to the fulfilment of those ends. In sermons, in talks by laymen who are scientists, and by scientific works in the library, this estimate and appreciation of science is emphasized.

Art is another field which makes profound appeal to modern men but traditional religion has been somewhat aloof from it, at least from certain of its forms for various reasons. The force of the old injunction, "Thou shalt not make unto thee any graven image," has been like a taboo against the arts. Art is sensuous, a work of imagination, and its classical expressions were of Greek and pagan origin. Protestantism, in its revolt from Catholicism, discarded the older ecclesiastical art as foreign to simple, New Testament Christianity. Yet art forms press for recognition. The most austere groups gradually feel the influence of surrounding culture. As wealth and education permeate society the demand arises for richer forms of service. In many denominations this change has been registered in controversies over instrumental music, vested choirs, candles, and the introduction of liturgical usage. There is now a widespread demand for this "enrichment of worship," but not always with consistency or effectiveness. A Methodist minister once confessed to me the difficulty he felt in preaching the type of sermon to which he was accustomed in the elaborate Gothic church his congregation had built. The warm, direct and intimate talks he had formerly given seemed out of place in the formal, stately edifice.

What seems to be needed is that religion shall come to terms with art in reference to their relation and significance for each other. A recent writer has said, "Art always represents the overcoming of difficulties." It sets forth a problem and its solution. In architecture, it is the problem of the support of the roof by walls and columns but with the appearance of strength and grace. In sculpture, the Greek athlete—the discus thrower, the runner, the gladiator, the archer—is shown in the posture and action of accomplishing his goal with well-coordinated effort. In the drama, the plot thickens with conflicting wills and interests to a tense climax where the hero conquers his enemy, or in tragic rôles wins admiration by suffering defeat with nobility and honor. Religion is also a struggle with opposing forces of evil. It is the battle of the soul with adversaries, with temptations, with the powers of darkness. The cross has with good reason become the great symbol of the struggle and the victory of Christian faith. It carries the whole meaning of man's failure and of his redemption. What was intended by the enemies of Christ to be His destruction becomes in the spiritual drama the instrument of triumph, the symbol of conquering love. No wonder it is the focal object of Christian art, in poetry and song, in painting, in statuary, and at the high altar of churches and chapels.

The danger of all symbolism is that it tends to settle into fixed forms that limit rather than free the imagination. Men are no longer literally crucified, and it is with difficulty that the imagery of the cross is made to carry the full significance of the moral struggle in which men are now involved. Other events in the life of Christ come nearer to the situations in which we live. Such were the encounters between Jesus and the theologians, His setting aside the old law of the Sabbath, His blessing of little children, and His scourging of the money changers. Just as the hymns of the church are rewritten from age to age, so the other forms of art demand revision and adaptation to growing experience.

Art expresses the natural, idealizing tendency of the human mind. It catches some event out of the complex field of life and sets it off in a frame of its own where its beauty is enhanced and magnified. A portrait by Rembrandt, a statue by Thorwaldsen, a landscape by Turner, selects out of the fulness of the world and fastens attention upon a significant face or figure or scene in nature. "Spiritual" values are not limited to "religious" subjects. Wherever loveliness of light and line reflect the harmony and fulfilment of striving forces, spirituality is manifest. Genuine works of art need no consecration to make them religious. Keats's *Ode on a Grecian Urn* and Browning's *Saul* carry in themselves a divine quality.

I have come to believe that it is the function of religion to discover the meaning and beauty in all spheres of life, and not to limit itself to those special experiences which we have traditionally conceived as religious. Beyond the areas of Hebrew and Christian traditions are many other aspiring, struggling, solving ways of the spirit of man. Outside the formal institutions and services called religious are the natural vocations of man which constantly reveal, through workmanship, comradeship, intelligence, sensitivity, courage and hope, the spiritual possibilities of the human mind and heart. Adjoining my church is the Unitarian Church of Von Ogden Vogt, whose artistic and religious feeling led him to give conspicuous place in his beautiful Gothic building to the symbols of man's daily pursuits—the steamship, printing press, dynamo, mason's, plumber's and carpenter's tools, the teacher, lawyer, doctor, scientist, painter and musician. They are not brought into the church to make them holy, they are brought because they are already sacred through the part they play in the total human drama. These are all ministering servants.

Some literally minded people may say that art and religion are just wish-fulfilments, that they move in the field of imagination above the hard realities of exact knowledge and strenuous endeavor. They are escape devices, utopian creations in the realm of unreality. But it is not difficult to show that human life everywhere utilizes the imagination in solving practical problems and in projecting more ideal conditions for contemplation and for direction of effort. All substantial achievements, those of business and science, are wish-fulfilments. But he is a dull soul who does not also go beyond such matter-of-fact practicalities. Who does not play games? Yet all games are make-believe. Who does not listen to music? But to what practical end? Why is there so much literature of fiction and poetry? In all these, as in mystery stories, there are plots, conflicts, and escapes.

Religion involves likewise this double play of the imagination. It undertakes through many agencies to solve problems by pointing distraught minds to ways of relief and healing; by cultivating friendliness for the lonely; by helping to reconstruct social attitudes and institutions. But it does more than this. It creates social groups which epitomize in ideal a society of blessedness and beauty. Here all are friends, all co-operate unselfishly for the common good, all seek to understand the marvels of life and the possibilities of mutual goodwill and great achievement. They live in the lines of a noble tradition whose heroes, martyrs, seers and sages strengthen faith and point forward to a glorious future. In imagination, and through the symbols of art, they quicken their spirits in an unselfish cause, and represent to themselves the fulfilment of their hopes.

We have sought to utilize the arts in the church to set forth and to enhance the highest values of life. We erected a building at a cost of two hundred and fifty thousand dollars to which Dean Sperry refers in his book, *Reality in Worship*, as a church built "for a non-liturgical, non-sacramentarian congregation." He describes it as follows: "The architect is said to have had in mind the old English moot-hall. The interior is undoubtedly successful. Brains went into the planning, and interest and affection into the actual stone

work of the masons. Moreover, there is clearly a religious idea behind it all. This is the meeting place of
the people, with a hint of the feudal hall of God the
Father. The church is simple, even bare; rough stone
work throughout the interior. On one side only there
is a series of heavy piers of Saxon stolidity. Beyond
these pillars an aisle, empty of pews, and at the end of
the aisle a great fireplace."

We maintain an excellent choir and have done something to encourage members of the church to cultivate
music, drama, pageantry, poetry, and dancing. A poem
is printed with the order of service each Sunday, and
this feature has elicited much appreciation. An eleven-
branched candelabrum with lighted candles rests on the
center of the communion table which stands in place
of an altar back of the pulpit. Far above, within three
deep arches, are stained glass windows by Charles J.
Connick, in memory of one of our boys who was killed
in the battle of the Argonne in the World War.

I conceive it possible to make religion as vital as the
day's work. Too often it seems quite the opposite.
Religion is identified with a day of rest. More and
more Sunday is celebrated as a holiday, a day free
from responsibility, given over to ease and pleasure.
So far from being the most vital and significant day
of the week as the theory of religion has implied, it is
for many just an interim between the real employments
of life. Even the churches are tempted to observe it
as such. They tend to offer entertainment, with attractive music, short services, and soothing sermons. Attendance is quite optional and easily foregone. In the
old day Sunday was held to be significant, to take people above "everydayism," to summon men to supreme
duties and to participation in the highest possible experiences. Half-filled pews, routine services, and the
absence of youth are evidences of listlessness. Few
daily papers take much note of what happens. Many

thoughtful men are heralding the decline of religion. Mr. Lippmann has shown how the "acids of modernity" have eaten away the foundations of the popular faith. The humanists of religion have rejected the supernatural, discarded God, and narrowed the horizons of faith. Mysticism, occultism, and cults revived from prescientific ages, parade their claims. Modernistic Protestantism wavers between the dead and the unborn.

The day's work suggests the vitality that religion needs, for the day's work at its best is productive and rewarding, serves insistent hunger and thirst, is creative and commanding. It holds its devotees day in and day out, is never to be slighted in fair weather or foul, in periods of discomfort or inconvenience. Deep laid habits sustain it, and it moves with the rhythm of the seasons through the long run of the years. A man's business is the foundation of his life and involves all his moral character. His honor and self-respect depend upon it as do his honesty, fidelity, workmanship and good nature. Fair dealing and the interest of those with whom he trades are essential to success, and a well-conducted office or shop contributes to the welfare of others as well as to his own. Upon a man's work rest his chances for participation in the wider life of the community. It is not strange that men often regard their work as their religion, and that doctors, lawyers, scientists and artists readily allow themselves to become wholly engrossed in their occupations.

Such concentration seems to me to rest upon a kind of unconscious conceit about one's vocation. It is a sort of professional selfishness. The claim of religion should be that the life of man cannot be adequately satisfied without a broader view and a wider participation in varied interests and in the concerns of the social order. It is common complaint that much of the evil in politics, in social maladjustments, in miscarriage of justice is due to the indifference of leaders in business and professional affairs. Real reasons may be cited, too, why all persons should share in the world of leisure, letters and art. It is in these realms that men live together and find the larger meanings of their existence. Here the tasks and labors of the day may be seen in some proper perspective. Without reference to these higher values what is a man more than a sheep?

Religion becomes as vital as the day's work when it recognizes the importance of that work not only as a job to be done but as a function of a larger and finer world of human relations and values. Work is the foundation of life but it is meaningless without something else built upon it. Man becomes absurd when he only lays foundations and does not utilize them to support some lofty and noble structure where his spirit may gain farther vistas, satisfying beauty and inner peace. We need religion that includes the whole of life, both the prosaic and the poetic, a religion that walks the earth and ministers to immediate needs, but which also rises to the stars and sweeps through the infinities of the imagination. To this end there must be whole-hearted acceptance of all that science knows, and all that art can symbolize.

I realize that the modern mind is preoccupied with intellectual problems about religion. It has been necessary for me to deal with these problems as a student and teacher of philosophy. But as the minister of a church I have had to understand religion as an experience. I could not think one way all the week and another way on Sunday, but there is a difference between teaching a class about religion and conducting a church for the practice of religion. The first requires some detachment, analysis, criticism and caution. The second demands all this and, in addition, significant interpretation and appealing presentation to create appreciation and action.

I am often asked how I can teach philosophy and be a preacher. Everyone seems to sense the difficulty. To some extent the acuteness of the problem is a reflection upon both schools and churches, for it suggests that they are both somewhat withdrawn from real life where thinking and action are closely interactive. In my experience the church has been a kind of laboratory for observation and cultivation of the living processes of religion, and the university has been a place for systematic study of them and of similar phenomena from many sources, in the light of psychology and philosophy. I have grown to have increasing appreciation of this rare combination and to feel the value of each interest for the other.

I have not been merely a "pulpit supply" in the church. I have done pastoral work, raised money, sat with committees, conducted marriage and funeral services, taught children, and listened to marital woes. No one can build up a church just by preaching. These other duties have never bored me. On the contrary they have taken me into the very heart of religious experience and given me an opportunity to share the heights and depths of the soul's life. I have not only learned to pity human beings; I have been inspired by the courage of the poor, by the fortitude of the sick and the bereaved, by the unselfishness and idealism of average people.

The universal yearning for understanding companionship and for a society of mutual sympathy and helpfulness has convinced me that religion should be as intimate as the home. Home is a place where one lives unrestrained, speaks his mind, meets various interests and opinions, and yet feels the deeper bonds which produce some kind of working harmony. A real home is one where you know your way around in the dark; where chairs and tables have individuality; where books and pictures have become part of your personality;

where you know voices and footsteps as well as faces; where you feel secure. Religion should create such feeling about the world until it becomes a "friendly universe." The home is not really perfectly secure, but a man strives to make it so. Sickness, accident, misunderstanding, even death may come in, but the heart clings to it. Similarly, in spite of imperfections, the religious soul feels the world to be a congenial place and strives to make it more completely such.

Ministers therefore must not only make religion scientific and æsthetic, but they must endeavor to make it hospitable, radiant, and friendly for particular individuals according to their need. It is amazing to what an extent people generalize their attitudes toward the whole world from a few instances. I have known persons to allow a single unfortunate encounter to destroy for them any religious feeling about life, and in other cases one happy hour has set the whole world alight. More than we usually admit, the quality of our feeling about the universe is determined by our particular relation to an immediate situation. Churches consequently exert enormous influence for or against this "cosmic emotion."

It has been said that many people are no longer religious in America because they have moved so far from their ancestral home, and have moved so often. They are not rooted in the soil and accumulate few heirlooms. Consequently they have little to give depth and stability to their personalities or to their feeling about life. When the Hebrews were exiles in Babylon their captors required of them one of the songs of Zion, but they replied, "How can we sing the Lord's song in a strange land?" The very sense of the reality and the presence of God is clearer for those who know the intimacy of a satisfying home. In the *Fire-Bringer*, William Vaughn Moody has Pandora sing:

I stood within the heart of God:

All was the same as once it was
Upon my hills at home.

I hold also that religion should be as inspiring as love. Love is the greatest force in the world. We talk about it as the heart of religion but we do not sufficiently recognize that the love that glorifies religion is identical with man's natural affections refined and sublimated into their noblest expression. The assumption that we must begin with belief in divine things, with supernatural realities, has been characteristic of Christianity in too large measure ever since its doctrines were shaped by the theologians. Why not begin with immediate experience, with the things right at hand, under our eyes, accessible to verification? Here within our grasp are the realities of love—love of companions, of children, of neighbors, of fatherland, and of mankind. This outreaching love knows no bounds. It encompasses the beauty of the seas and the wonder of the stars. It feels itself continuous with the distant past and with æons of the future into which its powers may be transmitted. The ranges of its ongoing influence may be as vast as the light years of the new measurements of space, so that we have reason to think in terms of the light years of love.

Scientists are convinced that in minute electrons titanic energy resides which some day may be released. There is also real ground for the conviction that in the love of the human heart are sources of energy beyond all the heroisms and devotion yet displayed. Here are potential moralities and idealisms of new magnitudes and intensities. Experiments for the release and use of this unfathomed dynamic might be made by more conscious and effective methods than any now employed. The elemental form of love is sex love, and the highest forms of love never lose that quality and pattern. Leuba has shown in his *Psychology of Mysticism* that the great mystics are genuine lovers though they are lovers of Christ and God. Their highest state is the ecstasy of spiritual marriage. It is this same love that makes a teacher devoted to her pupils, a nurse to her patients, a patriot to his country, a reformer to his cause, a saint to his vision.

Love gathers to itself knowledge and power in the service of the beloved. It builds institutions like the home, the school, the democratic state, social settlements, voluntary associations for peace, for art, and for religion. Justice flowers from it, and utopian dreams are the signals of its advancing sway. Already it has conquered many hatreds, austerities, cruelties, and slaveries. Old religions of authority have vanished before it, and new faiths are rising out of it. Celibacy and asceticism are too narrow for it. Exclusive sects cannot contain it. No fellowship is too inclusive for it. Love is the true life of man. God is love, and the kingdom of God is within us.

PRINCIPAL PUBLICATIONS

Books:

The Psychology of Religious Experience. Boston, Houghton Mifflin Co., 1910. (Now in Red Label Reprints.)

The New Orthodoxy. Chicago, The University of Chicago Press, 1925.

Religion. New York, Henry Holt and Company, 1929. (Now in Red Label Reprints.)

Articles:

"Social Consciousness and Its Object." *Psychological Bulletin,* 1911.

"Religious Values and the Practical Absolute." Presidential Address of the American Philosophical Association: Western Branch, *International Journal of Ethics,* 1922.

"The Mystics—Their Experience and Their Doctrine." *Proceedings of the Sixth International Congress of Philosophy.* New York, Longmans, Green and Co., 1927.

"Religious Values and Philosophical Criticism." *Essays in Honor of John Dewey.* New York, Henry Holt and Company, 1929.

Articles and Reviews in *The International Journal of Ethics, The Journal of Religion, The Journal of Religious Education, The Christian Century, The Philosophical Review.*

CONFESSIONS OF A TRANSPLANTED SCOT

By JOHN BAILLIE

(b. March 26, 1886, Gairloch, Ross-shire, Scotland)

Roosevelt Professor of Systematic Theology in Union Theological
Seminary

New York, N. Y.

CONFESSIONS OF A TRANSPLANTED SCOT

By John Baillie

MY THEOLOGICAL TRAINING began when, at the tender age of some five years, I was taught the first few responses of the Westminster Shorter Catechism. I was born in a Scottish Highland manse and all my early religious associations were with the more strictly Calvinistic type of Scottish Presbyterianism. The received creed was represented by the Westminster Confession of Faith, and my early boyhood was passed among men and women who knew and understood its elaborate doctrinal teaching through and through, and were well able to meet any difficulty which a boyish mind was likely to raise.

I have never since those days had the good fortune to live in a community that was, generally speaking, so well-informed in matters theological, so well acquainted with the contents of the Bible or so well able to explain and defend what it professed to believe. Not many systems of thought have been devised which (once certain initial premises are granted) hang together in so coherent a whole, or in which the vulnerable Achilles-heel is so hard to find.

But there were certain other features of this religion of the Scottish Highlands for which no mere study of its official symbols will prepare anyone who is a stranger to its inward life. There was here as deep and sincere a development of personal religion as could, perhaps, anywhere be pointed to in the Christian world. The practice of prayer, private, domestic and public, was

given a primary place in the daily and weekly round
and was a deep reality for men's thoughts.   There
was a strong evangelical note, so that one's mind was
constantly being turned upon the necessity of regenera-
tion, and yet any kind of sensational or over-emotional
"evangelistic" movement was looked at askance.

For never in any type of religion was there a greater
sense of solemnity than in this one.   Nowhere else,
however imposing and fitting may have been the ritual,
have I ever been so aware of the *mysterium tremendum*
as in these rare celebrations of the Lord's Supper.
Here, if ever, *das Numinose*, "the sense of the holy,"
was found prevailing; the comparative rarity of the
occasion giving to the sacramental feast that very same
acuteness of emphasis which in another tradition (that
I have since learned to prefer) is fostered rather by
the opposite rule of frequency.

In recent days and in certain other parts of the world
to which Scottish influence has penetrated, Presbyterianism has on occasion become a markedly unsacramental
religion, the "coming to the Lord's Table" being sometimes regarded as not very much more than a pleasant
piece of old-fashioned sentiment and therefore an
optional addition to one's central religious duties.   Nothing, however, could be a greater departure from original
Scottish religion as I knew it in my youth.

The whole year's religion then seemed to me to re-
volve round the two half-yearly celebrations, together
with their attendant special services stretching from the
"Fast Day" on Thursday (when no business was done
in the town and all the shops were shut) until the following Monday evening.   The Scottish sacramental
doctrine is a very "high" one, though not in the sense
of conformity to the too crude theory that developed
within the Latin countries.

It was through associations formed at school that
influences of another sort first began to play upon me,

opening my eyes to certain spiritual deficiencies in this
inherited system.   I was fortunate in my masters.   Since
those days I have made acquaintance with a kind of
schoolmaster who is greatly skilled in the mechanics
of his profession and knows all there is to know (up to
the very *dernier cri* in pedagogical theory) about how
to teach—but who has little or nothing to impart!   Of
this kind of dominie it can truly be said that, if only
he knew anything, his pupils would in time come to
know it also.

My kind of dominie had, for the most part, an opposite combination of qualities and defects.   My masters had minds richly stored with various knowledge,
but this knowledge was more or less *thrown* at their
pupils, to be taken or left according to one's tastes and
abilities; and the wiles of modern educational strategy
were left unpracticed.   I think there were a large number of us with whom the method worked and who drew
freely and eagerly upon the store thus set at our disposal.

In this way we became passionate explorers of some
of the main channels of English literature.   We were
deep in the poets, from Chaucer onward; and we were
always writing what we hoped might be poetry ourselves.   But above all, at this period, it was the great
Victorians that inspired us—Thackeray and Dickens,
Tennyson and Matthew Arnold and Charles Kingsley,
the Brontës, the Pre-Raphaelites, Carlyle, Ruskin.   I
can remember when the prose of *Culture and Anarchy*
seemed to me the most magnificent in our language,
and *Pendennis* the most absorbing story.   Perhaps in
all this the friendly interchange among the pupils
counted for as much as the guidance given by the masters; for there was a small coterie of us who shared
the same pursuits.   Nor was it only by the English
classics that our interest was awakened and our imagination stirred, but also by the Greek and Latin authors,

and by the whole glory that was Greece and grandeur that was Rome.

I can remember how deeply I was moved in these days by our reading of the *Apology* and the *Phaedo* in the Greek class. That indeed, must be a common enough experience. There must be thousands who can recall what it was like to come upon these pages with a virgin mind. But I, at least, coming to them from my particular background, could not read Plato and Carlyle and Matthew Arnold without being, even then, aware of a slowly emerging intellectual problem. Here was a new world of thought opened out to me, a very different world from the austere Highland Calvinism of my immediate surroundings. To others of a widely different tradition one of these three writers, the dour Scot frae Ecclefechan, may seem to echo a typical Calvinistic outlook, but it was of the difference—the difference that came to him so largely from the German and other romantics—and not of the resemblance that I was then aware. My difficulty was that through these new mentors I seemed to be becoming initiated into a certain region of truth and experience which could not easily be enclosed within the clearly defined frontiers of my traditional system.

And so—like many another lad from the North for many a century before me—to "the College of Edinburgh" with its many renowned teachers. There I studied many subjects, including English literature under Professor George Saintsbury, who has ever since seemed to me the soundest of all sound critics and the safest and surest guide to right reading. But during these college days all other interests were made secondary to my keenly awakened interest in what was virtually a new subject to me, namely, philosophy. I was much influenced by each of the four highly gifted thinkers who were then lecturing on philosophical subjects in Edinburgh. The training they gave us was, however, mainly in the history of thought and in the use of the tools of thinking, and sometimes almost scrupulous care was taken that we should be left free to form our own opinions.

I remember how once, in concluding the study of Kant's first *Kritik*, Professor Pringle-Pattison (then at the height of his influence) set very clearly before us the great alternative to which Kant's thinking finally led up—the alternative between the two very different lines of development followed by the Hegelians and by the neo-Kantians of the Marburg and other schools respectively—and then wound up his lecture and his course by saying, "At this point I leave you to your own reflections." At which one eager student (who was my great friend and who was killed in the war a few years later) so far forgot the dignities of the place and occasion as to cry out very audibly, "I've been at that point for two years!" At the time I sympathized with his impatience. The task of thought was an arduous one, and often I wished for more definite guidance. But how many times since then have I found myself deploring the narrow indoctrination into the principles and prejudices of a particular (and usually very one-sided) system which some American colleges offer to their students in the name of a philosophical training —to the virtual omission both of the study of logic (the theory of scientific method) and of a proper grounding in the history of thought in past ages.

But though in his lectures Pringle-Pattison was almost nervously careful to keep his personal views in the background, these were easily accessible to us in his published books, and my own mind was greatly affected by them. Certain other influences coming to me through my reading were, however, in those days even more powerful, and to some extent they were of a contrary tendency. Bradleianism was then a great power in British philosophy and, in particular, the name of Bernard Bosanquet was at the height of its prestige. One of the privileges of these years was the frequent opportunity they afforded us of meeting some of the distinguished thinkers who visited Edinburgh and joining in philosophical discussion with them. One of these was M. Bergson and another was Bosanquet. From the former I learned much but it was the latter who seemed to me the more reliable and careful thinker. And for a year or two I was inclined to follow his lead a little blindly, though not without much reliance also upon other writers too numerous to be mentioned here.

In this way it became inevitable that I should find myself faced with a religious problem. The problem was not, indeed, quite so acute as it would have been had I come directly from my earliest religious associations to this new philosophical atmosphere. Actually the transition was facilitated for me, not only by the wider humanistic leanings of my schooldays, but also by the prevalent temper of the church life of the northern metropolis. Robert Rainy and Marcus Dods were then well-known and venerable figures in its streets. Alexander Whyte and John Kelman (I must mention only those who are no longer with us) were at the height of their great powers. During several winters I was a keenly interested member of Dr. Whyte's famous Bible class (which in these years belied its name, since it was never about the Bible, but about the great figures of later religious history and the later classics of devotional literature). And who that ever saw or heard John Kelman can forget the fine manliness of his spirituality or the breeze of fresh air that he carried with him wherever he went?

Moreover, one was of an age to become deeply interested in the various arts, and to begin to entertain dreams of travel such as might give these interests greater opportunity of development. And one's exploration of general literature was as eager as ever, and

one's own scribblings as frequent.   Thus there was not
likely to be any entirely sharp cleft between one's general spiritual life and the philosophical conclusions that
were gradually taking shape in one's mind.   Yet a
serious enough spiritual problem did again and again
threaten to arise.   Not only did a system like Bosanquet's leave the least possible room for the development
of a vigorous and full religious outlook, but there were
many influences of an even more negative kind which
I was not always able to withstand.

This was in the first decade of the present century.
The bleak naturalistic outlook of the last quarter of the
previous century still had much power to persuade.   It
was far more difficult then than it is now to refute the
claims of materialism and mechanism.   The new developments in physics were only in their infancy and
their far-reaching significance was not yet grasped.   The
purely Darwinian (or rather ultra-Darwinian) reading
of biological evolution was the fashionable one to hold,
and its exponents had not begun to weaken even to the
extent of using the charmed word "emergent."

I remember that for long I could not decide how
much importance to attach to the book which now seems
more prophetic of the new era than any other that had
then appeared, James Ward's *Naturalism and Agnosticism*.   For as yet he must indeed have been a bold
man, and must have risked the sneers of all the emanci-
pated and knowing ones, who dared to speak a word
against the principle of universal causation or the in-
variability of natural laws or the conservation of energy
or the conservation of matter or the non-inheritance of
acquired characteristics or the point-for-point correspondence of mind with brain—we need not make the
list any longer.

So I descended into the valley of the shadow of the
negative.   Looking back upon it now, I can only rejoice that, if I had to pass through this valley at all, it

should have been given me to commence my journey through it at so early an age. I have since seen what seems to me far greater and more lasting harm wrought by the same experience coming to men at a later time of life.

Perhaps it was not so much by directly philosophical influences that I was ultimately guided toward a more positive outlook as by influences of a more theological kind leading to a deepening of religious insight itself. Of these I shall presently speak, but meanwhile let me note how I was more and more becoming convinced of the essential wisdom of my honored teacher (and later my very dear friend), Pringle-Pattison. These were the days of high (and now almost historic) debate between Pringle-Pattison and Bosanquet. I wonder if there are many who now doubt that the former, whether or not his own position be ultimately acceptable, at least carried off the honors of that controversy. The underlying principle of Pringle-Pattison's thought was clearly stated by him as early as 1883 in the essay contributed to the slim volume entitled *Essays in Philosophical Criticism* which he and R. B. (afterwards Viscount) Haldane conjointly edited in that year. His own essay was entitled "Philosophy as the Criticism of Categories," its contention being that our experience does not reveal itself to us all on one plane, but on a variety of planes, and that it is the business of a comprehensive philosophy to assign to each level of experience its true place and measure of importance, according to the degree of value and ultimacy which it finds it to possess.

The mechanistic categories of the inorganic world were thus accorded all proper recognition, but it was urged that when we pass from them to the categories of organic life we are passing to what is at once higher in the scale of value and deeper in metaphysical significance as being nearer to the heart of all being. It is

the same again when we pass from the categories of
life to the categories of conscious mind, and then again
to those of self-conscious intelligence. As organism is
more than mechanism, so is personality more than
organism. Such a line of thought plainly borrows much
from Hegel, but Pringle-Pattison's quarrel with Hegel
was, as is well known, that the latter never honestly
faced the implications of the fact that the most precious
of all our values are inseparably associated with personality.

The guiding thread of Pringle-Pattison's own system
was always "the principle of interpretation by the highest we know"—a phrase which appears in his book on
The Idea of God. It is not, he held, in our most elementary, but rather in our deepest and richest experiences that we have our best available clue to the nature
of the Absolute. The stream of evolution, he used to
say, is like other streams in that it cannot rise higher
than its source. Is is therefore the ripest fruits of the
evolutionary process rather than its germinal beginnings
that most truly reveal the nature of that from which
the process proceeds. The idea that the process was
itself ultimate, and that there was nothing behind it,
never seemed to him to make sense.

I remember sitting at luncheon with him in Edinburgh in 1928, three years before his death, and asking
him what he thought of Professor Alexander's *Space,
Time and Deity*.

"Well," he replied, "it is a very clever piece of
system-building."

"But perhaps," I suggested, "it is all on wrong lines.
Perhaps none of it is true."

"Of course it's not true," was his almost excited answer. *"It can't be true."*

"Exactly why," I asked, "do you say that it *can't* be
true?"

"Because," he replied, *it makes everything come out of nothing.*"

A little later, over our coffee, I spoke of the recent great popularity of Dr. A. N. Whitehead's contributions to philosophy. He said he had read only part of what Dr. Whitehead had written and asked me what I found in his books that was good. I said something to the effect that it was at least good to have it clearly recognized that the categories of organic life brought us nearer to the nature of reality than the categories of inorganic mechanism, these latter being highly abstract creations of the human mind. To which he replied, "But all that was in the little black book"—*i.e.*, in the symposium referred to above and published five-and-forty years before.

And then something was said between us about the impossibility of stopping short, as Dr. Whitehead seemed to do, at so half-way a conception as that of organism. The evolution of the categories (or the categories of evolution) seemed to proceed from those of physics through those of biology to those of ethics —from the machine through organism to personality. The view that reality was to be interpreted in terms of the simplest we know was at least plausible. The opposite view, that it was to be interpreted in terms of the highest was that which we both held. But what, we asked, could be said for the view that it was to be interpreted in terms of a conception like organism which was *half way up the scale?*

I still feel as sure as ever I did of the fundamental truth of these main outlines of Pringle-Pattison's philosophy. Of course, when so broadly stated, they cease to be the monopoly of any one teacher and many will feel that these same thoughts have come to them through entirely different channels. Indeed it was partly through other channels that they came to myself, at least in the form in which they are now established in my mind. Chief among such influences I should place the study of the two great philosophers of ancient and modern times respectively, Plato and Kant. These two seem to me to be the original sources of the outlook of which I have been speaking, and at these sources I have drunk deep and long.

I early became dissatisfied with the current English (and American) criticism of the Kantian ethic and in 1912 began a book on the subject, but the outbreak of war found it only half written and when, four years later, I had the opportunity to look again at what I had written, it was only to realize that it would never now be completed. A small part of it is, however, represented by "A Plea for a Reconsideration of the Kantian Ethic" which I printed in the *Hibbert Journal* in July, 1926.

As for Plato and Greek philosophy generally, we were excellently instructed at Edinburgh in this field, and yet it was only afterward, and more gradually, that I came fully to realize what matchless treasures of wise and disciplined thinking are at our disposal in the dialogues of Plato and the lectures of Aristotle and the scant surviving fragments of the other thinkers, both earlier and later. In later years I have found myself giving more and more of my time to the close study of this literature, and again and again I have offered a course of lectures on the development of theology in ancient Greece.

On my four years' life as an undergraduate in Edinburgh University there followed four years' theological training in New College, interlarded with summer semesters spent in Germany. During these years my philosophical interest was in no way abated. In Germany I attended the lectures of Rudolf Eucken, Hermann Cohen and Paul Natorp. Of the several other contemporary German philosophers whom I knew only through their writings I have no space to speak, though the course of my reflections was notably affected by them. Nor can I speak of the various problems which then occupied me, nor of my constant preoccupation with the principles of psychology, though it may be in place to refer to one article in which I have registered my opinions on the latter subject—"The Psychological Point of View," published in *The Philosophical Review* in May, 1930, and circulated also as an off-print.

I have already said, however, that in my progress toward a more secure mental outlook than I enjoyed in my undergraduate years these general philosophical adventures were less important than certain other influences of a more purely theological kind under which I now came and which seemed to show me that what was necessary for the solution of my problem was rather a deeper insight into religion itself than the successful construction of a lay system of metaphysics. A student of philosophy, who has been looking at religion only through gray-tinted metaphysical spectacles, and who then submits himself to four years of exacting and disciplined theological study, is bound to feel that whole new worlds of understanding are being opened out to him. And nowadays one is often painfully aware of the amateurishness of the references made to religion by certain philosophers whose competence in other fields commands one's deepest respect but who have plainly not devoted to the theological problem that long and hard labor of thought which, when conjoined to an intimate understanding of theological history, can alone lead to a wise and right-minded issue in this particular field.

One new world which was thus opened up to me was that of the historical study of the New Testament. During my first year as a student of theology a small group of us—most of whom were "philosophers"— made a habit of meeting together once a week for the

study of the Greek text of St. Mark. The following
year we received much stimulus from the lectures of
the very distinguished scholar who then occupied the
chair of New Testament in our college. And in the
summers I listened to the lectures of two equally distinguished New Testament scholars in Germany. I
have never since lost my interest in these studies. Sometimes for as long as a year or two I have found myself
neglecting them and seeking light in other ways, yet on
each occasion I have come back to them with something
of renewed eagerness; and most of what I have written
bears marks of the time thus spent.

More and more, indeed, as the years have gone by,
have I found myself being instructed by *history* rather
than by independent dialectical reflection. More and
more have I come to feel that, if I am to decide whether
such and such a belief be a true and wise one, my first
step must be clearly and deeply to understand its history—to know how it came into the world, from what
quarters it has encountered opposition and what have
been its fortunes in age-long debate. I do not claim
that I entirely understand why a knowledge of the history of an opinion should have this importance in
enabling one to judge of its worth. I have no pre-
conceived theory of the matter. I merely find it is the
case.

It will be seen, then, how differently I feel from a
distinguished philosophic friend who writes in his recently published *magnum opus* that "As a rule it will
be found that the historical introduction is very much
like the chaplain's prayer which opens a legislative ses-
sion: very little of the subsequent proceedings are decided by reference to it."[1] I should rather agree with
the reviewer in the London *Times* who pointed out that

---

[1] Morris R. Cohen, *Reason and Nature, An Essay on the Meaning
of Scientific Method,* p. 370.

this, "far from discrediting the historical method, proves only that the method is not used with sufficient thoroughness."

Yet the most important change of mind which came to me during these years in New College and in Germany was of another kind, and I think what it amounted to was the gradual realization that religion is in possession of an insight into reality which is all its own and cannot be reached at all without its aid. This is the change of mind, of course, which in European thought is represented in different ways by the two great names of Kant and Schleiermacher, and it was in close connection with my study of the Critical Philosophy and of *Der christliche Glaube* that it was accomplished in my own case.

For a general statement of its significance in contemporary theological thought I may refer to some carefully guarded words of Professor Clement Webb. "It was only gradually realized that . . . the existence of God, the object of religious experience and worship, could not be established by purely metaphysical considerations which took no account of specifically religious experience. . . . The significance of Kant's criticism is that it leads to the abandonment of the attempt to justify belief in the God of religion by other than religious arguments. God is known as such—so it comes to be held—only in religious experience"—so he writes in the course of an article entitled "Recent Thought on the Doctrine of God." [2] In the eighteenth century, he writes again in another publication, it was "very generally assumed that the reasonableness of acting upon a religious creed could be made evident to any man of competent intelligence quite apart from his possession of any specifically religious experience of his own." [3] In still a third place,

---

[2] *Expository Times*, Vol. XXXVII (1925-6), p. 360.
[3] *Religion and the Thought of Today* (1929), p. 36.

in the last words of his Gifford lectures, he warns us that "we must keep ourselves from rashly assuming that convictions we have reached by way of reflection upon the presuppositions of [religious] experience can be verified apart from it" and adds that "this is not to consent to such a divorce of theology from metaphysics as was recommended by Albrecht Ritschl, though it may serve to make his motive in recommending it intelligible to us." [4]

It was only at this time, then, that I left the eighteenth century behind me and availed myself of the newer insight of Kant, Schleiermacher and Ritschl. Yet I wonder if we need really go back as far as the eighteenth century in order to find the older view not only existing but flourishing like a green bay tree. Indeed in the earlier works of Professor Webb himself I can find no such clear recognition of the newer insight as appears in the passages I have quoted from his later writings. And with reference to Pringle-Pattison also my feeling is that only in his later years did he come fully to appreciate this aspect of the Ritschlian teaching (as of the teaching of Kant and Schleiermacher). But in fact can it be claimed even now that as many as half of our living teachers of philosophy in the English-speaking world have profited by the discovery of which I am speaking?

It seems to me that what multitudes of philosophers still believe about religion is somewhat as follows. They hold the study of metaphysics (some of them would even say the study of natural science) to be the only satisfactory and reliable avenue to truth about ultimate reality, and so to the knowledge of God. In the matter of religious belief none but the trained metaphysicians— a truly small band—can hope to stand on really solid ground. None but they can really *know* the truth about God and eternal life. Those who are

---

[4] *Personality and Human Life* (1920), pp. 268f.

not so trained may, and constantly do, attain to an "intuitive" grasp of the conclusions to which the metaphysicians are led by argumentation, and this intuitive anticipation of correct metaphysical results by quite unlearned people is what is meant by faith.

But if now it be asked, What is the use of metaphysics if the saints have already reaped its harvest in their own different way?—then it comes out clearly that the saint's faith is far inferior in certitude to the metaphysician's knowledge. The saint has an "intuition" (surely if ever word was overworked, this is the word!) that God exists, that He is omnipresent and omnipotent, that He hears prayer and forgives sin, and that "if our earthly house of this tabernacle were dissolved, we have a building of God, an house not made with hands, eternal in the heavens." But if this intuition is to be turned into an assured certitude such as will be secure against doubt, the saint has no alternative but to turn metaphysician. On this view, then, the function of metaphysics is to bring its own scientific criticism to bear upon faith's surmise and either expose its groundlessness or convert it into solidly grounded knowledge.

It will be realized at once that this doctrine can find much support in Plato, who taught that only a thorough training in philosophical kinetics and mathematical astronomy could lead to an assured conviction of the reality of God, and who believed faith to be definitely inferior to science in cognitive value (the successive divisions of his famous Divided Line in the *Republic*, going from lower to higher, being *eikasia* or guesswork, *pistis* or faith, *dianoia* or intelligence, and *episteme* or pure science [5]). It is here, as I understand it, that the Christian tradition has diverged from Plato; and it is here that I find myself parting company with his way

---

[5] *Republic,* 509-511 and 533-534.

of thought, which up to this point I am still so largely able to follow.

The Christian thinkers also have their Divided Line, but it is a line in which the relative positions of faith and scientific knowledge have been reversed. For St. Paul as for St. Thomas Aquinas faith is a higher exercise of the mind than reasoning and one that leads to greater certitude. For St. Paul as for St. Thomas faith stands for no mere preliminary glimpsing of results which scientific investigation can alone put securely in our grasp but for an *independent and even more reliable* source of insight into the nature of things. Unfortunately this very unplatonic claim that was made for faith was often embodied in a somewhat crudely conceived doctrine of revelation, the unacceptableness of which led after the Renaissance to the severe reaction which we now designate as rationalism.

A typical representative of this reaction is Spinoza who deliberately revises St. Thomas's doctrine of the three kinds of cognition (reason, faith, vision) by reverting to the Platonic order and putting faith lower than reason. Another representative is Hegel whose doctrine of the *Vorstellung* of faith as being inferior to the *Begriff* of metaphysics has been widely influential beyond the bounds of his own school. The recent change of mind which is described in the passages quoted from Professor Webb is in essence a return to the Christian position from which rationalism revolted, though its endeavor is to restate this position in terms that need give rise to no further difficulty.

I have already said that it was in great part through the reading of Kant's and Schleiermacher's own writings that this change of mind accomplished itself in my own case. Yet my reading was not carried out without the very valuable guidance of certain friends and teachers, both in Scotland and in Germany. Among these chief place must be given to Wilhelm Herrmann. When I went to Marburg in the spring of 1911 my mind was indeed already more hospitable toward some aspects of his teaching than it would have been a couple of years earlier. My confidence in the wisdom of the prevailing philosophic attitude to religion—as represented, say, by Bosanquet—was already seriously shaken. But as I listened to Herrmann and read his *Ethik* I was more and more led to agree that religion cannot really be important (and may profitably be replaced by philosophy in the lives of all who are competent to philosophize) unless it can offer us an insight into the nature of the unseen world which is quite specific in character, which can be obtained in no other way than by the practice of religion itself, and which is far superior in point of certainty to any of the conflicting theories defended by the various philosophic schools.

The axioms which were henceforth to serve as the presuppositions of my theological thinking may perhaps be set out in serial form as follows:

(i) That the truths for which religion stands are of such a kind as to be as accessible and as evident to those quite untrained in science and philosophy as to those who can boast the fullest scientific and philosophical training;

(ii) That, however, these truths can be brought home to us only through the discipline of religious experience itself and can consequently never be evident to anybody save in such measure as he is visited by such experience;

(iii) That the only means by which our hold on these truths can be made more secure is, not the pursuit of any independent scientific inquiry in which they can be buttressed from without, but the progressive deepening of religious insight itself;

(iv) That accordingly the only competent *criticism*

of religious convictions is one carried out, not in the light of knowledge obtained by some non-religious means, but in the light of advancing religion itself— leading to the discovery that the convictions in question are not as *religious* as they ought to be;

(v) That accordingly religious certitude, far from being a product of scientific metaphysics, or being in any way more fully enjoyed by scientific metaphysicians than by other folk, must be, for any scientific metaphysician who possesses it, the main (though certainly not the only) fact on which his metaphysical system will itself be built;

(vi) That while religious faith may communicate something of its own certitude to a metaphysical system in the formation of which it has been allowed to play its proper part, yet no such system can ever hope to possess the same degree or kind of certitude as attaches to the fundamental religious insights themselves;

(vii) That, as regards natural science, the most we have a right to expect of it is that, as Kant said, it should "leave room for faith," not that it should in any way provide a positive foundation for faith.

It will be realized at once that these are not really seven independent axioms but are all deducible from a single principle—the principle, already stated, that religious faith is not a dim fore-grasping of a reality which other and exacter processes of thought and research will afterward more clearly reveal and more securely establish, but a way of knowledge which is at least equal to any other in point of reliability and which leads us into the presence of a Reality that is not discoverable by any other means. It was this principle, and little else, that I took from the Schleiermacher-Ritschl tradition in which Herrmann stood—though I shall have to speak in a moment of another principle that I borrowed from the Kant-Ritschl tradition in which he stood equally.

I never had any sympathy with the subjectivist trend in Schleiermacher's thought, nor with his equation of religion with feeling, nor with his psychological doctrine of the primordial character of feeling as over against thought—doctrines to which William James and the American "psychology of religion" have given a new lease of life. Nor did I ever have much sympathy with the other aspects of Ritschlianism—its bitter anti-Catholic polemic, its narrow Lutheran Christocentrism, its inhospitable attitude toward whatever religious insight stands outside of the Christian tradition, its Marcionite tendency in regard to the Old Testament, its extreme opposition to mysticism, its disqualification of the Greek contribution to Christianity as embodied in the Catholic dogmatic and ecclesiastical system. Except in regard to the one great un-Greek insight described in my quotations from Professor Webb, I still remain a Christian Platonist.

At this point I may interject the remark that the so-called Theology of Crisis seems to me, as regards *one* side of its teaching, to have grown out of precisely those aspects of Ritschlianism which I found myself from the first rejecting; and this in spite of the fact that the Ritschlian system is in other respects the object of its direct and very bitter attack. Professor Barth listened to Herrmann's lectures at Marburg very nearly at the same time as I was listening to them, but we must have been attracted and repelled by very different sides of our teacher's thought.

A sentence from Von Hügel's posthumous volume will express more adequately than any words of mine the position which I feel obliged to defend both against Ritschl and against Professor Barth: "It has been, I take it, one of the greatest blessings vouchsafed to the Christian religion that it should have sprung historically from another historical religion, that it should be constrained by its very origins both deeply to respect and to admire another religion, and yet to consider itself, at its best, as bringing further light and help to the deepest places of the soul." [6] Or again I would subscribe to the words of Justin Martyr in his *Apology* that "whatever things have been rightly said by anyone belong to us Christians." But there is *another* side of the Barthian teaching which I can do nothing but warmly welcome and to which I feel myself, as time goes on, increasingly indebted. Its protests against our overweening humanism, our cheap evolutionism, our smug immanentism and our childish utopianism have been most challenging; and in what it has to say about our human insignificance as over against God and about our utter dependence on Him for our salvation it is difficult to do anything but rejoice.

In debate with my theological friends in this country I have, more often than otherwise, found myself defending the Barthian positions against the very opposite principles which are professed by perhaps a majority of them. Yet even here I am unwilling to follow Professor Barth all the way. There are indeed many things which he might have been the first to teach me, and in which I might be ready to follow him more unsuspectingly, had I not learned them first from Von Hügel—and learned at the same time to beware against understanding them in too one-sided a fashion.

Barth and Von Hügel have very much the same medicine to administer to our erring modernism, but only Von Hügel is careful to provide also a suitable antidote against an overdose. "Eternal Life," he writes, for example, ". . . will be found to include and to require a deep sense of human Weakness and of man's constant need of Divine Prevenience, and again of the reality of sin and of our various inclinations to it; but also to exclude all conceptions of the

---

[6] *The Reality of God*, p. 146.

total corruption of human nature, of the essential impurity of the human body, or of the utter debilitation of the human will. The Pauline, Augustinian, Lutheran, Calvinist, Jansenist trend, impressive though it is, will have to be explained, in part, as a good and necessary (or at least as an excusable, temporary) corrective of some contrary excess; and, for the rest, it will have to suffer incorporation within a larger whole, which, in appearance more commonplace, is yet in reality indefinitely richer—the doctrine and practice of Jesus Christ Himself. 'In my flesh abideth no good thing' will have somehow to be integrated within 'the spirit indeed is willing, but the flesh is weak.' " [7]

The other principle which Herrmann was largely instrumental in establishing in my mind was, as has been said, one which connected him (and his fellow-Ritschlians) rather with Kant than with Schleiermacher —I mean the rediscovery of the organic nature of the relation between faith and morals, between our religious belief and our consciousness of obligation. Yet here again the position to which I was ultimately led was one which my teacher would be very far from owning. Herrmann seemed to me to be admirably right in regarding an intimate acquaintance with the realities and difficulties and despairs of the moral life as the *Weg zur Religion*—the one indispensable preliminary to the attainment of religious insight; but I could not follow him in his insistence that such acquaintance was a *mere* preliminary or that religion, when it came, came as something *altogether* different and new.

My difficulty with such a view lay, and still lies, in my firm persuasion that in our moral experience we are *already* in real (though it may be unrecognized) touch with that Divine Reality of which religion discourses. The law may be only a "tutor," but its word is none

---
[7] *Eternal Life* (1912), pp. 391 f.

the less the word of revelation. In all our apprehensions of value we are, I believe, being apprehended of God. To feel, in however faint a way, the attraction of a higher ideal than that which has hitherto been realized in our actions is, I believe, to experience a direct visitation of the Holy Spirit, even though it may not always be acknowledged as such by him who receives it. Our sense of sin is itself the Spirit's work. As I have ventured to put it elsewhere, "In the experience of moral obligation there is contained and given the knowledge, not only of a Beyond, but of a Beyond that is in some sort actively striving to make itself known to us and to claim us for its own." [8]

I should therefore hold that the consciousness of value is itself a religious and—to use a word of which I am in no wise afraid—supernatural experience; that the central moral experience cannot in the end be correctly described without the introduction of some transcendent reality (as distinct both from non-transcendent realities and from transcendent idealities); and that accordingly no such thing as a "mere morality" can really exist. Yet almost all men will admit to having been visited by the moral experience; and so it has seemed to me that here we have the strategic point from which to undertake the interpretation and defense of religion in the contemporary world. It seems natural to begin from something which is not called in question and which may be taken as common ground. This is what, in much of my teaching and writing, I have tried to do.

The years—not much less than four—which I spent in France during the war were fallow years for me, as for so many others. I hardly read a page either of divinity or of metaphysic, and I had little time or opportunity for consecutive thinking. Yet the period brought with it a very great broadening of experience

[8] *Interpretation of Religion*, p. 462.

and, above all, such an understanding of the mind and temper, the spiritual needs and capacities, of average (perhaps I should rather say of *normal*) humanity as I at least had not before possessed. "He was only used to Cambridge," writes E. M. Forster about one of the characters in his fine novel, *The Longest Journey*—and, *mutatis mutandis*, I might apply the words to myself, "and to a very small corner of that. . . . That was what annoyed him as he rode down the new valley with two chattering companions. He was more skilled than they were in the principles of human existence, but he was not so indecently familiar with the examples." When I turned again to my old pursuits after the war was over, the khaki figures still seemed to keep their place in the background of my mind, and in much of what I have written since these days a clairvoyant reader may find them haunting the margins of the page.

But the years that have gone by since 1919 are still too near at hand to be seen in any true historical perspective. They have been so full of diversified study, and so rich in interchange of thought and opinion, that an adequate account of the formative and qualifying influences they have brought to bear upon me would, if attempted at all, have to be long and detailed. If I were to single out one contemporary writer rather than another whose books have really determined the direction which my thinking has taken, it would have to be Von Hügel. But old books have been as much in my hands as new ones and have counted for at least as much in respect of intellectual guidance and stimulation.

It remains only to add that no more during these later years than during the earlier ones has the philosophic quest, taken narrowly by itself, appeared able to afford me complete mental satisfaction. My interest in poetry, in the general literature of the few countries whose languages I could command, in history, in various forms of art, as well as in nature itself, has not lessened but rather increased as the years have gone by. Yet not one of these varied pursuits has ever been followed as a *mere* pastime. They have all, in some way, been parts of a single pilgrimage. In all of them I have, however mistakenly, seemed to myself to be seeking the One True Light, and I think that my interest in any one of them would have collapsed very suddenly if I had come to feel that it could in no way advance my central quest.

I remember with what delight I welcomed Professor Gilbert Murray's essay on *Literature as Revelation* on its first appearance, because it seemed to express with admirable felicity something I had long been trying to say to myself. A few sentences from it will form a fitting conclusion to these somewhat desultory pages. "There are among lovers of literature . . . some who like it for all sorts of other reasons, and some who demand of it nothing less than a kind of revelation. Most people of culture, I believe, belong to the first class. They like literature because they like to be amused, or because the technique of expression interests them. . . . And the other class—to which I certainly belonged all through my youth and perhaps on the whole still belong—does not really like the process of reading, but reads because it wants to get somewhere, to discover something, to find a light which will somehow illumine for them either some question of the moment or the great riddles of existence. I believe this is the spirit in which most people in their youth read books; and, considering their disappointments, it is remarkable, and perhaps not altogether discreditable, how often they cling to this hope far on into the region of gray hairs or worse than gray hairs." [9]

In writing what I have here written I have not regarded myself, and I hope the indulgent reader will

[9] *Essays and Addresses*, pp. 126 f.

not regard me, as making an essay in intellectual autobiography, which is perhaps the most difficult of all
literary kinds and has been essayed successfully by
hardly more than half a dozen people—by St. Augustine, Descartes, Rousseau, Newman, by Wordsworth
in the *Prelude,* and *perhaps* by Goethe.   No, I have
not written an autobiography: I have been "inter-
viewed"—that's all.

PRINCIPAL PUBLICATIONS

Books:

> *The Roots of Religion in the Human Soul.*   New York,
> George H. Doran, 1926.
> *The Interpretation of Religion.*   An Introductory Study
> of Theological Principles.   New York, Scribner's 1928.
> *The Place of Jesus Christ in Modern Christianity.*   New
> York, Scribner's, 1929.

Articles:

> "Belief as an Element in Religion," in the London *Exposi-
> tor,* January, 1915, pp. 75-92.
> "The Present Situation in Theology," in *Auburn Seminary
> Record,* November, 1920, pp. 209-229.
> "The Fundamental Task of the Theological Seminary," in
> *The Reformed Church Review,* July, 1922, pp. 259-275.
> "The True Ground of Theistic Belief," in *The Hibbert
> Journal,* October, 1922, pp. 44-52.
> "The Idea of Orthodoxy," in *The Hibbert Journal,* Janu-
> ary, 1926, pp. 232-249.
> "The Meaning of Duty: A Plea for a Reconsideration of
> the Kantian Ethic," in *The Hibbert Journal,* July, 1926,
> pp. 718-730.
> " 'Happiness' Once More," in *The Hibbert Journal,* Octo-
> ber, 1927, pp. 69-83.
> "The Mind of Christ on the Treatment of Crime," in *The
> Expository Times,* March, 1930, pp. 261-265.
> "The Psychological Point of View," in *The Philosophical
> Review,* May, 1930, pp. 258-274.

"The Fellowship of the Redemptive Quest," in *The Healing of the Nation:* A Symposium, edited by J. W. Stevenson. Edinburgh, T. & T. Clark, 1930, pp. 118-126.

"The Logic of Religion," in *Alumni Bulletin of Union Theological Seminary*, October, 1930, pp. 6-16.

"The Predicament of Humanism," in *The Canadian Journal of Religious Thought*, March, 1931, pp. 109-118.

SEEKING BELIEFS THAT MATTER

By WILLIAM ADAMS BROWN

(b. December 29, 1865, New York, N. Y.)

Research Professor of Applied Theology in Union Theological
Seminary

New York, N. Y.

SEEKING BELIEFS THAT MATTER

By William Adams Brown

(A part of the article which follows appeared in Volume I of *Religionswissenschaft der Gegenwart in Selbstdarstellungen,* a series of autobiographical studies of theologians, mostly, but not exclusively, German, which was edited by Erich Stange and published by Felix Meiner. I am indebted both to editor and to publisher for permission to use the material in this new context. I appreciate this permission the more as it enables me to direct the attention of the American public to what was not only the first collection of the kind to appear but one which contains material of great value to the student of contemporary theology.)

I. A WORD OF ORIENTATION

No one who undertakes to write the story of his intellectual life should delude himself into supposing that he is telling what that life has really been. The truth is rather that he is revealing to others, if not to himself, what he wishes it might have been. Inevitably as we look back over the past our dreams tend to take form and substance and we see ourselves and others not as we really were but as we might have been, had the conditions we faced then been such as we face now.

Nevertheless the enterprise has its fascination. For in trying to recall the past we come to understand the present better. We distinguish more accurately than we otherwise could which of the interests which engage our present attention really matter to us; to which of them we could bid goodbye without regret; which of them we wish we might carry with us into an indefinite, it may be, indeed, even into an unending, future.

It is in this spirit that I undertake the present retrospect. I have been asked in a few brief pages to tell the story of my intellectual life. I am not so vain as to believe that there is anything in the life story of a theological professor who for more than forty years has been engaged in the technical work of what many regard as the most unpractical of studies to interest men and women who have lived through the drama of the World War and the scarcely less dramatic events of the period of disillusionment which has followed it. This only is my justification for writing, that I, too, have lived through these momentous experiences; and it may not be without interest to some of my younger contemporaries to learn how they have affected one who came to them from a somewhat different background and had to effect a somewhat different reconstruction from their own.

Every man lives in two environments—an outward environment of space and time determined by his birth, home, nationality, race, profession, and religion, and by the major events which have transpired during his life; and an inward environment made up of the currents of thought and sentiment which play upon him consciously or unconsciously and furnish him with the thought forms through which his own ideals and aspirations are expressed. Inextricably interwoven in fact, they may yet be described separately.

And as every man's life is affected by the interplay of these two factors, so its quality is determined by two recurrent emphases, varying in intensity from period to period, sometimes even from hour to hour. From one point of view his inner life may be described as a quest, in which, as his experience enlarges and his insight becomes clarified, he perceives ever more clearly the problems by which he is encompassed and formulates the questions which life puts to him. From another point of view his life is a discovery, or rather a series of discoveries, as he reaches what is for him, at any rate for the moment, a satisfying answer to his questions. Men differ both in the number of the questions they ask and in the number to which they find answers. But there are few who find that the answers that first seemed to them adequate remain wholly satisfying and few who, if they are wise, do not recognize that the convictions to which they have come, however trustworthy as far as they go, are but partial and must be still further clarified and corrected by the insights and experiences of the future.

Such at least has been the experience of the present writer. In his search for beliefs that matter he has been fortunate enough to win a group of convictions which have maintained their validity for him in a world of change. But there is not one of them which he holds in just the sense in which it first came to him. And there is not one which he does not anticipate will be further modified and corrected by the experience which lies ahead.

To tell the story of the genesis and growth of these convictions is the purpose of the following pages. Like all theology that is true to its high mission, they are a report of progress to date.

II. STAGES IN THE SEARCH FOR A SATISFYING FAITH

As I look back over the more than sixty years that measure the span of my conscious life, four factors detach themselves as having had formative influence upon my intellectual development:

First, the religious environment in which I grew up in home and church—a home where the graces of religion were illustrated in lives of simple piety, and unflinching loyalty to duty bore its appropriate fruits in love, and peace, and joy; a church in which the great beliefs of religion were presented in forms that were intellectually satisfying and worship was privilege as well as duty.

Secondly, my first contacts with critical scholarship in college, seminary, and university, contacts which not only introduced me to the whole group of problems which are involved in the relation of religion to science but compelled me to face the personal question whether I could honestly continue in the ministry of a denomination whose practice, if not whose formal standards, seemed at more than one crucial point to contradict what I believed to be true.

Thirdly, the transfer of the argument from the academic field to that of applied religion, as I shared with others of my generation the thrill that came with the discovery of the social gospel and played my modest part in some of the early attempts that were made to translate that discovery into appropriate action.

Finally, the readjustment which began with the postwar period as we realized more deeply with each passing year the radical contradiction between the principles of the religion we professed to hold and the dominant spirit of our economic, industrial, and political life and were faced with the necessity of radical reform, not only in our conception of the task of the church, but in our ways of educating people to its service. These four determining factors may serve as signposts in the journey my story follows.

III.   FINDING A GOD TO TRUST

Unlike many of my contemporaries whose alienation from conventional religion may be traced in part to a reaction against the unlovely and incredible forms with which they were confronted in their childhood, my associations with religion both in home and in church were natural and uplifting.   What Norman Thomas has recently written of his own religious ancestry (in his essay "Puritan Fathers," *Atlantic Monthly* for November, 1931) could be transferred with slight variation to my own. On both my father's and my mother's side I came of religious stock and grew up in a home in which piety was taken for granted and the life of religion exemplified in characters of unusual simplicity and beauty. My parents were praying people and they believed that God answered prayer as directly as any earthly father answered his child.

As a boy I accompanied my mother to Northfield, the home of Dwight L. Moody, the noted evangelist of the day, and was deeply impressed by his vivid consciousness of God. I still remember the thrill which I felt when, fresh from this contact, I interpreted a sudden impulse to speak to a stranger about his soul as a direct evidence of the guidance of the Spirit. Later I used to go weekly to a rescue mission and have seen many a conversion of the old dramatic type. With such a background it was natural for me to turn to the ministry. I do not remember having seriously contemplated any other career.

To these early contacts I owe two convictions which have never left me during my later life: First, the conviction that religion is man's response in conscious acts of worship and service to a reality with which he is in first-hand contact, even during the times when he is unaware of that contact. Secondly, that the one satisfying proof of the existence of this reality and the fact of this contact is the transformation which it makes possible in the lives which it affects. Many and radical have been the changes that have taken place in my thought of God and in my understanding of the processes by which His presence is mediated. That religion is concerned with a real God and with real relationships, I have never doubted.

Yet though this conviction has never left me, its vividness has varied at different periods. My early reaction from the excessive emotionalism of the North-field type has made me distrustful of a religion which bases itself upon immediate feeling and is unwilling to submit to the tests of reason and controlled experiment. Yet later study and, still more, the acquaintance with persons of exceptional religious gifts have convinced me that at the core of all vital religion there is a mystical element and have made me sympathetic with forms of religion other than my own.

Painful experience of the aridness of a religion which is merely academic and critical has made me realize the importance of practical discipline for the training of the devotional life. I have found that even late in life it is possible by the practice of prayer to discover riches in the life of worship of which in earlier years I had made too little use. The desire to share this discovery with others is responsible for a group of books which, while the natural outgrowth and expression of convictions formed many years earlier, have been addressed to a different audience and were written in a different spirit.

IV. COMING TO TERMS WITH SCIENCE

But it is one thing to be convinced that religion brings men into touch with unseen reality, quite another to define to oneself the nature of that reality and to determine its relation to the more familiar realities which the senses make known and the different sciences study. The history of theology during the last four generations is the story of the progressive stages in the adjustment of religious faith to the new world made familiar to us by modern science, and my own work as a teacher of theology has made it necessary for me not only to follow this readjustment in its larger outline but to take an active part in it so far as it affected the group of individuals with whom I was brought into personal contact. For this I had exceptional advantages in the character of my education.

After three years at St. Paul's School, in Concord, New Hampshire, where I had a good grounding in classics, I entered Yale in the Class of '86, returning for a year of graduate study for the Master's degree. My subject of special study was economics; the teacher who influenced me most Professor William Graham Sumner, at that time the leader of the free trade school among American economists and the author of a work, *What Social Classes Owe One Another*, in which the position was defended that they owe one another nothing at all. My thesis, on *State Control of Industry in the Fourth Century*,[1] was based on first-hand study of the economic material contained in the Theodosian and Justinian codes and gave me my first introduction to a type of historical study which has ever since engaged my interest.

After leaving Yale I entered the Union Theological Seminary, where I studied under Dr. William G. T. Shedd, Dr. Philip Schaff, Dr. Charles Augustus Briggs, and Dr. Francis Brown. In Dr. Shedd I met an old-type Calvinist, a man who believed that we were all literally in Adam so that we were personally guilty of Adam's sin, and who held further that the Trinity was necessary in order to personalize the otherwise impersonal substance of God. In Drs. Schaff, Briggs, and Brown the critical spirit was active. From them I learned the newer views of the Bible and became familiar with the methods of historical criticism as they had long been practiced by German theologians.

Union Theological Seminary, an institution founded and controlled by new school Presbyterians, had from its foundation been the home of a liberal and comprehensive theology. During my student days it was en-

---

[1] *Political Science Quarterly,* September, 1887.

gaged in a theological controversy with the General
Assembly of the Northern Presbyterian Church, which
culminated in the trial and condemnation of Dr. Briggs
on an issue which involved the right of a Presbyterian
minister to apply the methods of literary and historical
criticism to the interpretation of the Bible. The result
of this trial was the withdrawal of the Seminary from
its official association with the Presbyterian Church, a
withdrawal which opened the way to its present position as an independent school of interdenominational
and international character.

While in the Seminary I resumed my study of
philosophy—which had been interrupted by the economic studies of my graduate year—specializing in
Kant, whose *Critique of Pure Reason* I read in a seminar conducted by Professor (afterward President)
Nicholas Murray Butler at Columbia University. My
philosophical interest was further stimulated by my
election some years later to the Philosophical Club, a
group of a dozen or more philosophers of different uni-
versities who meet monthly for the discussion of a paper
by one of their number. In this Club I had the benefit
of the criticism of such men as Dewey, Kemp-Smith,
Felix Adler, and others of equal eminence.

An essay on John Staupitz, written in competition for
the Hitchcock Prize in Church History, led me to study
the sources of Reformation history and still further
stimulated the historic interest which my graduate
studies at Yale had begun. This interest was accen-
tuated during the next two years which I spent as Fel-
low of the Seminary in graduate study at the University
of Berlin where, as a member of Harnack's seminar, I
came under the spell of that remarkable teacher and
made the study of church history, especially in its
earlier period, my specialty. A study of the Paulinism
of the Epistle of Barnabas, undertaken in Harnack's
seminar, first brought clearly to my mind the problem

of the distinctive character of the Christian religion, a problem which has remained central in my thinking ever since.

Returning to the United States in 1892, I joined the staff of Union Theological Seminary as Assistant to Dr. Schaff in Church History, and the year following, after Dr. Schaff's death, was transferred to the Department of Systematic Theology, which had been left without a teacher by the death of Dr. Worcester, the incumbent of the chair. Advanced to Provisional Professor in 1897, I became Roosevelt Professor in 1898, a position which I held until 1930, when I resigned to become Research Professor in the Field of Applied Christianity.

With my acceptance of a teaching position in the Seminary my formal education was theoretically over; but it has been my experience, like that of many other teachers, that the things I have found most useful in preparing me for my work were learned long after my classroom studies were over. Of some of these brief mention may be made to make the outward record complete.

Early in my career as a teacher I accepted the chairmanship of the Home Missions Committee of the Presbytery of New York. This Committee was charged with maintaining Christian work among the foreign-speaking peoples of New York City. During the early years of the Committee's existence the work was of a very modest character, consisting of one or two small missions for Italians carried on in rented stores after the usual evangelical fashion. My work with the Committee led me to make a thorough study of the conditions which obtain among the foreign-speaking population of our great cities, a study which my election in 1910 to the Board of Home Missions of the Presbyterian Church enabled me to extend to a national scale.

These contacts gave me a first-hand knowledge of the obstacles created for the work of the Church by an unchristian social environment and made it possible for me to study from the inside the efforts that were being made by the Protestant churches to include in their home missionary program forms of social service which had been hitherto confined to undenominational enterprises such as the settlements or the Christian associations. Incidentally I gained an understanding both of the possibilities and of the difficulties of institutional life which proved a valuable aid in understanding the facts of past history with which my work as a teacher obliged me to concern myself.

This understanding was further enlarged by my experience in interdenominational work, first as Chairman of the City Missions Council, an organization which brought together for stated conferences on their common problems the official representatives of the various organizations engaged in missionary work in New York City; later as Secretary of the General War-Time Commission of the Churches, the agency through which the Protestant churches of the United States functioned in the war. In my book, *The Church in America,* I have given some account of the origin and work of this Commission. Here it is sufficient to say that the experience was illuminating in two ways: first, as showing the extent to which the spirit of cooperation was present among American Christians when the occasion for it arose; secondly, as showing the practical obstacles put in the way of that cooperation by the present divided condition of Christendom.

In 1917 I was elected one of the Permanent Fellows (Trustees) of Yale University. This election, coming at a time when the University was passing through a serious crisis, not only made it possible for me to study the administration of a large modern university from the inside, but also gave me the opportunity to share in the discussion of the educational policies which were adopted. As Acting Provost during 1919-1920, and until 1931 as Chairman of the Committee on Educational Policy, I have been obliged to consider the relation of the special problems with which I have been concerned as a teacher of religion to the larger questions of educational method which affect all departments alike.

During the forty-one years of my life as a teacher I have had repeated opportunities to visit other countries and to profit by conference with men of other nations and races. The year 1903-1904 was spent largely in Germany and included a short trip to Constantinople and Palestine. In 1916 I attended the Congress on Christian Work in Latin America in Panama, and from there went to the Far East where, as Union Seminary lecturer, I visited China, Japan, and Korea, delivering lectures which were afterward published under the title, *Is Christianity Practicable?* A pamphlet privately printed, entitled *Modern Missions in the Far East,* summed up the impressions gained in my study in the mission field. Fourteen years later, as a member of the Lindsay Commission on Christian Higher Education, it was my privilege to spend five months in India in an intimate study of the Christian colleges of that country, a study which has been published by the Oxford University Press under the title, *The Christian College in India.*

The year 1922-1923 was spent partly in England and partly in Italy and France. During the year I lectured repeatedly, both in England and France. The Drew Lecture, delivered in the fall of 1922, was published under the title, *The Creative Experience;* and the Upton Lectures, also delivered in 1922, were published under the title, *Imperialistic Religion and the Religion of Democracy.* In 1925 I was a member of the Stockholm Conference on Life and Work and

Chairman of its Commission on Christian Education. In 1927 I was a member of the Lausanne Conference on Faith and Order and Chairman of its Commission on the Church.

In the spring of 1925, during the absence of President McGiffert, on furlough, I served as Acting President of the Union Theological Seminary.

In addition to the duties mentioned above, I have served on a number of other committees which have given me contacts which have proved of use in my professional work. I was one of the founders, and for many years a member, of the Board of Directors of the Union Settlement, one of the pioneer settlements of New York; a member of Good Government Club A and an active worker in the political campaign which resulted in the defeat of Tammany Hall in 1904; a member and for two years Chairman of the Committee of Fourteen, a committee organized for the suppression of commercialized vice. I was Chairman of the Committee on the War and the Religious Outlook, an interdenominational committee formed after the war to study the duty and responsibility of the Church in meeting post-war conditions. More recently I have become Chairman of the Department of Research and Education of the Federal Council of the Churches of Christ in America. I have also served for three years as President of the Religious Education Association. I have been a trustee and am at present President of the Board of Trustees of the Women's College of Istanbul (Constantinople).

These contacts and others of like kind have kept constantly before my mind the practical bearing of the theories I have been discussing in the classroom and helped to guard me against the scholar's temptation to identify his own specialty with the whole of life.

When in 1893, a young man of twenty-seven, without previous technical preparation, I was unexpectedly transferred from the field of church history to that of systematic theology, I was simultaneously confronted with two independent but closely related problems. One was the necessity of vindicating for my chosen department its right to a continued place among the disciplines of theology. The other was the demonstration that a scientific theology worthy of the name was possible within the limits allowed to thought in the Christian communion of which I was a member.

To begin with the first. Systematic theology, always the storm center of theological controversy, was at the time I was called to teach it facing a serious crisis. Its claim to independent scientific standing was simultaneously threatened from two different quarters. On the side of subject-matter its territory was being invaded by the more recent disciplines of Biblical theology and the history of dogma, in whose name during the last generation a series of brilliant scholars had been rewriting the history of Christian belief.

From the point of view of method, its procedure was challenged by the science of comparative religion, whose representatives saw no reason to grant the Christian theologian a privileged position denied to the Buddhist or the Mohammedan. It was presently to meet the competition of an even more popular rival, the psychology of religion, that new and fascinating study which professes to have discovered the clue to the origin of our most cherished beliefs in suppressed complexes of our emotional nature. Under the circumstances it was a fair question whether there remained for systematic theology any other place than that which Schleiermacher had assigned it two generations ago, as that branch of historical theology which expounds in constructive and sympathetic fashion the present beliefs of Christians.

It may seem indeed as if the issues thus raised were

purely technical and might have been left to be settled by those who were immediately concerned. But, as is often the case with academic questions, what was really at stake was something of much greater moment. It was the question whether the claim of Christians to possess a revelation of unique, and indeed of universal, significance could still be maintained or whether Christianity must be content to take its place, as Gandhi would have it, as one of the sisterhood of religions, each with an equal claim to mankind's interest and loyalty.

For such a view, even if I had myself found it satisfactory, the churches of the United States were not yet ready. To the great majority of American Christians, systematic theology was still what it had been throughout its history, the science of revealed truth, handing down from generation to generation the doctrines which it was necessary to believe for salvation in the form in which they had been recorded in the Bible and preserved in the classical literature of Protestantism.

Calvinist and Arminian might fight their battles about predestination and freewill, Episcopalians and Presbyterians dispute over the nature of the church; but these were family quarrels which did not affect the view of theology which all alike shared. They did not affect the central conviction that in the Bible we possess a revelation of truth differing in kind from any made accessible by natural reason and that that truth was preserved with substantial accuracy in the historic creeds. The most that could be conceded to the systematic theologian in his effort to come to terms with science was that he should reduce the area in which the supernatural was to be found, thus leaving an increasing territory open to the explorations of science.

Even in my own seminary, throughout its history exceptionally hospitable to new truth, the traditional

view of systematic theology was still dominant. Henry
B. Smith, a man of genuine philosophical insight, might
have done much to prepare the way for a view more
consistent with the method followed in other departments. But the promise of his inaugural was not fulfilled by his later writing, and his theology, in spite of
occasional flashes of insight, in the main followed the
older lines. Dr. Shedd, my predecessor in the Chair,
represented the most extreme form of scholastic
Calvinism. Under the circumstances it was natural for
students who had accepted the historical method to
conclude that systematic theology had had its day and
to turn to other disciplines for their intellectual and
religious stimulus. It was clear that if I was to maintain my position I must be able to show not only that
the teaching of systematic theology was *consistent* with
the results reached in the other disciplines but that it
had a field of its own from which no other study could
dislodge it.

Such a field, it seemed to me, was given by the very
nature of the Christian religion. In that religion God
reveals His presence to man in definite and recogniz-
able ways, and man responds to that revelation in worship and service. It is the function of the systematic
theologian, as I conceived his task, to formulate those
common convictions about God, as far as revealed,
which constitute the Christian gospel. He is not concerned with all Christian beliefs, even all true beliefs,
but only with essential beliefs, beliefs that matter. And
it is his task to set them forth in their simplicity and
purity, freed as far as possible from everything that is
transient and unimportant. So far I found myself at
one with my older colleagues, to whom Christianity
was before all things a revealed religion.

But in my conception of the way we gain our knowledge of this revelation, I found myself obliged to part
company with them. The theologian, though con-

cerned with divine realities, is still but man and must be content to use the tools that are open to him as man. In revealing himself to his human children God has not lifted them above the limitations of their humanity, though He has given them new materials with which thought can operate.

Scientific method, therefore, in all its rigor, is as open to the theologian as to the student in any other field and as necessary. There is no point at which he can use revelation as an excuse for dispensing with its use. To quote a sentence of my own, used in another connection: "In contrast to all attempts to secure the independence of theology by an artificial delimitation of territory, it is to be maintained that the real guarantee of its freedom is to be found in the distinctive character and inherent worth of its subject-matter. Philosophy and science are only methods. They cannot create, but only observe and interpret. In Christianity something is offered for science to observe and for philosophy to interpret, and the result is Christian theology."

In my book, *Pathways to Certainty*, I have discussed some of the consequences which follow from the acceptance of this principle and pointed out in what ways the technique of science is applicable to the solution of religious questions. I have there shown that in religion, as with the other realities that science studies, the final test of the truth or falsehood of any view must be its ability to unify and interpret our experience as a whole, and have tried to show what is the part played by faith and what by reason in defining the conditions of successful experiment in the field of religion.

Thus systematic theology, as I conceived it, is more than an historical study, telling what men believe as Christians. It is a normative study, helping them to define what they *ought* to believe. But it carries on its work within the limits set for all human enterprises by

the fact that they are human, as a progressive undertaking in which the formulation of each new individual
and generation is tested and corrected by the formulations of those who come after them.

This view of the function of systematic theology
helped me to a solution of the second of the two problems with which I was confronted, the problem of the
degree of freedom open to an American theologian
within the limits set for him by the creed of the church
to which he belonged.

This issue had been brought before me in acute form
by the controversy about Dr. Briggs. That controversy,
which on its face was concerned with the degree of
liberty open to the student of the Bible within a particular church, was in fact a phase of a far larger and
more fundamental controversy which affected in varying degree all the American churches. In this larger
controversy the issue at stake was this: how a generation
brought up in unquestioning faith in a God who had
revealed Himself in definite historic ways was to adapt
itself to a science which took nothing for granted and
asked of each alleged revelation what were its human
antecedents and conditions.

It appeared most clearly in connection with the attitude taken to the historic creeds. One party insisted
that every minister must take the creeds in their literal
meaning and that if at any point he departed from that
meaning his only honorable course was to resign his
ministry. Another party regarded the creeds as poetic
interpretations, having significance rather for their
revelation of the subjective attitude of those who put
them forth than for any contribution to our knowledge
of objective reality.

Neither of these positions seemed to me a tenable
one. The claim put forth in times of emotional stress
by the advocates of a conservative type of theology,
that the minister of the church was committed by his

subscription to the standards of that church to an acceptance of all the articles of the creed in their literal sense,
was not only a contradiction of the statement of the
great Protestant creeds themselves but was inconsistent
with the practice of even the most conservative church-
men. On the other hand the view of the creed as a
mere poetic dramatization of subjective attitudes, without claim to objective verification, seemed to me equally
untenable.

My study of history had convinced me that at the
heart of all the great Christian creeds were affirmations
concerning reality which I not only shared on intellectual grounds but which I believed to be of the highest practical importance. But these affirmations were
couched in language taken from the thought of a bygone age and needed constant restatement and redefinition in the light of the new knowledge of the present.
The fact that that redefinition had not yet taken place
in any official manner, far from depriving the individual minister of the right to undertake it on his own
account, was the strongest of all possible reasons for
his doing so, and I regarded it as my duty as a churchman, no less than as a theologian, to contribute as far
as I could to this reinterpretation.

In this conclusion I was further confirmed by my
study of history. For this study showed me that in
every great branch of the Church, not excluding the
Roman Catholic, this process of reinterpretation had
been ceaselessly going on. In each branch of the
Church, including my own, there have been two schools
of thought, one suspicious of change because of its un-
settling effect upon religious conviction, the other eager
for change because believing it the most promising
means for providing fresh channels for religious faith.
Both by conviction and experience I belonged to the
latter group and have found it possible therefore to
work for progress within the church of my fathers.

V. TESTING FAITH BY PRACTICE

So far I have been speaking of the problems which I confronted in my effort to come to terms with science on its more theoretical side. But there was another phase of the adjustment of the relation between religion and science which was even more difficult and in its consequences more far-reaching. I mean the adjustment of the practice of the Church to the radical social changes brought about by applied science.

The effect of these changes is apparent not only upon practice, but even more upon thought. They accentuate men's consciousness of what has always been the most formidable obstacle to religious faith. I mean that which is the result of the contrast between the type of life lived by those who profess the Christian religion and what we should expect it to be if God were really such as they assume. God, we are told by the theologians, is love, and in Jesus Christ has given us not only a redeemer from sin but an example of what the life of man should be.

But while there are many individuals who take Jesus' teaching seriously and exemplify His principle of sacrificial love in their own lives, our social life as a whole has been organized on very different principles. Whether we consider industry or business or politics, the assumption has everywhere been made that enlightened self-interest is the highest law and the function of religion is discharged either in furnishing men with courage to undertake the struggle or in repairing the damage which they have suffered when the struggle has resulted in defeat.

Such a view has become increasingly unsatisfactory to multitudes of religious people. If God be the God of all life and not only of a part and if His nature be love, how can we be content with a gospel which is addressed to individuals alone and has nothing to say of the social order of which they are a part? It may be possible for Hindus, with their pantheistic faith, or for Buddhists, who see in desire the root of all evil, to be indifferent to the nature of the existing social order; but for Christians, who profess to follow Jesus who came preaching the Kingdom of God, such neutrality becomes increasingly difficult.

During the years when my work as a teacher began, this enlarged view of the social responsibility of Christians was winning many adherents. Those were the days of the nascent social gospel. Arthur Toynbee had introduced the university men of Oxford and Cambridge to the dwellers in Whitechapel, and his example was being followed by Stanton Coit in New York, by Miss Addams in Chicago, and a few years later by the founders of the Union Settlement in New York. In Rochester a young professor, Walter Rauschenbusch by name, was winning the experience which was presently to bear fruit in *Christianity and the Social Crisis* [2] and *Prayers of the Social Awakening*,[3] and the fruits of his work were soon to become apparent in the churches in their formation of social service commissions and their adoption of the *Social Creed of the Churches*.

The new spirit made itself felt in the missionary work of the Church, both home and foreign. It led to a redefinition of the missionary objective. It is not enough, we were told, to make Americans Christian. We want a Christian America. It is not enough to convert individual Chinese or Indians to Christianity. We want to see the principles of Christ regnant in all phases of our national and international life.

With this new spirit I was early brought into contact, at first through the Union Settlement, of which I was one of the founders; later through active participation in the home mission work of my own church, the Pres-

---

[2] New York, 1907.
[3] Boston, 1909.

byterian, both in its local and in its national aspects: As Chairman of the Home Missions Committee of the Presbytery, a position which I assumed in 1909, I had the opportunity to take part in more than one practical experiment of exceptional interest. In the American Parish on the Upper East Side of New York City a number of foreign-speaking churches under their own native pastors were affiliated in a single parish under an American chairman—at that time my former student and friend, Norman Thomas, then the pastor of the East Harlem Church. In the Labor Temple (on the Lower East Side) an abandoned Presbyterian church was taken over by our Committee and made the center of an unconventional work which brought together large numbers of industrial workers and through its open forum and lectures furnished a meeting place for conservative and radical, Jew and Christian.

Two convictions stand out in my mind as the outcome of those early years of social experiment: the first, of the limitation of any attempt at social betterment which takes its departure from an uncritical acceptance of the existing social system and is not based upon a comprehensive study of the underlying causes which have produced the unfortunate results we deplore; the other, that of the inadequacy of any attempt which the churches may make to cope with these conditions while they still remain divided. Many years' experience as a worker in the cause of Christian unity, in its local, its national, and its international fields, have given me a painful consciousness of the incongruity of a Church calling others to unity which is itself divided, while at the same time my work in the field of applied Christianity has revealed the even greater incongruity of a Church pledging its allegiance to the ideal of a Christian society, while at so many points contradicting in its practice the law of social brotherhood.

These convictions, slowly ripening through years of

experience, were brought to a head by the war. Through the war we learned not only the nature of the social peril to which we were exposed but also the extent of the social resources on which we could count when great issues were at stake, and we had the courage to demand of men the supreme sacrifice. As Secretary of the General War-Time Commission of the Churches, a body through which the Protestant churches functioned together during the war, I had the opportunity to study at first hand both the extent of the peril and the greatness of the resource. Seen in this new perspective, our early experiments in the social gospel, useful though they were as palliatives, were seen to be wholly inadequate. The time seemed ripe for a new departure, a departure that should visualize the responsibility of Protestantism as a whole and, upon the basis of an adequate induction of facts, attempt in the field of social ethics a program which should do for the Church of tomorrow what the individualistic ethics of the Catechisms had done for the Church of yesterday.

As Chairman of the Committee on the War and the Religious Outlook, a committee set up by the churches immediately after the Armistice to study post-war conditions and problems, it was my privilege to collaborate in a preliminary survey of the field which needed investigation. In one of the volumes of this survey (published by the Y. M. C. A. under the title *The Church and Industrial Reconstruction*) the ethical principles of Jesus were used to test the present industrial order as well as the different methods by which it is proposed to replace or to improve it. Attention was called to certain elementary distinctions often overlooked in contemporary ethical discussion, as, for example, the distinction between the end sought and the method by which it is to be realized; between the steps on which all agree and which are immediately practicable and the more radical changes as to which men, equally intelligent and sincere, may differ; between the responsibility of individuals and that of the Church as an institution. Special emphasis was laid upon a number of particular problems as to which we do not now possess adequate data, and the hope was expressed that those who were in a position to do so would join in a concerted effort to secure these data.

Unfortunately this slow and painstaking method proved too tedious for a generation which through five years of war had become accustomed to living in an atmosphere of excitement. In the enthusiasm which swept over the nations with the coming of peace it was easy to overlook the fact that the war, which had seemed to come upon us so suddenly, was no isolated or arbitrary occurrence but the result of causes that were deeply rooted in our social and political order.

The disastrous failure of the Interchurch World Movement showed to be sure that it is not easy to carry over war-time methods into the tasks of peace, but the lessons which that failure should have taught were quickly forgotten, and it was only as the extravagant optimism induced by the artificial boom of the years 1927-1929 was followed by its inevitable disillusionment that we came to realize the true nature both of the task and of the problem of the teacher of religion. The problem is to distinguish from the many competing interests which press upon him the one central fact that matters, that he may concentrate upon it all available resources both of mind and of will. The task is to share the discovery so far as made with as many persons as possible so that the next advance attempted in the name of religion may be so wisely planned as to reach its objective and so firmly based as to require no retreat.

This conception of the problem and of the task of the Christian teacher, forced upon me by my post-war experience, was confirmed by what I learned as a member of the World Conferences at Stockholm and at Lausanne. These conferences revealed the existence, among Christians of different name, organization, and intellectual and religious tradition, of a body of common convictions which made them spiritually one.

But they revealed also the fact that as the churches are at present organized there is no way in which the nature and extent of the existing unity can be adequately expressed or its appropriate consequences drawn in action. It revealed further the fact that the leaders in the different churches are closer together than the rank and file they represent and made it clear that if the unity that seems theoretically possible is ever to be realized in fact a long-continued process of education is necessary. Thus, whether we consider the need of defining the objective of the church or of creating the will to achieve it when recognized, the work of the Christian teacher seems more than ever essential.

VI.   TAKING STOCK OF LIFE'S DISCOVERIES

It is against the background thus briefly sketched that the basic convictions which constitute my philosophy of life have gradually taken form and substance. What these convictions are, I have expressed in a series of books and articles [4] which discuss in detail the major problems in the field of religion and define my agreements and disagreements with the contemporary thinkers whose work most closely parallels my own. Here it will be sufficient to indicate my attitude on certain

---

[4] *E.g., The Essence of Christianity,* 1902; *Christian Theology in Outline,* 1906; "Changes in the Theology of American Presbyterianism," 1906; "Is Our Protestantism Still Protestant?" 1908; "Calvin's Influence Upon Theology," 1909; "The Covenant Theology," 1911; "The Old Theology and the New," 1911; *The Christian Hope,* 1912; "Expiation and Atonement," 1912; "The Place of Christ in Modern Theology," 1912; *Modern Theology and the Preaching of the Gospel,* 1914; "The Permanent Significance of Miracle for Religion," 1915; *Imperialistic Religion and the Religion of Democracy,* 1923; *Beliefs That Matter,* 1928; *Pathways to Certainty,* 1930.

questions of central importance in my working philosophy of life.

Every Christian theologian is obliged sooner or later to define his position on four major issues: (1) The nature of religion; (2) the distinctive contribution of Christianity; (3) the genius of Protestantism; (4) the function of the Church. He must have a clear conception of the field which he is to cultivate, the historical tradition in which he stands, the type of thought and experience to which he belongs, and the institution in whose service he has enlisted.

And first of my view of religion. As I have already explained, I early came to the conviction that in religion we have first-hand contact with superhuman reality. Most definitions of religion are at fault in that they restrict the area of this contact too narrowly. They make a part do duty for the whole: dependence as with Schleiermacher, responsibility as with Kant, enfranchisement as with Ritschl. Religion is all this and more. It is submission to the will of a greater; gratitude for the experience of deliverance; loyalty to the call of the unseen; adoration of the supreme excellence. In different individuals, different phases of this experience receive emphasis. In the historic religions they are combined in different proportions and crystallize into the institutions we call churches. Religions differ not only in the elements they include, but in their capacity for self-reformation and renewal; and what is true of each religion is true of the lesser divisions within each.

In the history of theology, we find two interpretations of religion persisting side by side. One attempts to bring the phenomena of religion wholly under law, and conceives of religion as man's final reaction to the universe as a whole. The other thinks of the religious experience as something immediate and inexplicable, something which may indeed bring order and meaning into a world otherwise confused and dark, but which is

itself irreducible to anything that has gone before. To
thinkers of the first type religion is natural—understanding by nature the universal, the normal, the uniform. To those of the second, it is supernatural—
understanding by supernatural the exceptional, the
original, the creative.

While any adequate philosophy of religion must do
justice to both these aspects of the religious experience,
I believe that the second is the more primary and fundamental. Otto is right in reminding us of the non-
rational element which enters into the making of religion. Wherever it is a living thing and not simply
the memory of a past experience, it is always awe in the
presence of mystery. Miracle (in the psychological if
not in the metaphysical sense) is of its essence. To
understand a religion like Christianity, therefore, we
must not explain away the sense of mystery but discover in what context it comes to pass and what effects
it produces.

In my essay on "The Permanent Significance of
Miracle for Religion," I have called attention to the
fundamental place which the belief in miracle holds in
living religion and analyzed the recurrent experiences
to which it owes its continuing vitality. As long as
man's experience brings him face to face with mystery,
surprises him with flashes of insight, keeps alive his
longing for certainty, and refreshes him with the consciousness of renewal, he will continue to believe in
miracle. Our theoretical explanations of this belief
may indeed alter with our larger knowledge, but no
change in our theory will prevent the recurrence of the
experience or make it reasonable to minimize its importance. In the future as in the past, religions will
differ not in affirming miracle, but in the kind of event
to which they attach supernatural significance—whether
in the outer world or in the inner; whether experiences
that remain purely mysterious and inexplicable or that

lend themselves to ethical and rational interpretation. Christianity justifies the claim of its adherents to supremacy most of all in this, that it makes the greatest moral teacher of all time the object of its worship and attributes to His person supernatural significance.

The two tendencies which meet us in the interpretation of religion in general reappear in the interpretation of the Christian religion. To one school of thinkers, Christianity is the crown of natural religion, the goal to which the whole process of the universe is inevitably tending. Jesus, the individual, is an incident. He has significance as the incarnation of an idea existing independently of Him and destined sooner or later to come to expression in the very nature of things. To another school, history is a stage on which personality plays the dominant rôle and the human spirit experiences a genuine salvation. Christianity as the religion which mediates this salvation is in the fullest sense of the term the supernatural religion; and Jesus, its central figure, is something *sui generis*, the world's Savior, the Founder of the Kingdom of God.

For the reasons already stated I believe that those who take the second position are in the right. Christianity is more than the crown of natural religion. It is mankind's response to the impact of a fresh personality—not wholly explicable by its antecedents—of creative significance for the life of the individual and of the race. As the name implies, it is the religion of men who find in Jesus of Nazareth the supreme revelation of God.

When I began my study of theology, Albrecht Ritschl was the best-known advocate of this Christocentric theology. In making the person of Christ central in his thinking he was only repeating a commonplace of historic theology. What was original was his association of this exalted estimate of the Founder of Christianity with the Jesus of the critics. Previous

theologians had sought to safeguard the uniqueness of
Jesus by pointing out exceptional qualities in His person, the Virgin Birth, the resurrection, the miracles, at
the least His sinlessness.   Ritschl insisted that His
uniqueness consists just in the way in which He fulfils
His function in the particular station in which He finds
himself.   His sovereignty is not something added to
His sacrifice on the cross but the effect which His
sacrifice produced upon those who came under His
influence.   To separate person and work as though one
could be complete without the other is therefore to
Ritschl illegitimate. We know the person only through
the work.

This desire to safeguard the genuine humanity of
Jesus led Ritschl to reject the high Christology of the
creeds.   He saw in this Christology a corruption of
primitive Christianity due to the influence of Greek
thought upon the second generation of Christian thinkers, the first-fruits of that speculative interest which,
whether expressed in a Justin or a Hegel, it was his
life mission to combat.

I could not follow Ritschl in this rejection, and this
for three reasons.   In the first place, I did not believe
that the reconstruction of the critics offered us a firm
enough basis on which alone to build a theology.   The
historic Jesus, as presented in the pages of our contemporary critics, is itself an imaginative construction
in which the meager data of the Gospels are fashioned
into a picture which reflects the sympathies and the
prejudices of the artist.   What the Gospels give us is
not a scientific account of what Jesus did and said, but
the impression produced by Jesus upon those who came
nearest to Him; and this impression includes features
to which no single later interpretation has done or can
do full justice.

In the second place, I was convinced that if Christianity was to prove itself the universal religion it must

rest its case upon its present power to inspire and to renew, not on the record, however glorious, of its achievements in the past. The Savior the world needs is indeed the historic Jesus, but the Jesus who has become the Christ of faith—the living Spirit with whom we have direct communication in our present need. Finally, it did not seem to me that Ritschl's theology made adequate provision for the varieties of the Christian experience. Like Ritschl, I saw in Jesus not the unworldly saint of mystical theology, but a man among men, virile, courageous, uncompromising, the enemy of selfishness in every form, the founder of the new society whose law was service and whose driving power was love. But I did not think that I had the right to make my understanding of Jesus the test by which to judge other men's Christianity. In a universal religion there must be place for all kinds of men: the mystic must find his home, as well as the practical man of affairs; the speculative thinker, as well as the man who comes to God by way of the categorical imperative.

To be a Christian, as I conceived Christianity, was not to imitate Jesus' conduct, still less to accept the letter of His teaching. Rather was it to yield one-self to His spirit, and under the guidance of that spirit do one's own thinking and follow one's own conscience wherever that might lead. This I conceived to be the true meaning of the high Christology of the creed: not as Ritschl interpreted it, a device for replacing the human Jesus with some metaphysical construct of the schools, but the recognition of the fact that the God who reveals Himself in Jesus is still at work in the world, speaking to us today as directly as He spoke to Jesus and leading His disciples, as He promised, into ever new truth.

This conception of the continuing influence of Jesus was reinforced by my contact with other religions. In repeated visits to the mission field—in China, in Japan,

in India, and in the Near East—I have had the opportunity of studying Christianity in its impact upon other
faiths, and that study has convinced me that in bringing
Christianity to men of other religions we are not coming to men who lack first-hand knowledge of God, but
only sharing with men who have no acquaintance with
the particular revelation which has come to us through
Jesus the new insight and inspiration which He has
brought.

It is true that the language in which we describe this
revelation is symbolic, pointing to a reality transcending
our experience which each must interpret for himself.
But this is no more true of our Christian witness than
of any other attempt to share experience with others.
All language has symbolic character. It is a device by
which we make vivid to consciousness the aspects of a
reality which cannot be completely expressed in words.
Words are a part, the most important part it may be,
but still only a part, of that universal sign language
which expresses itself most directly through gesture and
the dramatic arts. That is why ritual as well as doctrine must always hold its place in the vocabulary of
religion.

But the fact that we express our experience of God
in symbols is no more reason for doubting that we have
immediate experience of God than the fact that all our
language is symbolic should lead us to question the existence of any of the lesser realities with which we have
to do—ourselves, other persons, the earth on which we
stand, the sky to which we look up, the physical universe itself. There is always a residuum in experience
which can never be completely expressed, and of no
experience is this more true than of our experience of
the supreme reality of religion. To say that we believe
in the deity of Jesus is only another way of saying that
we find in His person a symbol of inexhaustible meaning.

This conception of the nature of the Christian religion gave me my standard for evaluating the various types of Christianity which have emerged in the course of history. I could no longer claim for any one of them a monopoly of the Christian name, not even for my own. In each I could find some traces of the influence of the Christian spirit. In none had that spirit come to complete expression. One and all were partial forms of Christianity, stages in our progress to something better.

But I found it equally impossible to arrange them in an ascending series according to their approximation to the goal, as was the fashion in the prevailing philosophy of history. To me, as a Protestant, it was natural to think of Protestantism as representing a higher and purer form of Christianity than Catholicism. As a Modernist it is equally inevitable that I should think of the later Protestantism as presenting a truer interpretation of essential Christianity than the earlier. But I had no right to conclude that the Protestant type of Christianity would ever completely supersede the Catholic, or that the Modernist interpretation would be universally accepted.

Whereas I had once conceived the different forms of historic Christianity as so many steps in an ascending series, succeeding one another in logical sequence (as Hegel had pictured them), I came to regard them as a group of parallel types which had their roots in fundamental differences in human nature; types which made their appearance in Christianity indeed, as they had appeared in each of the other historic religions, but which differed from their counterparts in other faiths in this, that in Christianity they had been exposed to the influence of Jesus. My task as a theologian was to classify these types, to point out their similarities and their differences, to show what my own type could offer which the others lacked and what it needed which they could supply, and to test one and all by the spirit of Jesus as that spirit had revealed itself to me in my study of the history of His Church.

There were two points in particular at which this testing needed to be made. The first was in connection with the Modernist controversy within Protestantism; the second in connection with the older controversy between the Protestant and the Catholic.

The issue in the Modernist controversy is in substance this: whether in accepting the results of modern criticism, liberal Protestants have abandoned the fundamental principles of the Reformation, or whether they still have a right to the Protestant name. The question is differently answered by different scholars. Harnack denies the break. Sabatier affirms it. To Harnack, Protestantism is one of the three great historic forms of Christianity. He finds its essence in the re-emphasis of the autonomy of the individual as expressed in the doctrine of justification by faith. Great as is the difference between the older and the newer Protestantism, to Harnack they are both species of the same genus. He is convinced that no new form of the Christian religion has appeared since the Reformation. Sabatier, on the other hand, associates the older Protestantism as the religion of the book with Catholicism as the religion of the church, and contrasts both as religions of authority with the religion of the Spirit. In this he speaks for the radicals of all schools who believe that we are witnessing a new Reformation even more far-reaching than the old.

In my essay, "Is Our Protestantism Still Protestant?" I have tried to mediate between these two positions. With Harnack I conclude that, as opposed to Catholicism, Protestantism in both its forms represents a different principle; namely, the principle of the direct approach of the individual to God over against the principle of churchly authority. But I believe that

Harnack minimizes the difference between the older and the newer Protestantism. As Roman Catholicism differs from Greek Catholicism in admitting the principle of progress through its provision of an organ through which the Church can speak today, so the later Protestantism differs from the earlier in substituting a dynamic for a static conception of Christianity.

To men like Luther and Knox, the differences between Christians presented an insoluble puzzle. They could not conceive how two men who were both led by the Spirit of God could come to different conclusions on any important matter of doctrine. The modern Protestant conceives of God as progressively revealing Himself through an historic process in which each generation corrects the mistakes of the past. He does not expect uniformity of belief and, therefore, is not surprised by its absence. It is enough for him to know that those from whom he differs agree with him in seeing in Christ the supreme revelation of God and finding in Him the answer to their questions and the satisfaction of their needs.

More perplexing than the question raised by the different types of Protestantism is the older and more fundamental question of the relation between Protestantism and Catholicism. What is one to say of that ancient church which through so many ages has claimed the right to speak as the infallible vicar of Christ? What is to be its place in the Christianity of the future? As a student of history I had been concerned with the Catholic Church primarily as one of the historic stages through which Christianity had passed in its development, a stage wonderfully interesting to the historian, no doubt, but, so far as present Protestantism was concerned, negligible. My work for church unity taught me that such a position is untenable.

No one who desires to understand the world in which he lives can ignore a religion which commands the whole-hearted allegiance of some of the most acute and devoted spirits of our time. The more I studied Roman Catholicism, the more I came to know its living representatives, the more clearly I perceived that at the back of its organization, with its claim to absolute authority, lay a core of vital experience which I dared not neglect. The motives to which Catholicism appealed were human motives; the sources from which it drew its strength were in the men and women with whom I had to do.

I could not even study contemporary Protestantism as I saw it in actual operation without perceiving that the Protestant church included many individuals whose experience by no means conformed to the theories they professed; who were indeed, by every test I could apply, of the Catholic rather than of the Protestant type, just as there were not a few Modernist Catholics who approximated to the Protestant type. Was one then to conclude that Protestantism and Catholicism must forever stand opposed to one another? Was there no third possible form of Christianity in which the excellencies of both could be combined?

In my book, *Imperialistic Religion and the Religion of Democracy*, I have suggested a possible answer to this question. With the authoritative religion which finds its most signal expression in Catholicism and the individualistic faith which has hitherto been characteristic of Protestantism, I have associated a third type, which finds its principle of unity in a common spirit expressing itself in different forms. This third type I have called Democratic Religion. By democracy in the sense in which I here use the term, I do not mean the rule of the majority over the minority, still less the doctrine that all men are equal in powers and attainments. I mean rather the conviction that since God speaks to every man directly according to his capacity each personality is to be respected by every other.

The democrat, as I define him, believes that each should be willing to learn from his neighbor, however uncongenial that neighbor may be, that through the cooperation of many men of many minds society as a whole may make progress toward the ideal. This conviction lies at the heart of modern Protestantism, but it has not yet found consistent theoretical expression, still less has it created the institutions through which its genius can express itself in action. The task of the theology of the future is to supply this lack, to substitute for the sectarian conception of the Church which has hitherto been characteristic of Protestantism a conception of the Church as comprehensive and many-sided as that of Roman Catholicism but at the same time consistent with the principles of freedom and of progress for which the newer Protestantism preeminently stands.

This recognition of a common core of agreement across areas of difference does not mean that I regard the differences between these types as unimportant or the theologian as discharged from responsibility for trying in every proper way to make his own view prevail. But I do believe that in this effort he must recognize that, however convinced he may be that the truth which he affirms is true and that the reality to which he witnesses is real, his own definition of the truth is partial and his own appreciation of that reality inadequate.

I am a Christian, not a Hindu or a Mohammedan, and I believe that in Jesus Christ, God has given a revelation that mankind needs and that it is my privilege so far as I apprehend it to share. But I realize also that the God who has revealed himself to me through Jesus Christ is ever at work in His world and

I expect to find, as I have found, traces of His presence and light from His truth in the devout men whom I have met in other religions.

I am a Protestant and as such I believe that in the principle of private judgment Protestantism holds in trust for humanity something which loyalty to the truth will not suffer me to surrender. But I recognize also that Catholicism has precious truth, and to study of its teaching and fellowship with its devout exponents I owe priceless insights and stimulus for which I cannot be too thankful.

I am a Modernist, and as such I am committed to follow the scientific method to its limit wherever it shall take me. But I recognize in some of my Fundamentalist colleagues a first-hand acquaintance with God which I covet for myself and which my scientific conscience as well as my spirit of fellowship constrains me to recognize.

As I contemplate the Church of the future I think of it not as fashioned after my own idea of what a Church should be but as embracing within its catholic fold, on terms consistent with mutual self-respect, men of types different from my own, with whom I would gladly work and, above all, with whom I would humbly worship.

PRINCIPAL PUBLICATIONS

Books:

Musical Instruments and Their Homes (with Mary E. Brown). New York: Dodd, Mead & Co., 1888.

The Essence of Christianity. A Study in the History of Definition. New York and Edinburgh: Charles Scribner's Sons, 1902.

Christian Theology in Outline. New York and Edinburgh: Charles Scribner's Sons, 1906.

Morris K. Jesup. A Character Sketch. New York: Charles Scribner's Sons, 1910.

The Christian Hope. A Study of the Doctrine of Immortality. London and New York: Charles Scribner's Sons, 1912.

Modern Theology and the Preaching of the Gospel. New York: Charles Scribner's Sons, 1914.

Is Christianity Practicable? New York: Charles Scribner's Sons, 1916.

The Church in America. New York: The Macmillan Co., 1922.

Imperialistic Religion and the Religion of Democracy. A Study in Social Psychology. London and New York: Hodder & Stoughton, Ltd., and Charles Scribner's Sons, 1923.

The Creative Experience. London and New York: Hodder & Stoughton, Ltd., and Charles Scribner's Sons, 1923.

The Quiet Hour. New York: Association Press, 1926.

The Life of Prayer in a World of Science. New York: Charles Scribner's Sons and Association Press, 1926.

Beliefs That Matter. New York: Charles Scribner's Sons and Association Press, 1928.

Pathways to Certainty. New York and London: Charles Scribner's Sons and Christian Movement Press, 1930.

Articles:

"State Control of Industry in the Fourth Century." *Political Science Quarterly,* September, 1887.

"Christ the Vitalizing Principle of Christian Theology." Inaugural Address as Roosevelt Professor of Systematic Theology in the Union Theological Seminary, November 1, 1898. New York, 1898.

Review of Ladd's *Theory of Reality* in *New World,* September, 1900.

Articles on "Millennium," "Parousia," and "Salvation," in Hastings' *Dictionary of the Bible,* 1900, 1902.

"Adolf Harnack as a Theological Teacher," *The Outlook,* August 10, 1901.

"Changes in the Theology of American Presbyterianism," *American Journal of Theology,* July, 1906.

"The Pragmatic Value of the Absolute," *Journal of Philosophy, Psychology and Scientific Method.* August 15, 1907.

"Is Our Protestantism Still Protestant?" *Harvard Theological Review*, January, 1908.

"The Reasonableness of Christian Faith," *Hibbert Journal*, January, 1908.

"Calvin's Influence Upon Theology." An Address delivered in Commemoration of the 400th Anniversary of the Birth of John Calvin, on May 3, 1909, at the Union Theological Seminary, New York. Privately Printed.

"The Theology of William Newton Clarke," *Harvard Theological Review*, April, 1910.

"The Task and Method of Systematic Theology," *American Journal of Theology*, XIV, 1910.

"Christianity," pp. 201-213 in *The Unity of Religions*, ed. Randall, New York, 1910.

"The Old Theology and the New." Lectures delivered at the Summer School of Harvard University, 1910. Reprinted in the *Harvard Theological Review*, January, 1911.

"Changes in Theological Thought During the Last Generation," *Methodist Review*, January, 1911.

"The Christian Demand for Unity: Its Nature and Implications," in *Essays in Modern Theology and Related Subjects*. New York, 1911.

Articles on "Covenant Theology," and "Expiation and Atonement (Christian)" in Hastings' *Encyclopædia of Religion and Ethics*, 1911, 1912.

"The Place of Christ in Modern Theology," *American Journal of Theology*, XVI, 1912.

Review of Hocking's *Meaning of God in Human Experience* in *Journal of Philosophy, Psychology and Scientific Method*, April 24, 1913.

"Problems and Possibilities of American Protestantism," *Constructive Quarterly*, June, 1913.

"Theological Education," reprinted from Monroe's *Cyclopædia of Education*, Vol. V., New York, 1914.

"God in History. With special reference to the present War." The Drew Lecture for 1914, delivered in Memorial Hall, London, October 16, 1914.

Review of Royce's *Problem of Christianity*, in *Journal of Philosophy, Psychology and Scientific Method*, October 22, 1914.

"The Permanent Significance of Miracle for Religion."
The Dudleian Lecture for 1915. *Harvard Theological
Review*, July, 1915.

"Modern Missions in the Far East." A Report prepared
for the Directors of the Union Theological Seminary.
Privately Printed, New York, January, 1917.

"Christianity and Industry." An Address given to a group
of industrial secretaries of the Young Women's Christian Association, New York, 1919.

"The Seminary of Tomorrow," *Harvard Theological Review*, April, 1919.

"The Responsibility of the University for the Teaching of
Religion," *Yale Divinity Quarterly*, June, 1920.

Report as Acting Provost of Yale University, 1919-1920,
Yale University Press, 1920.

"The Future of Philosophy as a University Study," *Journal
of Philosophy, Psychology and Scientific Method*, 1921.

"The Common Problems of Theological Schools," *Journal
of Religion*, May, 1921.

"How We May Unite. A preliminary analysis of Problems
and Possibilities," *Constructive Quarterly*, June, 1921.

"The Claim of the United Church on Man's Allegiance,"
Constructive Quarterly, December, 1921.

"Movements of Promise in the American Churches," *Congregational Quarterly*, London, July, 1923.

"The Problem of Classification in Religion," *Proceedings
of The Aristotelian Society*, 1923.

"A Protestant View of the Anglo-Catholic Movement,"
Christian Union Quarterly, New York, 1924.

"La Religion Democratique," *Revue d'Histoire et de
Philosophie Religieuses*, Juillet-Aout, 1924.

"The Ministry and Sacraments of the Reformed Churches,"
Proceedings of the Alliance of the Reformed Churches,
1925.

"The Stockholm Conference on Life and Work: An Impression and a Forecast," *The Review of Reviews*,
December, 1925.

"The Church and Christian Education," *The Christian
Union Quarterly*, October, 1925.

"After Fundamentalism—What?" *The North American
Review*, September-October-November, 1926.

"A Century of Theological Education and After," *The Journal of Religion*, July, 1926.

"Our Educational System and Education as a Christian Problem," in symposium, *An Outline of Christianity*, Vol. IV., New York, 1926.

"Accomplishment at Lausanne," *The American Review of Reviews*, November, 1927.

"The New Note in Religion," *The Yale Review*, September, 1927.

"Basic Assumptions of Religion in Their Bearing Upon Science," *Religious Education*, April, 1928.

"Second Thoughts on Lausanne," *The Review of the Churches*, July, 1928.

"Needed Emphases in Religious Education," *Religious Education*, May, 1930.

"Church Union in Southern India," *The Review of the Churches*, January, 1930.

"What Jesus Means to Me," *The Christian Century Pulpit*, December, 1930.

"A Retrospect of Forty Years," *The Expository Times*, December, 1930; also, *The Methodist Review*, March-April, 1931.

CHRISTIAN THEOLOGY AND A SPIRITUALISTIC PHILOSOPHY

By EUGENE WILLIAM LYMAN

(b. April 4, 1872, Cummington, Massachusetts)

Professor of the Philosophy of Religion in Union Theological Seminary

New York, N. Y.

CHRISTIAN THEOLOGY AND A
SPIRITUALISTIC PHILOSOPHY

By Eugene William Lyman

WHEN one hears theology preached from Sunday to Sunday, as was apt to be the case with one reared in the New England of my boyhood, one cannot date the acquiring of theological ideas and convictions with the definiteness that may be possible with respect to one's more formal philosophical views. What one, in looking back, can identify is of the nature of attitudes and dispositions of mind rather than tenets of a theological position. But, in general, the affiliations of the Christian teaching in the little hill town in western Massachusetts in which I grew up were neither with the Calvinism of Jonathan Edwards nor with the Unitarianism of William Ellery Channing, but with the liberal Evangelicalism of Horace Bushnell. Washington Gladden, who acknowledged Bushnell as his spiritual father, was preaching in Springfield in my youth, and Theodore T. Munger was minister in North Adams, and while I did not hear either of them I read books by each in my early teens. Washington Gladden's *Who Wrote the Bible* essentially solved the problem of Higher Criticism for me before seminary or college days.

My early religious attitudes, then, were molded by a Congregational church of liberal orthodox type which was in effect a community church. Not only was it practically without competition from other denominations, it also touched and influenced all sides of life in that little town. Revivalism played a certain part in the church life. The time when I most clearly remember our meeting-house being crowded to the doors, galleries and aisles being filled, was during a series of meetings conducted by an eloquent temperance evangelist. Nevertheless, the part of the revival was a minor one. Educational methods on the whole prevailed, and the distinctly liberal preachers among our succession of ministers were the ones who left the deepest impression upon my mind.

My mother was a stalwart Christian of conservative feeling and of much moral force, and an awakener of intellectual ambition. Her reading aloud to the family was a regular and much enjoyed part of every Sunday, and included not only Bible stories, *Pilgrim's Progress*, and later, *Paradise Lost*, but a pretty wide range of novels and other literature. My father was a man of liberal temper, genial and public-minded. Our town-meeting government, with which my father had much to do, ingrained democracy in my mind. The *Springfield Republican*, then as now one of the few really independent newspapers in this country, was a powerful educational influence. Thus my early religious attitudes took shape in an atmosphere of positive Christian faith, moral earnestness and civic spirit, which was colored by the inevitable provincialism of a New England hill town.

My early philosophical reading was limited, so far as I now recall, to *Sartor Resartus* and Emerson's *Essays*. The effort to prepare for college left little leisure time for such reading. There was no high school within reach, and going away to a preparatory school was not financially feasible. Hence it was necessary for me to study chiefly by myself, and also to teach school in order to earn money for going to college. The awakening of my interest in philosophy came in Amherst College with taking the course in philosophy taught by Professor Garman, who stimulated so many of his students to become teachers of philosophy. Professor Garman was a most skilful teacher and preferred, as he often said, instead of writing books, to follow the example of Socrates and "write on the fleshy parchments of men's hearts." His method was to develop basic philosophical problems in such a way as to render them vital for students, and then to make the students wrestle with these problems in class discussion and by means of brief papers which all of the class wrote on the same topic.

In carrying out this method he used the unique device of his "pamphlet system." Pamphlets, privately printed and sometimes freshly composed over a week-end to meet the needs of the class, took the place of classroom lectures. By this means problems, and the data deemed most important for dealing with them, were presented to students apart from solutions, and the students were summoned to a "weighing of the evidence." It is an adaptation of this method, made possible by the mimeograph, which I have used throughout my teaching.

The view of reality as a whole in which Garman's course culminated was that of an ethical metaphysics of the Lotzean type. This view I heartily embraced, finding in it an interpretation of religion which stood the test of reason and a philosophy which had vital and inspiring meaning. I felt that it made possible the solution of the problems arising from biology and psychology as they were then taking shape. On the basis of this metaphysics the Darwinian doctrine of evolution could be combined with man's moral and spiritual interests through the idea of the immanence of God. And, taken in conjunction with the psychology of William James which I then began to study, this metaphysics could do full justice to the facts of physiological psychology and at the same time maintain the reality of psychical causality and of human freedom.

I came to believe quite firmly in the power of the

mind to gain the objective standards of thought requisite both for natural science and for man's moral and spiritual life. Professor Garman's course at that time ended with a discussion of "the Atonement," in which self-realization through self-sacrifice was presented as the Christian principle which contained the highest ethical ideal, and which at the same time was the highest metaphysical principle—one that made possible grappling effectively with the problem of evil.

No systematic instruction in the history of philosophy was given at Amherst at that time, which resulted in a handicap that I only slowly overcame; but I still feel that the unified treatment of the problems of philosophy which Garman's comprehensive course gave was of the highest value, and that many departments of philosophy in the present fall short at this very point. At all events the teaching of Professor Garman has been one of the most far-reaching influences in my life.

Although I had gone to college with the ultimate purpose of preparing for the ministry, that calling and the teaching of philosophy were being balanced in my mind during two years spent as an instructor in Latin in preparatory schools. Then I turned to theology because the religious interest was uppermost in my mind. At Yale Divinity School I came to appreciate Christianity as an historical religion, especially through the teaching of Professors B. W. Bacon and F. C. Porter. They presented the most significant results of German as well as British and American scholarship; but more important still were the contributions of their own scholarship and insight. Professor Porter's courses in Biblical theology were of the utmost value to me, both historically and philosophically. In these courses the Hebrew prophets were interpreted in relation to the historical development of their people, and yet the spiritual discovery of each was made to stand forth clearly. Jesus was portrayed in connection with the movements and forces of His nation, and at the same time that which was new and universal in His teaching and in the meaning of His deeds and personality was presented with convincing discernment. Paul was shown to be much greater than theology and ecclesiasticism have for the most part understood him to be, because he more than any other Christian possessed and interpreted the mind of Christ.

These teachings and points of view have remained with me as a permanent possession and have been to a very large extent normative for my thought of religion and of God. And while this apprehending of Christianity as a genuinely historical religion took me into a quite different realm from that into which I had been introduced by philosophy in college, yet there was a real continuity in the influences by which my thought was being shaped. For I occasionally glimpsed in Professor Porter's way of interpreting things some of the features of a Lotzean metaphysics.

It was during two years of study in Germany that I first felt that I was coming to have a systematic theology. This development in my thinking came through the study of the theology of the Ritschlian school. At that time in Germany theology seemed to me to be far more vital and fruitful than philosophy. While the history of philosophy was being diligently cultivated, few were venturing on constructive philosophy. The Ritschlian theology, on the other hand, was at the height of its development and influence. It combined the brilliant historical scholarship of Harnack with a constructive reinterpretation of Christian doctrine which was fresh and vitalizing. Its interpreters manifested much more warmth of piety than did either the representatives of the older speculative theology which derived from Hegel or the orthodox Lutherans.

I studied with Reischle at Halle, Kaftan and Harnack at Berlin, and Herrmann at Marburg and became convinced of the *Selbständigkeit* of Christianity. I felt that inherent in Christianity itself was not only a way of life and of salvation adequate for human needs but also a world-view which could give to our experience as a whole its most significant interpretation. And I believed that all of Christian theology should be organized around the supreme values to be found in Jesus as a moral and religious personality, without a special ontology concerning Him which sets Him apart from mankind, and around the kingdom of God as an ethical, social, and religious conception. Thus the watchword "Back to Christ," from the Christologies of the creeds and the ecclesiastical doctrines of salvation, seemed to me to be justified and to stand for a forward movement in theology.

At the same time the rejection of all speculative theology by the Ritschlians, and the doctrine that all religious truth belonged in the realm of value-judgments, ran counter to my previous thinking and produced considerable tension in my mind. I felt that a kind of religious positivism was involved in this side of Ritschlianism, with its indifference to any metaphysics of personality, or philosophy of evolution, or idea of divine immanence, and I believed that religion could have a basis in a reasoned theory of the nature of things. A diligent reading of all of Kant's *Critiques* followed, and in the end I became convinced that the Ritschlian watchword, "Back to Kant," should be adopted. It was, however, Kant's autonomous ethics, including his doctrines of the person as an end-in-itself, of the realm of ends, and of the primacy of the practical reason, which impressed me most—far more than his doctrine of the limits of the theoretical reason. And I remained dissatisfied with his phenomenalistic view of the self. Still, for the time being I accepted a philosophy of faith and of postulates in place of a metaphysical interpretation of reality; and while this position no longer satisfies me, I continue to hold that faith is one of the philosophically valid pathways to knowledge.

After Ritschl and Kant I turned to Schleiermacher, and from his *Discourses, Soliloquies,* and *Glaubenslehre* I gained a view of the *Selbständigkeit* of religion, which the Ritschlian exclusive emphasis on Christianity had obscured. As Kant had shown me the autonomy of ethics, so Schleiermacher showed me the autonomy of religion. I came to see that religion was a relatively independent, integral factor in human experience. I say, "relatively" independent, for autonomy did not mean to my mind—and does not now—that no federation of the autonomous realms was desirable and possible. It means, rather, that no realm of experience which can be called autonomous is simply derivative from the other realms, and therefore reducible to one or more of the others. Religion, then, cannot be equated with ethics, nor with ethics plus philosophy. It is a unique, characteristic mode of human experience, which has a right to make its own report concerning the nature of reality.

Schleiermacher's pantheizing tendency, however, seemed to me to endanger the ethical and social meanings of Christianity and not to be congruous with the essential nature of the Christian world-view. And his method of assigning to so many historical dogmas a symbolical meaning, after having criticized them as being untenable in their original intent, was to my mind unacceptable. Thus when I returned to America and began teaching philosophy and psychology in Carleton College, Minnesota, the very principles and points of view which I had found to be illuminating and stimulating, but which were only partly reconciled in my thought, presented me with a series of problems.

The first of these problems which I studied was the meaning of mysticism. Stimulus to this study came not only from the contrast between the ethical theology of

Ritschl and the mystical elements in Schleiermacher's theology, but from the large place given to mysticism in James's *Varieties of Religious Experience* which had just been published. The same problem has occupied me often since, but the position arrived at then, which found expression in my *Jugundschrift,* "Faith and Mysticism," has remained with me as an essential part of my understanding of religion and its philosophy. This position was that mysticism in its milder forms is a normal constituent of religion, but that it is not, as such, normative for religion. That is to say, mysticism, taken by itself, is not the essence of religion, and it must submit to norms of truth and value which arise from other sides of our experience. But mysticism, I urged, is not incompatible with the mediation of religious ideas through history or with faith in historical revelation. There is something mystical in all our profounder personal relations and in all vital religion which is expressed in personal terms. Though such experiences are mediated by past knowledge they have also a quality of immediacy which results in accessions of insight and of energy.

During the eight years which I spent at Bangor Theological Seminary—following upon three years of teaching at Carleton College and one in Montreal—I was teaching systematic theology, but my personal study continued to be largely in the field of philosophy. This was because theology had already been vitalized for me by the Ritschlian interpretation of the content of Christianity—that interpretation being enlarged by a positive appreciation of mysticism; whereas I was dissatisfied with the isolation of theology from philosophy, and of Christianity from other religions, which the Ritschlian position involved.

In those years William James, whose lectures at a Harvard summer school of theology I attended, was developing his pragmatism, and I found it contributing much to the solving of my problems. His psychology was authoritative and at the same time it was accompanied in his philosophy by a doctrine of metaphysical freedom. His criticism of the "sectarian scientist" was in no sense hostile to science as such, coming as it did from one who himself was a trained experimental scientist as few of our philosophers have been, and it helped to lay bare metaphysical assumptions and dogmatisms often put forward in the name of science. His recognition of faith and religious experience as being a doorway to metaphysical truth, his meliorism, his conviction that the "axis of reality" runs through personal entities and entities akin to the personal, all these were to me prepossessing aspects of his philosophy.

It seemed to me impossible to derive absolute idealism from epistemology, as Royce was doing, and I felt that absolute idealism subordinated ethical and religious values to rationalistic speculation. Pragmatism appeared to me more in accord with psychology, with the evolutionary view of man, with the historical spirit, and with ethical and religious values, and I accepted it as a method and a theory of truth.

Though I since have come to think pragmatism inadequate as an account of the nature of truth, and as only one method among others for gaining truth, its contribution to philosophy is in my judgment very important. Its insistence that ideas, if significant, must make a difference in our experience, both receptive and active, and its consequent treatment of philosophy as by right an active constructive force in the world, have widened the scope of philosophy and increased its grasp of reality. For my own thinking pragmatism overcame the dualism which Kant developed between the theoretical and the practical reason and restored unity to the conception of truth. It also helped me to see that the habit of giving a parallel treatment to the categories of space and time, which derives from Kant but which he did so little to justify, is not rational; and that time, being the form of both our outer and our inner experience, has a greater objectivity than space which is the form of our outer experience only. Pragmatism, too, connotes a dynamic conception of ultimate reality and a universe in the making, and hence gives metaphysical significance to the aspirations and strivings of men and the issues of human history.

Thus to me pragmatism opened the doorway again to metaphysics which Kantian criticism had seemed to close. The pragmatism which I set forth in my *Theology and Human Problems* included an empirical metaphysics in which religious experience had full parity with other types of experience. It was theistic pragmatism and presented a combination of cosmological and teleological reasoning as uniting with religious faith in grounding the conception of God. I dissented, however, from James's pluralism as failing to account for the unity which characterizes the universe, even though it be still in the making. And I likewise dissented from his doctrine of a finite God, not in order to maintain the philosophical conception of the Absolute, but to uphold a pragmatic and religious conception of God's infiniteness.

In the more specifically theological field the writings of Troeltsch were interesting me much. As the theologian of the *religionsgeschichtliche Schule* he showed the fallacy of isolating Christianity from other religions, after the manner of Ritschlian apologetics, and he made clearer in my mind the need that systematic theology be approached through a philosophy of religion after the manner of Schleiermacher. But there was a relativism in Troeltsch's thought by which I, as a pragmatist, should not have been troubled, but which I could not accept, being convinced of the normative value of the religion of Jesus and of the congruous Kantian doctrine of the realm of ends.

At this time the reading of Rauschenbusch began to make a strong impression on my mind. Christian ethics, I was coming to realize, called not only for the supremacy of love in the life of the individual and for a world-wide human brotherhood, but also for a Christian social order in respect to the production and distribution of wealth. Garman's comprehensive course in philosophy had included a doctrine of the State, designed to give religious and philosophical meaning to the duties of citizenship, and the Ritschlian theology made one's ethical vocation an essential part of the life of sonship to God. But in both instances there was a too uncritical acceptance of existing social institutions as vehicles for Christian ideals. Christian ethics must be more searching and must demand the criticism and reconstruction of the institutions of property, of business and industry, and of political life. The Christian must strive for social justice no less than for personal righteousness. An ethics and a religious consciousness which thus could challenge social institutions and supply norms for their reshaping could not be fitted into a thoroughly relativistic philosophy. Some of the implications of this fact, however, remained for me to think out at a later time.

A furlough shortly before the war made possible for me study with Troeltsch at Heidelberg, Eucken at Jena, and Bergson at Paris. The greatest mental quickening came from Bergson. Already the reasoning of James Ward had convinced me that the authority of the principle of the conservation of energy was not of such a nature as to require that biological evolution be understood as nothing but a mechanical process. On the contrary, as he had shown, the up-hill tendency of the evolution of life—the very opposite of the down-hill tendency of mechanical forces—required psychical, teleological factors for its explanation. Bergson's *Creative Evolution* emphasized still more the immanent psychical creativity at work in all forms of life, distinguished this type of teleology from a radical finalism in which all is predetermined, and grounded the creative process in a metaphysical conception of Time and of Freedom.

In these respects Bergson's thought was in line with that of William James, while Bergson's doctrine of intuition was what helped James to his theory of "the compounding of consciousness" and to his view that individual conscious spirits may be at the same time internal parts of God. Bergson's opposition between intuition and intellect I could not accept, but on its positive side his theory of intuition seemed to me to be important for understanding our psychical nature and the deeper things in our moral and religious life. And his doctrine of creative evolution gave both a biological and a metaphysical grounding for principles which are indispensable if we are to comprehend evolution in its higher ranges—in the development of man and his history.

It was congenial to the main interests that were occupying my thought that I was called to a chair of the philosophy of religion and of Christian ethics in the Oberlin School of Theology. Most of my five years at Oberlin fell within the period of the war. Ethical questions were inevitably to the fore. While not a theoretical pacifist, I took the pacifist position to the extent of opposing, in local prints and public addresses, America's entrance into the war. My sympathies were with the Allies, but I held that war had become a greater evil than the evils it was invoked to rectify, and that when a war was under way Wilson's "peace without victory" was the valid principle. In my book, *The Experience of God in Modern Life*, I upheld the ethics of democracy and of internationalism. Democracy as an ethical ideal, I was coming to see, called for industrial democracy, because in our present system the ethics of privilege works powerfully against the ethics of progress.

In respect to the theistic problem, I sought, in this same volume, to express anew both the meaning of God and the grounds for belief in Him. If the purpose of God for men is to bring them into the relation of sonship with Himself, this should be understood to involve the creating of creators. God is thus understood to be an Eternal Creative Good Will with whom men can be co-workers, and the experience of God and a life of moral creativity should interpenetrate. The grounds for belief in the reality of God as thus conceived I held to consist in a union of intuition, and of the higher ranges of man's spiritual achievement, with an interpretation of cosmic evolution.

A conception of purposive evolution is needed here as well as Bergson's conception of creative evolution. Moreover, the reality of evil must be steadily faced. The facts of evil require us to recognize that there are limiting conditions for the purposive, creative activity of God. But these limiting conditions are best understood as being inherent in a creative process and an ethical goal. The idea of a finite God is apt to mean a God who is struggling with a refractory external environment. Hence it is better to affirm the infiniteness of God, meaning that He is the ground of all finite existence and that His wisdom and love are infinite.

Thus I found the belief in the existence of God to rest upon the vast upward trend in the portion of the universe that we know best, which has made possible creative personality and a spiritual community for man; upon a critique of the ultimacy of mechanical, non-teleological categories as being explanatory of the cosmos in its total extent; and upon man's intuition—made classic by prophetic personalities but experienceable by the many—that the deepest reality is Divine, or more fully expressed, is Creative and Redemptive Love.

The problems which have occupied me during my thirteen years of teaching the philosophy of religion in Union Theological Seminary may be grouped as belonging to the following areas of thought: the theory of religious knowledge; Christian ethics and the metaphysics of personality; the bearing of the new cosmology on religious faith. To the problems which have concerned me in these areas I wish now to give special discussion in order to bring out the relation proposed in the title of this chapter between Christian theology and a spiritualistic philosophy. It is perhaps evident from the foregoing account that the traits of what may best be called a spiritualistic philosophy have been emerging, though not always in consistency with each other, in conjunction with the development of my understanding of religion and theology. But it will be well now to subordinate the chronological outline and proceed to a more systematic sketch.

The pillars of the house of Christian theology, as I conceive it, are four: (1) historical continuity with the spirit of Jesus, such that the life of sonship to God seen in His teaching, deeds and personality is recognized to be that which can fulfil man's deepest religious needs and aspirations; (2) an ethical mysticism, which sonship indeed implies, in which the sense of an immediate relation to God imparts the freedom, freshness of insight, and power that belong to a religion of the spirit; (3) acceptance of the normative character of the ethics of love in its intensive and universal meanings, so that love is recognized to be the supreme test and goal for man's psychological nature, his social institutions, and his world-wide relationships; (4) a theistic interpretation of the cosmos.

Continuing the figure, the architraves of this house constitute the main features of a spiritualistic philosophy. They are: a religious realism; a metaphysical view of personality; objectivity in ethics; a spiritualistic metaphysics. Let me give to each of these structural principles of a spiritualistic philosophy a brief consideration.

Religious realism is in one aspect a part of the reaction against subjectivism which has been taking place in many fields of thought. Subjectivism—that is, the notion that whatever truth and reality we get are mainly the product of our own states of consciousness, emotional attitudes, desires, and habits of thought—had considerable justification when individual minds were asserting their powers against dogmatic systems of thought and of society, and when such capacities for objective knowledge as we have were being used largely to buttress those systems. But in the end subjectivism lost not only its objects but its subjects. It could give us neither things nor selves. And when the monistic idealists sought to establish the objective reality of God on the ground that there must be one subject who sees all our subjective experience in its true perspective and meaning, the pluralistically minded subjectivists could reply: "Why this preference for the One as compared with the Many? Is it not merely an intellectual bias, or a desire for the accompanying sense of security?"

When these extremes had been reached, it was inevitable that there should be a reaction toward objectivism. For knowledge itself implies that we have some measure of capacity for grasping things as they are. The knowledge which science gives, for example, in geology concerning the earth

"Before there were the first of us around,"

can hardly be given a subjectivist treatment, else how could the subjects have arrived later? Historical events have a way of disillusioning us and insisting that we take them realistically. Philosophic criticism is indistinguishable from skepticism unless it is able to lay hold of objective truth and structural principles of reality.

In short, the scientist's faith in experiment, the pragmatist's faith in practice, and the idealist's faith in
reason require for their vindication a realistic view of
knowledge.

But there are still many today whose attitude toward
knowledge in general is objectivist, and yet who relapse
into subjectivism when they think of religion. Often an
arbitrary standard of objectivity is set up, and when it
is found that religion cannot conform to that, the conclusion is reached that it is merely subjective. One
might as well insist that the only evidence for the
objective reality of the planets and stars is the fact that
the earth is being hit from time to time by meteors;
whereas the earth is being played upon constantly by
forces from the planets and stars.

As I have maintained in my essay in the volume,
Religious Realism, we need an understanding of intuition as a source of objective truth if we are not to
continue in respect to religion a subjectivist way of
thinking which we are abandoning elsewhere. Two
forms of intuition should be distinguished, the perceptive form and the synthetic form, and each can be illustrated by the ways in which we know human personalities. A perceptive intuition occurs in moments of
special *rapport* between persons when one swiftly and
freshly apprehends another's unique quality or deeper
intent. Georg Brandes wrote after his first meeting
with John Stuart Mill: "A quiet nobility and perfect
self-control pervaded his presence. Even to one who
had not read his works it would have been very evident
that it was one of the kings of thought that had taken
his seat in the red velvet arm-chair near the fireplace." [1]
A synthetic intuition is gained, for example, when a
biographer, who has assembled abundant data, pene-
trates to the inner meaning of the life of which he is
writing and grasps it as a unified and living whole. It

---

[1] *Creative Spirits*, p. 185.

is for lack of such a synthetic intuition that so many biographies fail to make us know the lives of which they treat.

In religious intuition, as Professor Montague has explained, the whole self is engaged, and thus an indispensable condition is provided for a wider and richer apprehension of objective truth. "Even ordinary perception and reasoning," he writes, "is largely based upon the subconscious stores of memory and instinct. They furnish the meaning with which our sensations are clothed, and the motives by which our reasonings are driven." But "in normal experience . . . there is evoked only that part of the subconscious which is relevant to that situation, while in the real mystic intuition the inner self in its entirety is the controlling factor." [2]

Religious intuition of the perceptive type is exemplified when, after conscientious examination of life's complexities and attentive brooding upon them, one swiftly and clearly sees that "*Now* is the accepted time," "*This* is God's will for me," "Lo, God is here." In religious intuition of the synthetic type there is an apprehension of a totality as having such inner relations as give it divine significance. Such an intuition is expressed in the words of the apostle Paul: "For the earnest expectation of the creation waiteth for the revealing of the sons of God." Such penetrative and synthetic insights are not substitutes for detailed analyzed knowledge; but they add to our possession of objective truth as really as does the analyzed knowledge, for it is by such insights that comprehensive wholes and inner principles of unity are grasped. At the same time these insights are not to be withdrawn from further testing. They are subject to such testing both by critical reflection and by practical living.

Thus a body of organized truth can be built up, which

---

[2] *Ways of Knowing*, p. 57.

can be brought into comparison with organized truth from the special sciences. So far as these bodies of truth make a coherent whole they meet the final test of objectivity. We often talk about "our world" or "this universe of ours" as though we knew what these terms meant. Usually the meanings they have for us are tacit and are taken over unreflectively from some intellectual or social group. A far higher objectivity than our vague common sense world-views can claim belongs to a world-view which has gained inner coherence and meaning through the interpretive power of religious insight.

The metaphysical view of personality which forms a part of a spiritualistic philosophy involves many difficult problems which cannot be considered here. But the meaning of this metaphysical view may be indicated by pointing out that it stands in contrast both to the phenomenalistic view and to the naturalistic view. The phenomenalistic view turns upon regarding time, the form of all our inner experience, as lacking in full metaphysical reality. If this be true, the self as we actually experience it must be a non-essential appearance of something timeless—an unknowable or the Absolute. But this timeless somewhat is no longer the self about which we are talking. That self is by its very nature acting in time. There is no valid reason for calling in question the full reality of that self or of the time-aspect which it shares with many other things. We may recognize timeless truths, but whatever they are, they cannot cover the entire nature of existence, to which time inseparably belongs.

The naturalistic view of personality holds that whatever personalities do is the doing of their bodies. If thinking, appreciating, purposing are going on, these events are actions of some bodily organism. The mind as a whole consists of such actions plus the bodily habits which have resulted from similar actions in the past.

In contrast to this naturalistic view the metaphysical view finds personality to be essentially an inner psychical reality, manifesting awareness of things present, memory of things past, and anticipation of things to come. It finds this inner psychical reality, even in its inchoate infant stages, actively going out to meet and explore environing objects including its own individual body. And to this outgoing psychic activity there belong from the start some simple patterns of action or response, *Gestalten*, which make possible the discovery of objective structure in the environment and consequently growth in knowledge. A self thus understood has an inherent unity from the start, and particular sensations and impulses are abstractions from this unity. As the self becomes developed and articulate its unity becomes richer and more meaningful; but its unity is never a mere derivative from the body, nor is it merely due to some outside organizing agency, as is the unity of a book. Such a self can be intelligibly thought of as a seat of intrinsic value, of cognitive discovery, and of creative action and as a being capable of worshipful response to and cooperation with a higher spiritual Reality.

If one asks the inevitable question, Whence comes a reality so unique as this psychical self even in its inchoate early stages? the reply is that if we go on to a more comprehensive spiritualistic metaphysics, this question ceases to be troublesome. But that matter aside, one should not stumble at the emergence of selves if one recognizes emergent evolution at all. The emergence of selves is no more anomalous than the emergence of psychic functions in general, or of life as a whole, or of the higher chemical properties. Moreover, from the fact that the self has a beginning it does not follow that it is a transient entity nor that its fortunes are inseparable from the body.

We are not bound to suppose that the whole of

emergent evolution must in the end sink back into mere space-time; nor are we bound to suppose that the highest emergents we know, namely selves, must relapse into simpler elements. On the contrary, emergent evolution is a name for the fact that new emergents may establish permanent relations with the rest of the universe. Nor should we assume that emergents must forever be tied to the conditions from which they emerge. Such has not been the case in the emergence of birds from reptile types. Selves as they emerge are conditioned upon bodily organisms, but it does not follow that they must forever be conditioned upon the type of organism from which they emerge. The metaphysical view of personality does not forthwith establish personal immortality, but it takes radical issue with those views of personality which rule out immortality in advance.

The philosophy here being outlined includes objectivity in ethics. By this term I mean that ethical values are not determined solely by desires and choices, nor by a merely experimental organization of desires and choices, even though they be taken collectively as well as individually. Rather, there are certain objectively valid principles according to which ethical values must be judged and by which, or by approximation to which, ethical values must be constituted. Such principles are the Kantian one that every personality is an end in itself and can never rightly be made merely a means to other ends, and the corresponding principle that the goal of ethical living is the achievement of a Realm of Ends. These principles are the ethical equivalents of the Christian teachings, at once ethical and religious, of the human soul's infinite worth and of the Kingdom of God.

Other such principles, implied in the foregoing or supplementing them, are justice, equality, the intrinsic worth of all creative capacities, and love as inclusive of

all the other principles and as also requiring them in
order that it may be the supreme ethical value.

If it be said that such principles are general and
abstract, and that the ethical thing to do in a particular
situation cannot be simply deduced from them apart
from examining the requirements of the situation—
that is quite true. But neither can the requirements of
a situation be determined in ethical fashion apart from
such principles. They are "tools for analysis" of situations, and they are more than that; they are structural
to any treatment of situations that can be called genuinely ethical. They subsist, not in the sense of deriving
their authority from some remote abstract realm of being, but in the sense of being eternally valid for thinking, purposing, social beings whenever they arrive on
the scene. And they have to be discovered, whether
slowly and painfully or not, if the life of such beings
is to attain to rational, ethical organization.

The acceptance of such objectively valid ethical principles does not mean, as is often supposed, the rejection
of the ideal of creative thinking and action in the ethical
life. The recognition of basic principles of harmony in
music does not impair the creative talent of the musician. Rather, it is the possession of such principles
which liberates and makes significant whatever creative
talent he may possess. So in the ethical life it is
precisely when the basic principles for such a life have
been discovered that creative thinking and action become possible. If passion blind us to the principles,
the higher levels of ethical living become impossible
for us, no matter how ardently we desire to escape from
present evils and to attain a fuller freedom. And must
we not think that the creativity of God himself is the
expression, not of sheer sovereignty and unqualified
will, but of the principles of Goodness, Truth, and
Beauty which are inherent in his eternal nature?

A spiritualistic philosophy, I have affirmed, should

include a definitely spiritualistic metaphysics. This position stands in contrast to the naturalistic metaphysics so widespread today, which denies that we have reason to believe in a Supreme Divine Spirit, but with which some thinkers are endeavoring to connect a portion of the values of the Christian religion.

A naturalistic metaphysics as a rule holds that the idea of God is untenable. But if on such a basis the effort is made to retain the idea, it will mean the personification of certain valuable processes in nature, or it will be used to denote such processes without any personification. The strength of this position is its insistence that religion must be neither hostile nor indifferent to the valid results of the physical and social sciences. On the contrary, religion should assimilate these results, promote their increase, and function with and through them. This is well. But the idea that a religious interpretation of the cosmos can be thus secured, even though a psychology of worship and social fellowship be added, is a grave error.

Of course there are always some processes which make for good with which we can and should take sides. But are these prepotent, and does religion establish a vital relation with them? If we say, yes, upon what does this answer rest? Upon the optimistic feeling that nature must be such that, though there are many maladjustments in the world, intelligence and effort, plus a cultivation of the right emotional adjustments, are bound to win? The dualisms and conflicts and evils of the world are far too serious to be met in this way. Christianity, except in the case of certain secularized forms of liberalism, has always faced these issues in their more tragic meanings, and has enabled men to transcend them because it has found that faith and reason establish a living relation between men and a Cosmic Creative Spirit who is the ground for the existence and ongoing of a world in which moral effort, intelligence, faith and love can triumph. But in this aspect Christianity goes quite beyond the bounds of naturalism.

A spiritualistic metaphysics will include a view of nature which accepts the doctrine that man is a part of nature without leveling down his psychic functions, his unity, and his higher capacities to merely physical or physiological processes—or if these aspects of man be recognized as unique, without treating them as non-efficacious with respect to the rest of nature. Such a view can be expressed by a union of the doctrines of panpsychism and emergent evolution. Panpsychism expresses the continuity between man and the physical and biological orders in the midst of which he has arisen and upon which he is continuously dependent. It discards the idea of dead, purely inert matter and affirms that there is some spark of spontaneity in whatever individual reals science and philosophy may justify us in accepting. Emergent evolution affirms that, notwithstanding the continuity, there have come to pass unique levels of being in the world, which cannot be treated by the leveling-down process. And if these two doctrines are really combined, the genuineness of immanent teleological causation is recognized; which at the level of man means that the moral life has full significance.

But more important for a spiritualistic metaphysics than the foregoing view of nature will be a view of the whole world as being grounded in God. Such a view goes beyond naturalism because it finds God, as a purposive creative Spirit, to be immanent in the world and yet to be transcendent of it since He possesses all supreme values in His thought and is ceaselessly at work to give them actualization. The order and progress of the world, according to this view, are not taken for granted but receive their explanation through the purpose and creativity of God. Man's rational, moral and religious life is not an anomalous episode but a participation in and cooperation with the life of God.

And because God is the ground of the order and creativity of the world, He is the ground also of its redemption from evil. Evil cannot be precluded from a world-process the higher levels of which demand the increasing cooperation of finite creative spirits. In indeterminate but tragic ways ignorance, sloth, wilfulness, pride will alienate human spirits from each other and from God. But religion in its profoundest experiences knows that God's love is inexhaustible and, working even through suffering and sacrifice, can effect the reconciliation of man with man and with God. And these same experiences make known to men their highest destiny—as sons of God to be sharers in both His creative and His redemptive work. Thus when God is known to be the ground not only of the world's order and its creativity but also of its redemption He becomes the ultimate explanation and interpretation of the world.

That this spiritualistic metaphysics appeals for its completion to religious insight should not prejudice it, for when has a significant metaphysics not been in part at least a matter of vision?

Theologians have often sought to dispense with metaphysics altogether, holding that to present God as the explanation of the world involves at best too much difficult theorizing, upon which a religion that is to meet the needs of the common man should not be dependent. These thinkers have held that it is enough to establish the primacy of ethics and religion among the functions of the human spirit, leaving the reality of God to be an affirmation of faith. But really to establish the primacy of ethics and religion involves an epistemology which is as remote from the common man as are theories of the cosmos. If what has been said about religious realism is right, none of us has to wait upon either cosmology or epistemology for a vital knowledge of God.

But neither should any of us wish to withdraw this more intuitive knowledge from the testing of reflective thought and the interpretations of a synthetic philosophy.

Religion in all its most developed forms offers man an interpretation of the Ground, the Way, and the Goal of Life. If the profoundest interpretation of the Way of Life is to be found in the creative and redemptive love embodied in the teachings and personality of Jesus; and if the true portrayal of the Goal of Life is to be seen in the ideal of the Kingdom of God on earth—a world-wide community in which brotherhood prevails —and in an immortal spiritual destiny; then the most adequate interpretation of the Ground of Life must be sought in a God who gives triumphant meaning to this Way and this Goal because he is the Ultimate Reality of the universe.

PRINCIPAL PUBLICATIONS

Books:

> *Theology and Human Problems.* New York, Charles Scribner's Sons, 1910.
>
> *The Experience of God in Modern Life.* New York, Charles Scribner's Sons, 1918.
>
> *The God of the New Age.* Boston, Pilgrim Press, 1918.
>
> *The Value of Belief in God.* New York, Association Press, 1919.
>
> *The Meaning of Selfhood and Faith in Immortality* (Ingersoll lecture). Cambridge, Mass., Harvard University Press, 1928.
>
> *The Meaning and Truth of Religion.* New York, Charles Scribner's Sons, 1933.

Chapters in cooperative volumes:

> *Studies in Philosophy and Psychology,* Garman Commemorative volume. Boston, Houghton Mifflin Co., 1906,

Chap. VIII, "The Influence of Pragmatism Upon the Status of Theology."

Religious Foundations, Rufus M. Jones and others. New York, The Macmillan Company, 1923, Chap. IX, "How Shall We Think of Progress?"

Religious Realism, D. C. Macintosh and others. New York, The Macmillan Company, 1931, Chap. IX, "Can Religious Intuition Give Knowledge of Reality?"

Articles:

"Faith and Mysticism." *American Journal of Theology,* July, 1904.

"The Ultimate Test of Religious Truth; Is It Historical or Philosophical?" *American Journal of Theology,* January, 1910.

"What Is Theology?" *American Journal of Theology,* July, 1913.

"Social Progress and Religious Faith." *Harvard Theological Review,* April, 1914.

"Must Dogmatics Forego Ontology?" *American Journal of Theology,* July, 1914.

"The Religion of Democracy." *Union Theological Seminary Bulletin,* November, 1918.

"The Ethics of the Wages and Profit System." *The International Journal of Ethics,* October, 1920.

"The Philosophy of Religion," in *The Dictionary of Religion and Ethics,* edited by Shailer Mathews and Gerald B. Smith, The Macmillan Company, 1921.

"The Rationality of Belief in the Reality of God." *The Journal of Religion,* September, 1922.

"Religious Education for a New Democracy." *The Journal of Religion,* September, 1923.

"The Faith That Is in Us." *Union Theological Seminary Bulletin,* July, 1924.

"Ritschl's Theory of Value-Judgments." *The Journal of Religion,* September, 1925.

"A Revival of Philosophy in Religion." *Alumni Bulletin of Union Theological Seminary*, June, 1927.

"The Living God and the Christian Purpose." *Alumni Bulletin of Union Theological Seminary*, October, 1927.

"Mysticism, Reason and Social Idealism." *The Journal of Religion*, April, 1928.

"The Place of Christ in Modern Theology." *The Journal of Religion*, April, 1929.

A BELIEVER IN "CHURCHIANITY"

By DANIEL ARTHUR McGREGOR

(b. October 30, 1881, Ottawa, Ontario, Canada)

Professor of Dogmatic Theology, Western Theological Seminary;
Recently Appointed Executive Secretary of the Department of
Religious Education of the Episcopal Church

Evanston, Illinois

A BELIEVER IN "CHURCHIANITY"

By Daniel Arthur McGregor

THE aim of this symposium, as I understand it, is not to present a number of different systems of theology, but to have each writer tell something of what he believes today and how he came to his present position of belief. We are asked to mention the various influences, situations, prejudices and interests which have played a part in our thinking. I find myself in hearty accord with this plan of presenting beliefs. I am not of those who are sure that they have a source of beliefs free from the influence of their own environment. Nor am I of those who are made skeptical about all beliefs because they see the environmental factors in theologies.

I am enough of an absolutist to believe in God and in truth, and enough of a pragmatist to believe that God reveals truth and Himself to man in and through man's wrestling with his environment. If God is Love it would seem natural that He should be apprehended by purposeful living, rather than by impartial thinking, if indeed there be any such thing as impartial thinking. Environmental factors and passionate desires do not come as a distorting influence in our quest for God and for truth, they are the necessary conditions of the quest. A belief is not to be set aside when it is shown to be the rationalization of a desire or an attitude; this may be its best title to consideration.

I acknowledge, therefore, that desire and taste have had an important influence in bringing me to the theological position in which I now find myself. I can see such influences at work in the lives of other men, and

I am quite sure that I have also been affected. Nor do I wish to discount my own views or those of other men by making allowance for such human deflection. Human desires do not lead away from truth, they lead to it. We come to our beliefs by the pathway of our need, we hunger for satisfaction and we come to believe that to be true which ministers the satisfaction that we find.

Of course, this position may not be held in an individualistic way, or we shall have as many truths as there are persons in the world. We are social beings, and a rationalization which is shared by no other than myself cannot minister satisfaction to me in a social world. It is useless to me in the world that I live in. I must come to terms with other people and find solutions that meet common problems. But this does not mean that we must find a truth independent of human needs and desires; it means that I must go back of my own individual needs, find needs that are common to many or all men, and then find common satisfactions for those common needs. We may not seek to be free from anthropomorphism, but we must seek to be free from the individuality of the separate life. As a social being I cannot use a rationalization if I am the only one to adopt it; I can only use it if it is a satisfactory rationalization of the experience of many others. Ultimately a universal rationalization would be a universal satisfaction and a universal truth.

Therefore I turn for my theology to the needs of men and to their efforts to rationalize the attitudes which they have adopted in seeking satisfaction of those needs. I am very skeptical about the ability of the pure reason to reach absolute truth; I am most skeptical about my own ability to do so. But I am a man with many and great needs. I am one of a people with many needs, and I look out on history and present life to see what methods and approaches have led to the fullest satisfactions of those needs. I do not think that the universe was made for me, and I do not expect it to conform to the demands of my life and my desires. But it is a legitimate supposition that it was made for man and that it can supply the satisfactions for his needs.

At any rate, human life is an experiment to test the truth of this supposition. "Mere Humanism," someone says. Not necessarily. If the universe has a deeper meaning than man (and I believe that it has) it may well be that the path to the understanding of God is the path of finding the meaning of the universe for man. This is a faith, a prejudice, which I freely acknowledge. I can form rationalizations to support it, but I cannot prove it. It probably springs from the desire to save together the values of Humanism and Theism. This faith or prejudice has had a great deal to do with my religious wanderings. As I have stated it, it is probably a rationalization of those wanderings.

The Evangelical Stage

I was born and brought up in a deeply religious home. The religious life was evangelical, the theology a mild Calvinism. I am not able to agree with those persons who speak of this type of religious life as tyrannical and oppressive. It was a firm discipline, but I never felt it as a burden, and all my life I will be thankful that I had it. Of course we went to church on Sundays, three times, but this was not a task, it was a joy to which one looked forward during the week. The Bible was believed to be literally true and we were well trained in it. God was prominent in our thoughts, and our lives were steadied by our belief in Him. Conversion was emphasized and every effort was made to bring the unconverted to a saving knowledge of the truth.

This whole system of thought and practice ministered to us great values. In the church a community was created which felt itself to be the people of God. This church possessed the Bible which was the very Word of God, the final truth. In reading the Bible and in listening to the preaching of the Word one was having communion with God. In reliance on the truth contained in Bible and sermon, one had a guarantee of certainty, a rock of assurance in an uncertain and bewildering world. This assurance gave poise and confidence to life. It set the transitoriness of the visible world in the setting of the eternal and invisible world and it made the believer at home in the greater cosmos. It lifted man out of his littleness and gave him the consciousness of dignity by teaching him that he had an eternal destiny. By its doctrine of God, by its reading of the Word of God and by its practice of prayer this religious system gave to the believer the sense of being in living fellowship with the supernatural and infinite. Above all the changing world was an unchanging God, and we were His children. In this evangelical religion man was not degraded, he was lifted to the proud position of being an heir of God and joint-heir with Jesus Christ.

There were rich emotional experiences in this religious life. If the sense of sin was strong, yet the sense of forgiveness was sometimes stronger; if one sometimes felt lonely in this world, one's imagination could picture the city which hath foundations; if one was discouraged by difficulties and failures, one could gain hope and strength by looking to the invisible God and by resting back upon His everlasting arms. Those who stigmatize Calvinism as a religion which makes man a slave and which gives no place to the emotions must have seen a type very different from that which I knew.

But in spite of all the satisfactions which it ministered, we were not able to hold to it. The promises and assurances had been presented to us as guaranteed by the Bible, and doubts arose as to the authority of this Book. It is hard for man to believe all that Christianity says about him, its estimate of man is so high and its promises so glorious. It is only possible for a rational man to believe the Christian message if support is given to his faith. Christianity is almost too good to be true. And the young men of my generation were assailed at the same time by the new teachings of biology as to the animal ancestry of man, and by Biblical criticism showing the human origin of the Bible. We used to talk a great deal about "doubt" in those days.

He who doubts has put himself outside the system which he questions. And from this new position we were able to see faults in the old system of which we had not been conscious as long as we were within it. We saw that it did not give sufficient recognition to the new science which was becoming so important. It had shut our eyes to much of the beauty and wonder of the world around us. By focusing our eyes on the world beyond, it had kept us from seeing much of the glory of this present world. It looked backward and inward, backward to the days of the Bible, inward to the experience of the soul. While living within the system, sharing its characteristic attitudes, we had found satisfaction; but now that we stood without, in new attitudes, we became conscious of new hungers that the old could not satisfy. Within the churches men and women felt themselves needy and looked to the God of the churches to give them satisfactions to their needs. But outside the churches a new life was sweeping on, lusty in its self-confidence. We had doubts of the old, and the new was glowing with promise. We stepped over into Liberalism.

The Liberal Stage

How fresh and free the air seemed in this new country. We stepped out of a sense of the need of divine help into a confidence in human power. We threw away the old religious supports as a healed man throws away his crutches. We were sure that the new learning showed that the crutches were weak anyway. Literary criticism demolished the divine authority of the Bible. When this foundation of Evangelicalism fell, the whole structure of the plan of salvation fell also. Psychology took away the miraculous element from conversion. Science was the new Messiah.

The new religion was very human and very confident. We did not discard God, that would have been too cruel; but we practically superannuated Him since science could do everything that man needed. We did not deal with beliefs but with conduct, and we prided ourselves on being concerned with actualities of experience rather than with the uncertainties of belief. I am not at all sure that we were really more concerned with moral conduct than were the Evangelicals, but we talked more about it. We had a glowing faith in progress. We could see that science was producing more goods, and we were quite sure that it could also produce richer life for man.

We opened our eyes to the world of nature and we found it so wonderful and beautiful that we did not mourn our loss of a world of grace. We justified ourselves for forsaking the traditional religious attitudes by making the appeal "Back to Christ." We knew so little of New Testament criticism that we thought we were quite justified in taking the Sermon on the Mount and interpreting it in a purely individualistic way. Our religion was a morality touched by emotion.

I must deal briefly with Liberalism for I do not love it, and therefore will probably not be fair to it. It was a pleasant companion for a few fortunate people for a short time; but many of us feel that we were deceived. It failed to render either the outer or the inner satisfactions that we sought. There had been great inner values in Evangelicalism, the sense of needs met, of

forgiveness vouchsafed. But now we were not conscious of neediness and had no experience of saving
grace. We talked a great deal about "ideals" but after
a while we found that unspecified ideals were empty.
There was no sense of a great destiny to be achieved,
nor of great woe to be avoided. Life was no longer
a mighty tragedy, it lost its tension. The goal seemed
to be the fulfilment of comfort.

I remember about this time spending a few days in
a town made up principally of retired farmers and discovering to my dismay that such a social condition was
what I was hoping for all men. It was too horrible.
We had thought that we had support for our beliefs
in the liberal interpretation of the Gospels, until we
read Schweitzer and found that we had lost our back-
ing of New Testament scholarship. And then some
of us began to see that this whole liberal religion was
merely a comfortable rationalization of middle-class
prosperity, and that behind the scenes a great industrial
civilization was keeping the workers of the country in
poverty and hopelessness.

The religion of which we were so proud was not true
to the ethos of the New Testament, nor was it capable
of meeting the needs of the great mass of men. During part of this time I was in college work in India,
and then, after returning to this country, was pastor
in an Illinois town where the main industry was steel.
My religion had plenty of beautiful truths, but it could
not meet the terrible needs that were all around me in
either place.

I became a convert to Socialism and found in this
movement some of the things that were lacking in liberal religion. Socialism gave us a great goal to live for
and perhaps to die for. It filled life with the sense of
destiny, it enabled us to believe that we were working
for the Kingdom of God and that all the forces of social
evolution were working with us. There was a social

ideal that glowed before us, and in the light of that ideal we could recapture some of the lost religious experiences of the past. Socialism was an evangel, it was the good news of the good time coming. It had a dogmatic system which seemed to be sound.

Then came the World War, and the weaknesses of Marxian Socialism were revealed. I was bewildered; life was not worth living without a faith and I had no faith. Evangelicalism, Liberalism and Socialism, all had failed to meet my needs or the needs of the men and women among whom I lived. I had no guidance to give, I could not find my way myself. I resigned from my pastorate, not without strong suggestions from my leading people; I slipped out of the denomination in which I was enrolled, and for five years I hardly stepped into a church.

THE WILDERNESS YEARS

These years were barren and unhappy. During the war I served in America as an official in the American Red Cross, and after the war I held a business position. I always think of the years 1916 to 1921 as "the wilderness years." I was making a living, but had put aside the problems of life. I could not find an answer. Orthodox Christianity seemed unbelievable and Liberal Christianity powerless.

Meanwhile the world was racking itself to pieces in war or was facing a post-war future without a principle or guide. Faith was lacking, and only faith could save men. We could not believe in the facile optimism which prevailed in the first decade of the century. We had enough faith in reason to believe that the undirected and uncontrolled functioning of human instincts could not lead to life. Science was not a Savior, science was a tool which could be used to destruction as well as to salvation. Reason was utterly unable to cope with the strong tides of human passion. Wherein was our hope? Some of us had no hope, we walked in the darkness without guide, compass or chart. We wanted to believe something but we could not find anything believable. We wanted to be saved but could not find a Savior. We wanted to be converted but could not find anything with the power to convince reason and sway emotion to which we could surrender.

If at any time we dared to hope we were stopped by the grim realities of mechanistic physical science. It seemed that the whole of reality was a deterministic system in which the hopes and ideals of men had no place. There was but one God visible, determinism, and Bertrand Russell was his prophet. Science was certain, all else might be illusion, and we could not surrender to illusions.

We needed a rational faith in the reality of God; not only did we need it as individuals, but the world needed it desperately. The grounds on which the Christianity of our early training had based this faith were seen to be insecure; science was advancing, it had the certainty of mathematics, and it had no need of such an hypothesis as God. Faith is not speculation, faith is confidence. We might speculate about God, but the ground of confidence was gone just at the time when we needed it most. We looked to the Christian Church. It had had the power in the past to create the type of character in the individual and in society which our day needed. But it could only create this character if there were utter faith in the teachings of Christianity. We needed this character, the Christian Church could create it if we would believe, but we could not believe.

And then came a breach in the stone wall of deterministic science. Poincaré pointed out the relative nature of the classical mathematics, and soon Einstein appeared with his new doctrine making relativity regnant in all fields of thought. The autocratic right of physical science was denied by those men who knew most about it.

The new teaching did not establish the truth of religion but it put the whole question of faith in a new setting. The old foundations were not reconstituted but the character of some of the objections had changed. We could not base our beliefs on an absolutely authoritative book, nor on the necessities of reason, but we were free to adopt such beliefs as we chose in the form of hypotheses and to uphold them as the truest truths if they proved the most valuable hypotheses for life. Science became the servant of man's life and justified its hypotheses by the service rendered. Religion might do the same if it would accept the same pragmatic criticism.

THE PATHWAY TO FAITH

On this basis it has seemed to me possible to make my approach to the problems of religion and life. The reason that prejudiced us in favor of Christianity was that in the past it had produced values in living that could not be produced otherwise. Could we not analyze Christian history, isolate those factors or beliefs which were evidently necessary for Christian living, and then hold these as hypotheses? We could believe, even if we could not prove. In fact, would not this way be really the way of faith? Such an approach is not unbiased or intellectual, it is predicated on a value-judgment; it begins frankly with an assumption that that which is necessary for the richest values in human life is true. It is an assumption of the identity of the *ens necessarium* and the *ens realissimum*. It is pragmatic, not in the sense that we will treat the useful as true, but in the faith that genuine truth is reached by the efforts of human striving after value.

Such an effort must be social. Truth must be that

which ministers life and highest satisfaction to all men
in all times. We begin with the historical judgment
that the technique of thought and practice called the
Christian religion has ministered the highest values to
men. We are then called on to accept as our hypothesis in practical life those elements in the Christian
religion which are necessary for this achievement. We
are not trying to prove theological truth, we are trying
to solve human problems of living. And we are not
the first persons to deal with the problem; men have
been working at it for centuries. The results of their
efforts must be considered, the relationship between the
most successful efforts and the hypotheses assumed in
those efforts must be noted. That assumption has the
greatest claim to our acceptance as true which has rendered the greatest service to human living. The first
acceptance, of course, must be merely as the scientist
accepts an hypothesis, as a guide in further experiment.
But it is improper to ask for *a priori* proof of an hypothesis; the proof must be in experience, it must prove
itself true by its value.

We have tried to prove the Christian view of God
and the world. We have tried to prove it by Biblical
authority and by reason, and we have failed. Yet this
Christian teaching is an essential part of a complex
technique, the Christian religion which has solved
man's problems of living as no other technique has
done. We want to believe it because we want the values
that it alone can render. We have not proved it, perhaps we cannot prove it; but we can accept it as an
hypothesis and believe it until it fails.

What is the Christian hypothesis? To answer this
question we must survey the history of Christianity,
we must not accept the statement of it made by any
chance person or in any particular time. The Vin-
centian canon is our guide. *"Fides est quod semper,
quod ubique, quod ab omnibus creditur."* The Chris-

tian hypothesis is that complex of assumptions which is implicit in the functioning Christian life. I do not claim that I am able accurately to state what these basic assumptions are, to do so is a task of great difficulty; but I believe that this method is the legitimate method for our quest. Neither Bible nor church councils profess to state these assumptions. The Bible is a collection of more or less random literature of Christian authorship; and church councils state the point of view of the Church on specific questions. Neither claims to be systematic. The real Christian hypothesis can only be discerned by a process of historical analysis. We must go to the continuity of Christian life to learn what it is by which this life has been lived.

We do the best that we can in our effort to state what the historical Christian hypothesis is. We believe that this Christian religion as a continuity of culture has shown its capacity to produce the values which we desire in individual and social life better than any other technique which humanity has tried. It is, then, a legitimate belief that the Christian apprehension of the basic realities of life and the universe is the one best adapted to these realities, that is, it is the truest, it is the hypothesis by which to order our lives.

In this connection there are two considerations that must be faced. First, the accepted Christian hypothesis must not conflict with beliefs held in other fields of thought; or, at least, if there is a conflict, an adjustment of views must be found. But it is quite inadmissible to insist that all the accommodation must be on the side of Christian belief. If the moral and social values vouchsafed by religion are the highest values in life, then we have a perfect right to demand that conflicting hypotheses found in other disciplines of thought should recognize the rights of the religious life. The day of dogmatism in science is past.

Second, we must discover what in the Christian hypothesis is of temporary importance and what is permanent, that is, what is necessary in order that the Christian culture shall produce in our day the same values as it has produced in the past. The Christian culture is not identical with any of its past forms.

When we have thus isolated the hypothesis by criticism, we are then called on to take up a new attitude toward it. Our acceptance of the hypothesis in practice must be ungrudging. We are not seeking the irreducible minimum of belief, but the maximum of efficiency in the creation of individual and social character. Our interest is very practical. This does not mean that the theoretical is ignored, but that the theoretical is reached by the way of the practical. Truth is not divorced from value, and the highest value is moral character. Thus, as scientific discussion begins with an hypothesis and proceeds in terms of this hypothesis, so religious discussion and practice will begin with that hypothesis which is the correlate of the highest achieved religious value and will proceed in terms of that hypothesis.

Expressed in religious terms, this means the authority of the Church. One must be careful not to introduce under this heading more than is proper, that is, more than is actually necessary in fact to the continuity of Christian experience in society and in the individual. But one may not disregard this authority of the facts of the past any more than one may in science disregard the results of the researches of others. One may claim that official ecclesiastical statements of the implications of Christian experience are improper readings of that experience, but one's own understanding of the Christian life must be drawn from the facts of that continuous experience. And, at the least, those expressions of the Christian faith which have been recognized as satisfactory statements of the implications of the experience by large numbers of Christians deserve respectful and humble consideration.

Taking this position I find myself very much of a conservative, but I do not believe that I am an obscurantist. This method seems to me to be scientific. It is an appeal to the valuable experience of the past, and to the words of the past so far as these are expressive of the experience. The one who takes this position needs sharp criticism always or he will smuggle in all kinds of intellectual bonds under the cloak of his liberty. But every position has its corresponding dangers, and the danger of the position of the man who does not so love the past is that he will miss the rich values therein and become a provincial of the present age.

Thus far I have dealt with the progress of my own life as a quest for a basis on which I could believe the Christian faith. I have come to the position described and believe that I have a rational faith. I confess myself, as the title which I have chosen shows, a believer in "churchianity." I draw my faith from the historic Christian Church; I take as my hypothesis for life that hypothesis which is implicit in her life. I must now state what are some of the outstanding elements in this hypothesis.

REVELATION AND REASON

A basic difference between the conservative and the liberal today is as to the question of revelation. Is the content of religion something which man finds by his own efforts, or is it something that is revealed by God? This issue may be confused by the claim that all discovery of truth is the apprehension of the revelation of God. This seems to me to be avoiding the question. The question is, is there anything specific in the Christian life and message that is not the discovery of man's reason?

On this question I must declare myself a conservative. We must distinguish between reason and creative, imaginative insight. There are insights into the meaning of life and reality which are much more akin to the artist's vision than to the deductive processes of the rationalist. And these glimpses of meaning do not need to be repeated to every generation; they can be transmitted from one generation to another. They are gifts from the moments of high uplift in the life of the race. They are henceforth normative for thought and aspiration. We may call these visions, these adventures of faith, by the name revelation; we have no better name for them. Of course, every claim to revelation needs to be criticized, but criticism is not destruction, criticism is distinguishing the true revelation from the false claimant. Revelations are real, and the content of revelation is something that could not be gained by the ordinary processes of reason.

Reason is not constructive and creative. Reason is negative, critical and selective. The love of values which is faith is creative; faith is demanding and adventurous in its attitude to life and reality. Religion does not spring from reason, it is criticized by reason; religion springs from imagination, faith and love. Religion is the evidence of things not seen. Reason is properly critical of faith, its function is to point out contradictions in the content of faith. Faith is biased, prejudiced by love; reason criticizes the bias. But bias is direction. There is no absolute direction; reason is not the possessor of an absolute direction from which faith veers at a tangent. Faith is adventuring out in some *positive* direction in quest of the highest values, faith is daring.

The work of the critical reason is twofold; first, experimental, and second, analytical. By the experimental work of reason I mean the work of inquiring as to whether the values of life are or are not attained by the venture of faith. Such criticism is always necessary, for religion's only claim to belief is on the score of the values which it can mediate to the life of man. Reason must constantly ask the questions: "Are the experienced results of religious living really valuable to life?" and "Is religion really producing the values which it claims to produce, or is it justifying itself by talking about one set of values while really producing another set?"

The analytical work of reason is that of criticizing the rationalizations of religion. Life must strive to be rational, and religion always rationalizes its attitudes by a system of doctrines. Reason must ask whether these doctrines are free from internal contradiction, and whether they are in opposition to the rationalizations that man uses in other spheres of life. Man must adopt some social attitude which seeks certain particular highest values, and man must adopt such rationalizations as support this attitude. Then he must accept pragmatic criticism of the attitude and logical criticism of the rationalizations. If a particular venture of faith, in advance of reason, realizes the highest values, then the postulates implicit in this venture become authoritative for us so long as they are value-giving and are not irrational.

The great teachings of religion have always been put forward as revelations, not as rational deductions. I see every reason why one should criticize the claim to revelation, but I do not see valid standards for such criticism except the pragmatic criticism of value and the logical criticism of contradiction. I do not see that there can be an *a priori* rejection of the possibility of revelation as such, especially as we see such a similar psychological functioning in the case of the artist. And I see in the Christian life the achievement of such supreme values and something so non-rational (to use the word in its narrowest sense), as to deserve to be called the revelation of God.

It is not primarily a revelation of doctrine but of life; Christianity is the emergence of a new human life in society and individual. This life is not merely a rational criticism and correction of other life, it is a new pattern, a new coordination, a new creation of the immanent Spirit of God, it is a revelation. And if, in religious language, this is the revelation of God, or if, in modern scientific language, it is the emergence of the next step in the evolutionary process, it becomes authoritative for my life. I must subordinate my life to this life, and I must demand of my thought that it give adequate recognition to this new reality.

The Christian Church

It is evident from the foregoing that I place very great emphasis on the Church and its authority. By the Church, of course, I do not mean the official hierarchy but the continuity of Christian living. I suppose I might properly be called a liberal Anglo-Catholic, but I would spell the word liberal with a small "l" and I would emphasize the word "Catholic." I am indebted, both for the pattern of ideas in my religion and for the opportunity to practice that religion in a social group, to those who have gone before me, to the great multitude of Christian people who through all ages have wrought out and thought out this life in which I am privileged to participate. I am dependent on this tradition, without it I am lost; I do not know how to live nor am I such an artist as could create a pattern for life. It is in the life of this continuity, the Christian Church, that I find life.

It is a commonplace to say that religion is not a system of belief, but a social life. However, although we all acknowledge this, I doubt if we work it out thoroughly. This doctrine means that salvation is achieved by us in, or is mediated to us through, a social life. Since we are molded by our social environment and are made, to a large extent, in its image, it is of the utmost importance that we be integrated into the best society.

Every society is a definite structure, the incarnation of a particular principle or pattern. This social pattern is not created anew with every generation, it persists through the whole life of a culture. And every particular social pattern has, and must have, its own rationalizations, so that a doctrinal system is always taught with the pattern of life. We do not believe in a religion because we reason out the truth of its doctrines; we believe in a religion because the social group which is the bearer of the religion appears to mediate to us the highest values. And we believe the doctrines because they appear to rationalize the beloved social system.

Christians believe that the Christian religion ministers richer values to our life than any other group can minister. But the Christian religion is a very complex whole; it has social, ritualistic and doctrinal parts. The values are not in any one part, they emerge in life from the working in due measure of each several part. The doctrinal cannot be judged apart from its place in the religious system, nor apart from its character as a rationalization of that system.

The primary factor in religion is not its doctrines but its social life. To be a Christian is not to believe Christian doctrines but to be a part of the Christian society. People do not join the Church because they come to believe its doctrines; they believe its doctrines because they have become a part of its life. Any pastor can testify to the truth of this statement from his own experience. And we do not create this social life of the Christian Church, we are absorbed into it, into this social continuity which enfolds us.

Thus social continuity is essential to the Christian life and religion. And this is not easily gained. The continuity of a social process is different from the perpetuity of its forms. But the forms are very important, for if the form is changed there is great likelihood that the content will be changed also. The apostolic succession cannot guarantee the retention of the life, but the rejection of continuity will certainly mean the loss of the life.

A religion is more closely akin to a national or racial culture than it is to a philosophy, and a culture finds its home not in books but in a continuity of living people and in their institutions. One cannot enter into the reality of Greek culture by believing the philosophy of Plato, but only by immersing oneself in the stream of Greek mores. We cannot be Greeks today because the continuity of Greek culture has been broken. We may pick up beautiful fragments from the wreck, but we cannot reconstruct the whole. The pattern in terms of which the social lives of the Greek people were coordinated is broken and we cannot recreate it.

I repeat that the retention of no one form can guarantee the continuity of the culture. The emphasis on the apostolic succession by Catholics leads to the danger of trusting to a tactual succession of bishops rather than to a continuity of culture; but the rejection of the same apostolic succession by Protestants seems to me to face a greater danger, that of ignoring the necessity of cultural continuity. Continuity is essential, but it is not a continuity of creeds or administrators, it is a continuity of social life of a particular kind and pattern. It is the continuity of a society, which is a Church.

We are not saved by a Church, but in a Church; not by a society operating on us and for us, but by our being assimilated and assumed into a society which has an enduring and saving pattern. I cannot create a culture such as that of the people of France, but I can be assumed into French culture; I can be made French by a process of social conditioning. And I cannot create the Christian life in myself by any effort or belief; I can be made Christian by being assumed into a Christian society.

For these reasons I believe in the Church and acknowledge myself a devout believer in "Churchianity." I have little faith in the unchurchly Christianities that are being presented. They make for good writing and for striking preaching, they appeal to some of the radicalism of our day, they form contact on today's craving for freedom. But they leave the individual alone to work out his own destiny. And I am convinced that the individual as individual cannot work out his own destiny; he does it in and as a part of a definite society. I do not believe in social determinism, nor do I believe in individual freedom. We are social beings and we find ourselves not in our own individualistic freedom but in a social life. Individualistic religion is not what man needs or wants today; what his life is seeking is a fellowship in which he can lose himself and find himself. Man cannot find the salvation of his soul until he finds a saving fellowship. And the message of Christianity, as I understand it, is that there is such a fellowship in communion with which, in spite of its many defects, he will progressively find the fulfilment of his life.

CHRISTOLOGY

When one lays so much stress on the Church as I have been doing he is likely to meet with indignant objections from two quarters. The Liberal will point out the faults of the Church and will say "Surely you cannot expect man to be satisfied with such an institution as it is." And the Conservative will say: "You are giving up belief in Christ. You are substituting the Church for Christ. You claim to believe in continuity, but you are departing from the most definite statements of the position of the Christian Church in the creeds."

In reply to the Liberal one may simply point out that the Church is not seen in its true character in any single generation. The Church is not only what appears today. The Church is a culture growing in the world, it is to be evaluated by its past and future as well as by its present. It does not claim to be perfect but to be the power of God. The Church is to be believed in because of the power that worketh in her. The Church includes Jesus Christ, it is the continuity of the working in human life of the new pattern that emerged in Him. The Church is faulty, but by virtue of the fact that she is a living culture she is not to be judged by what she is but by that which she has the potency to become.

The answer to the objection of the Conservative will take us into serious questions. In the first place, it is the mere historical fact that the Christian Church has never been primarily interested in the historic figure of Jesus of Nazareth, nor in Him as unrelated to the Church. Early Christianity did not look back to Nazareth but forward to the Parousia. There is a modern Jesuolatry found among both Liberals and Conservatives which finds no counterpart in early or mediæval Christianity.

Such religion is backward-looking and morally antiquarian; Christianity has been forward-looking in hope and faith. It has lived, not by looking back to the earthly Jesus, but by looking forward to the coming of the Kingdom of God or to the glory of heaven. And in either of these two forms of the Christian hope the Church has occupied a large place. To the early

Christian the Church was the nucleus of the Kingdom of God; to the mediæval Christian heaven was the glorification of the Church. I do not claim that Jesus did not have a large place in this hope, but I point out that He was seen as the Messiah *of the Kingdom,* as the Savior *of the Church.*

Christian theology has not taught that in the Incarnation God became a man, but that God became Man. The Athanasian Creed states that Christ is one "not by conversion of the Godhead into the flesh, but by taking the manhood into God." In Jesus Christ manhood is assumed into the divine life. The conventional conservative understanding of the Incarnation is that the man Jesus of Nazareth was God; the conclusion of the Church is that in Christ God takes humanity into Himself. The Incarnation is not in *a man,* but in *humanity-in-Christ.*

Jesus Christ is not an isolated divine Being standing unrelated in the long process of human history; He is the beginning, the emergence of the new divine humanity. And the Incarnation is not complete in Him, else would our lives be Godless today. Christ was on earth incarnate in Jesus, and He is still on earth incarnate in the continuity of life that emerged in Jesus Christ, He is still in His Body the Church.

In Jesus Christ we have the incarnation of the eternal Son of God; but we must make a sharp distinction between the mythical individual Jesus and the actual personal Jesus. There is no such thing as an individual-in-himself; every person is what he is in the social environment which he chooses and to which he feels that he belongs. And there never was any such person as Jesus-the-individual; there was a person whom we call Jesus who was the focus and center of a social group. Apart from that group life He was not Himself. He found Himself in the group life of His people and particularly of His nearest disciples. He cannot be understood out of relation to His chosen group; He was what He was in and as a part of it. It is heresy to say that God became a man; it is orthodox Christian theology to say that God assumed humanity into His divine life in the person, the life and the work of Jesus Christ.

The Incarnation did not cease nor pass away when Jesus left this earth. It carried on. Human life in Him and by Him and through Him was so transformed that the incarnate life of the eternal Christ continued through the years. The Church, the Christian fellowship, is the continuity of the Incarnation. It is not an appendix to the Incarnation, nor a result of the Incarnation, it is the living Incarnation, the Body of Christ today.

I think of it in terms of a strain in plant or animal life. The new pattern of life, the divine-human life emerged in Palestine nineteen hundred years ago in the person, the life and the work of Jesus of Nazareth. And this strain is still operative in life, it is multiplying itself. It is not an isolated phenomenon in life standing alone in time or space; it is a life which is cross-fertilizing with the whole of life until the day when it shall be dominant. As a strain in life it is present today. All its expressions are the result of its entry into ordinary human life, but it is not overcome by these ordinary strains; it will yet become dominant and have the rule in all life. And this strain in life which emerged in Palestine in Jesus and His fellowship and which is present today is the very life of God, it is the Christ, the eternal Son of the Father.

Thus to believe is not to set the Church in place of Christ; it is to exalt the Christ whose body the Church is. It is not to ignore Jesus, it is to see Him as the pioneer of our salvation, and not only as the pioneer, but also as the author of eternal life to as many as believe in Him. He is not only the guide to salvation; since He is the *locus* of the emergence of the divine and saving life among men, and since we find our salvation by assimilation into this life as into a culture, He is our salvation. But He is not adequately thought of as a person who lived nineteen hundred years ago. He is a life that is active today, He is the living Lord of the Church. He is the vine and we are the branches.

SACRAMENTS AND ESCHATOLOGY

It has often been charged against those who magnify the Church that they tend to emphasize the material and institutional aspects of religion. I plead guilty to this charge; my religion is very materialistic. I know nothing of a spiritual which is not also material, I do not even know what the word means apart from its material expressions.

I look for a material Kingdom of Heaven such as the Hebrew prophets foretold and such as the early Christians expected. I think that it will come through the application of science under the influence and direction of the Christian fellowship rather than through miracle, but I genuinely believe in its advent. I think that the doctrine of the Parousia, of the Messianic Age, of a coming Christian world-order, is a doctrine that greatly needs to be believed and preached today. Primitive Christianity was a hope of the Kingdom of God, mediæval Christianity was a hope of heaven, modern Christianity can only be true to its past when it is abounding in hope. At present our Christianity is not rejoicing in hope; this is because we have tried to get away from the concrete and material and have tried to seek the "spiritual."

I believe in sacraments because I believe in the reality of the material. Man's salvation is from God, and God mediates it to man through a social continuity, the

Church. This Church, any Church, is not merely a
spiritual continuity. It is a continuity of souls, it is
also a continuity of bodies, of buildings, of hymn-books
and prayer-books and water and bread and wine and
furniture. I cannot know the Christian life, the Christian culture, unless I have contact with these material
parts of the process, any more than I can know my
friend if I do not have contact on him through material
means.

The eternal saving life of the Christ is mediated to
me in and through the acts of the Body of Christ, the
Church. If one believes in psycho-physical parallelism
in nature, then one will express his theology in terms
of a spiritual-physical parallelism, the sacraments will
be of little value in themselves except as channels of
the divine. But we are coming to see that life cannot
be adequately described in terms of psycho-physical
parallelism, the physical is more important than we
have sometimes been inclined to think.

And in the social sphere we must recognize that the
ordinary material contacts are not merely agencies of
a super-ordinary spiritual. We cannot separate the material from the spiritual and personal. My friend is
not a mystic presence who hides behind his visible attributes, he is known to me in and through these. And
the Christ is known to us in and through material
things. The sacraments are the actions of Christ in
His Church mediating Himself to us.

By the waters of baptism persons have actually been
brought into the new social relations of the fellowship
of Christ's Church; it is not magic, it is the mere report
of what is actually happening socially. And our social
life is our real life. In the fellowship meal of the
Christian family the very life of the new culture, of
the Christ, is actually mediated to the individual, and
this is done not by the preaching of a leader, but in the
humble reception of the sacred elements. Whatever be

our theory, these elements in such a situation actually are the Body and Blood of Christ. They are the material embodiment of that divine-human life as it exists today in the world. I do not believe in magic, but I do believe in the continuous life of the eternal and now incarnate Christ in the world.

And so I come to my conclusion, I am a believer in "Churchianity." It is open to anyone to say that this whole system of belief is a rationalization of my desires. I frankly admit it. But I do not think it is the rationalization of desires that are peculiar to me; I believe that it deals with the deepest desires of man, not merely of myself. If I did not believe that the Christian continuity has actually produced the richest values in the life of man, and if I did not love those values very dearly, I confess that I should not find the arguments which I present completely convincing. But I do not base my belief on arguments, I use arguments to help myself in holding beliefs which make a beloved position and attitude rational. Christianity is hard to believe, it is almost too good to be true. I should not be able to believe it were I not moved thereto by the authority of a continuity of life which has shown its power to bring to men the greatest values of life, values greater than they have ever asked or thought.

PRINCIPAL PUBLICATIONS

The Anglican Communion in India, 1930. (National Council Episcopal Church.)

Articles:

"Contemporary Theories of Primitive Religion." *Anglican Theological Review,* April, 1929, p. 343.
"What Do We Mean by a Personal God in the Light of Modern Science?" *Cincinnati Papers,* 1931.

THEOLOGY AS GROUP BELIEF

By SHAILER MATHEWS

(b. May 26, 1863, Portland, Maine)

Dean (emeritus) of The Divinity School; Chairman of the
Department of Christian Theology and Ethics; Professor of
Historical Theology; The University of Chicago

Chicago, Illinois

THEOLOGY AS GROUP BELIEF

By SHAILER MATHEWS

T HE New England of today preserves few traces of mid-Victorian Evangelicalism. It has lost most of that provincialism which the Evangelicalism demanded. A mobile civilization like today's does not rest upon the niceties of life controlled by social conventions and limited means of transportation. The life that I knew as a boy probably had no purer morals or any higher commercial honesty than that of today, but respectability was more clearly a social asset. Theology, like one's conduct, needed respectability. There were, of course, heretics, but a real New England Evangelical had no doubt as to their future. He might do business with them, but he did not expect to spend eternity in their company.

God had his plan of salvation, and New England theologians, especially if they were Congregationalists or, as were my family, Baptists, knew precisely what it was. The only debatable question of theology was whether the death of Christ was vicarious or substitutionary. Criticism had been heard of as one of the dangerous characteristics of far-away Germany, but the real enemy of religion was not German theology —the Unitarians could use that—but the teaching of such men as Darwin, Huxley, and Ingersoll. But Evangelicalism was not greatly concerned even over them. Did it not have for its philosopher Joseph Cook, and for its representatives Moody and Sankey?

I grew up in this atmosphere. On my mother's side for generations there had been ministers and teachers.

My grandfather was our pastor and my father was a Baptist deacon. Our family life was simple, and Evangelicalism was in its very atmosphere. As children we never danced, went to the theater, or played cards. But our life was not somber. We knew the wharves of Portland, the islands of Casco Bay, and the forests and hills of Maine; we had our sports and our reading. We went to church and Sunday school, and after we joined the Church went to prayer meeting as much as a matter of course as our father went to his business. There were no serious doubts and, thanks to wise family discipline, no serious temptations. It was a healthy life in which religion was a natural element. God could be trusted to order the affairs, especially the business and health, of Christians. Sickness and misfortune were His discipline. God was very real.

In college I experienced no particular change in this attitude. The student body in Colby was like the citizens of Portland. Religion was taken as a matter of course, but students were divided into those who were notoriously "wild," those who were studying for the ministry, and those who had neither promising virtues nor condemning vices. I suspect there was a touch of snobbishness on the part of those of us who were conscious of our virtues, for almost without exception the men whose future we distrusted turned out to be successful teachers, lawyers, or men of affairs. Naturally this attitude of mind perpetuated our evangelical self-complacency. The Y. M. C. A. was just beginning to develop in colleges, but the chief religious duties consisted in going to church and prayer meetings and occasionally seeking to convert some of our less pious comrades. We had no serious anxieties about the social order. Indeed I do not remember that we knew there was a social order. We knew God had been good to New England.

True, there was one disturbing factor; evolution. I

remember that when we were studying biology by committing Huxley's *Physiology* to memory, I went to my
professor and asked him for a book to prove that evolution was untrue. He asked me the reason for my request; I replied that it was contrary to Christianity.
Thereupon he told me that, if science showed that any
Christian belief was incorrect, Christianity would have
to be modified at that point. I can still feel the shock
which such a statement gave me. But I am inclined to
think that it was the beginning of what independent
thinking I may have done. At any rate, without any
direction I read everything I could find in the college
library on evolution. I found I could still believe
evangelical theology. There was, therefore, no particular change in my intellectual outlook, but, in the
attempt to face a real problem, there was something
more than classroom recitations of books I had committed to memory.

I went to Newton Theological Institution as a matter
of course. I was expected to become a minister, and,
although I had never announced that intention, I did
what the family expected me to do. Many of the men
of my generation who became university teachers did
the same. Johns Hopkins was just founded, but the
theological seminary was the graduate school for those
who did not want to go into law or medicine. At Newton there was little to stimulate original thought.
Theology was the exposition of the teachings of the
Bible; church history was a record of an institution
divinely established. Naturally we studied the Bible.
I remember that I read the entire Bible through in its
original languages. We had a few lectures about
Higher Criticism, but we were given to understand that
it was a matter which was dangerous to our faith, and,
while we needed to know about it, our real mission was
to show that it was false. I cannot remember that it
was ever used for any purpose whatever. Biblical in-

struction was little concerned about the pentateuchal or the synoptic problem beyond the fact that questions which had arisen about the authorship of certain books had all been answered. There was no serious difficulty we had to face beyond that which was naturally involved in the effort to get sinners to repent.

Yet I remember that I repeatedly put one question to our professor of theology. Might not Paul, who had been educated as a rabbi, have carried over some of his rabbinical thought into his writings, and if so, ought it not to be recognized when interpreting his teaching? Here was a question of historical relativity which the professor did not take very seriously, or much less did I understand. To quiet me I was told I had better write a paper about it. This was the only instance in my education up to that time I can recall when I was asked to prepare a paper other than those set by classroom tasks. I wrote the paper and thus quite unexpectedly came upon what was to be an enduring interest, that is to say, historical study as a means of understanding and evaluating Christian doctrine.

The interest in the foreign missions which sprang up in the late '80's almost carried me into the foreign fields, but circumstances so shaped themselves that upon my graduation from the theological seminary I had decided not to be a minister and began to teach rhetoric and public speaking in my *alma mater*, Colby College. I supposed that my connections with theological thought were ended, and in consequence I was not— and never have been—ordained. Yet for parts of two years I taught the New Testament in Newton Theological Institution, during the illness of my teacher and life-long friend, Ernest DeWitt Burton.

At the end of these two years I was transferred to the field of history and political economy, and spent a year at the University of Berlin studying in those fields. So far was I then removed from theological interests that I heard but one theological lecture during my entire period of residence. I have never regretted the fact that I learned historical method in a field where there were no temptations to apologetics. On my return to America I published in Latin a source book, *Select Mediæval Documents,* wrote articles on political economy for a newspaper, organized university extension centers, and undertook to raise ten cents per member from the young people of the Baptist denomination to support a Biblical professorship in the college.

In 1894 my historical interest was diverted toward Biblical fields, and I came to the University of Chicago as associate professor of New Testament History. It was a new field about which I knew next to nothing, and for that reason I was unhampered in the application of historical method to the recovery of what we then called the background of the New Testament. The Germans had already entered the field, and Schürer's great work had already been translated, but historical material was handled as illustrative rather than as creative. In my case new influences were at work. I had been told to get ready to come to the University of Chicago to teach sociology, and for several years I had been making the necessary preparations for that office.

It was natural that with the encouragement of Professor A. W. Small, my debt to whom it would be difficult to overstate, I began a series of papers for the *American Journal of Sociology* on "Christian Sociology." So far as I knew, there was no systematic treatment in this field. These studies were published in 1897 under the title, *The Social Teaching of Jesus,* and were continually reprinted until 1928, when I withdrew the book from circulation and issued in its stead the volume, *Jesus on Social Institutions,* which embodied conclusions which I could not have reached at the beginning of my study of the subject.

I now see that when Jesus is viewed in a true his-

torical light, he has no social program. His immediate
purpose was relative to His situation but His real message is a call to service to men because of faith in the
fatherliness of God. In 1899 I published *A History
of New Testament Times in Palestine*, which was an
attempt to set forth the rise of the Jewish social order
in which Jesus lived. At the request of the Chautauqua
Institution I wrote *The French Revolution—A Sketch.*
In so doing I pioneered into the field of the presentation
of history from the point of view of social psychology.
I can see the importance of this study, for when I came
to rewrite the book in 1926 I found that unconsciously
I had laid a foundation for what seems to be the true
method in theology.

During the first ten years of my teaching in the
Divinity School of the University of Chicago, I thus
found my chief interest outside the field of theology
proper, in that of a study of the New Testament as an
historical document setting forth the beginnings of a
new group consciousness and in revolutionary social
change. The two fields of investigation led me to give
particular attention to the rise of the social psychology
of the Jews expressed in messianism, and I published
a book under the title, *The Messianic Hope in the New
Testament*. In it I attempted to describe the messianic
scheme as it appeared in Jewish literature, especially
the Apocalypses as well as in revolutionary movements,
and to show the results of the use of these current messianic expectations by the early Christian community
as an interpretation of Jesus. Such an attempt led to
a distinction between the form and the function of early
Christian beliefs, and thus gave materials which later
were used in constructive theology. The first bearing
of such a study of social minds, however, was naturally
in the field of social morality, and I published *The
Church and the Changing Order, The Individual and
the Social Gospel* and *The Social Gospel* as attempts

to carry the ideals of Jesus into our present social order. When I was transferred to the chair of systematic theology I began at once to organize the results of this historical and sociological study of the literature of the first stages of our religion as a basis for theology. For several years I taught courses setting forth the content of the gospel. So far as I knew there were no precedents for the attempt except a volume by Hyde, *Social Theology*. But its method was very different from mine, which was simple. Each one of the doctrines of orthodox theology was treated under three heads, (1) Biblical material, (2) historical evaluation, and (3) a constructive statement.

Such a method, I can now see, involved a number of methodological weaknesses, but it was a step in the right direction. The chief weakness seems to me now to have been the neglect of the historical process which lies between New Testament times and our own day, and the unconscious assumption that Christianity was a body of truth rather than a religious social movement. The New Testament thought was to be transformed into a positive theology without the recognition of the fact that our Christian religion is itself an aspect of a social process and is not to be identified with the teaching of the New Testament. There was the further difficulty that there was no well-organized technique for the historical evaluation of the Biblical material.

The only method that I could see at the time was that of the equivalence of function between the messianic interpretation of Jesus and the presentation of His ideals in thought forms to an entirely different situation. The discovery of these thought forms was made from a study of modern life. Their equivalence with messianic forms was based upon the study to which I have already referred, but it lacked definite method. There was in this conception, however, an imperfect technique which, as far as it went, still seems to me to be an advance over that romanticizing of orthodoxy which without any distinct method endeavored to set forth orthodox doctrines in such a way as to make them acceptable to the modern world.

In a way it answered the basic problem of theology, the relation of the Bible to doctrine. As long as the Bible was considered the source and content of Christianity, some sort of method had to be found by which it could be accepted by those who had adopted the results of Higher Criticism and the evolutionary interpretation of nature. It was natural that during the latter years of the nineteenth century and the opening of the twentieth century men whose training and point of view had made the Bible central should have endeavored to preserve it as the norm of Christian beliefs. What was needed, and what I was trying to find, was a method by which the values of Christian doctrines— particularly the Biblical as I then thought—could be conserved in our own moral and religious systems without dependence upon a discredited doctrine of inspiration. In 1907 I published *The Gospel and the Modern Man,* which set forth the outcome of such methods as I had then been able to organize, and which I elaborated in an article in *The American Journal of Theology* in 1911, "A Positive Method for Evangelical Theology." My loyalty to the Church determined the apologetic quality of the method.

Other influences, however, than the academic were at work. As editor of *The World Today,* a popular magazine devoted to current events, I lived for eight years in quite another atmosphere from that of the University, although I continued my teaching. Politics, social reform, and general literature gave me a sense of the reality of the world with which religion had to deal. The academic and professional aspects of religion were thus set in a perspective of human needs. What was equally important, it led me to see that religious ideas, like those of politics and economics, get their real significance only when they are institutionalized. Therefore, a theologian ought to be an active churchman if his thought is to be more than technical and speculative.

Partly by intention and partly by the action of others, I was carried into active church life not only in the reorganization of religious education in the Sunday school, but in local, municipal, national denominational and interdenominational organizations. Official responsibility in such large interests put my theology into a realistic social perspective. It became increasingly clear that theology was a phase of a religious movement and that as such it could not be understood as if detached from the operations of social groups. A theology which serves as a basis and test for the integrity of a group life is very different from truths abstractly considered. It must be approached from the social and historical facts rather than from metaphysics.

This participation in a wide field of religious activity in which I have always been involved made it impossible for me to think of theology as a mere academic discipline, or of the Christian religion as concerned only with truth. Years of experience in committees composed of all sorts of men of Christian and non-Christian faith inevitably affect one's attitude toward religious beliefs. One comes to feel that in religion one is dealing with highly complicated social situations and histories. The history of doctrine becomes the history of people who make doctrines. The theologian seems to be less a philosopher and more a social engineer and, one had almost said, a social psychoanalyst. Christianity as a religious social movement comes to have a wider meaning than a religious philosophy or a body of infallible beliefs.

The evidence that a religion is a phase of civilization grew upon me as I studied the history of dogma. I began a series of studies looking toward the discovery of the extent to which the creative social minds that had found expression in Western civilization were also to be seen in the shaping up of the doctrines. It soon became evident that this was the key to an understanding of the history of Christianity. It was a religion rather than merely a system of doctrines.

Originating, as it did, in a social group within Judaism, it had, without any intention on the part of its leaders, expanded into an independent religion and gradually, by virtue of its own needs, had developed its rites, its organization, and its formulas. This process had continued as social experience had given rise to difficulties in theological conformity, the rise of new needs and resulting conflicts, and the methods by which an inherited religion was held and utilized by a Christian community in new situations. In other words, theology was a product of social minds, relative rather than final.

I may have stated the elements of this thesis too sharply, but I have no question that it expressed a fact verifiable by anyone with historical insight. Dogma, therefore, is not of the nature of philosophy, but like all formulas which a social group makes in the interest of self-preservation. The history of Christianity shows that orthodoxy is the group belief organized by a dominant group, and that heresies, so far as they are more than individual beliefs, are group beliefs of repressed minorities. Put in another way it would appear that orthodoxy was the formulation of a dominant social mind and heresy that of a counter-social mind.

An inevitable consequence of such a reading of history is that Christian theology is functional rather than scientifically accurate, inseparable in its origin and development from the history of Western civilization. Its authority has been coextensive with the authority of the group which enforced it. Its truthfulness is another matter, to be determined by other methods than appeal to authority.

It is clear that a description of Christianity as a phase of Western civilization is far from a precise definition. It is also clear that it involves the question as to the worth of religion as a form of human behavior and of the acceptability of Christianity in our own day. In any evaluation of historically derived doctrinal formulations, there would always be a question whether there was within them anything of permanent value. However orthodox the authority of history might make a belief, it could furnish no guarantee of its permanent acceptability. Judgment as to its value would still have to be passed. This in turn could be possible only as one saw Christianity in its relation to scientific facts. What should the modern church do with inherited beliefs which did not square with scientific conclusions and social needs?

As a result of historical critical study the Bible had already lost its authority as an infallible revelation to be used as a theological oracle, but now the basis of religious loyalty itself was subject to examination. If one accepted evangelical orthodoxy it could only be because of the authority of a group or a literature rather than because of any demonstration of its truth. But if the decisions of the group themselves were functional, a method by which the social mind of a given period adapted religion for its own good, what was there left of Christianity for our own day? The only answer that I could see would be that ecclesiastical authority must be replaced by some intelligible method by which one would be able to distinguish between the form and the content of an inherited religious group belief, and then determine as to the truth of its content by such criteria as were applicable.

This tension in the Christian religion is one which

has recurred repeatedly in the history of human thought. A change in civilization brings about a tension between new situations and inherited beliefs, and as a result there follows skepticism on the part of some, an attempt at enforced conformity on the part of others, and search for a new method of appraising and expressing the inherited beliefs on the part of others. So it was in the case of the Sophists in the days of Socrates; so it was in Christendom in the second decade of the twentieth century. On one side there was the current belief that religion was passing out of the picture; on the other extreme was the Fundamentalist, insisting upon the authority of the Bible and of the doctrinal formulas of the past.

Between the two were two classes of theologians in sympathy with the Church; those seeking to modernize orthodoxy by a more gracious exposition of its content, and those who felt that the real task was the organization of a method of evaluating our religious inheritance and discovering whether or not it could actually serve our modern world. Roughly speaking, these two latter classes might be called Liberals and Modernists. Though often confused, they really differ. Liberals are interested in formulations while the Modernists are primarily seeking for a method in religious thought which is justifiable from the point of view of modern needs and tenable when examined from data acknowledged to be real.

The Fundamentalist movement was a defense of the methods of an orthodoxy which had been developed by past ecclesiastical authority. It introduced no new doctrines. Its very insistence upon premillenarianism was logical since the Bible was treated as outside the historical process, a source of canonized truth, and there is no doubt that the speedy coming of Christ is definitely and continually expressed on the pages of the New Testament. It was logical also that its leaders should have been opposed to modern science and especially evolution. The doctrines which they were championing had been drawn up long before men had any definite scientific knowledge even upon such elemental matters as the revolution of the earth, the circulation of the blood, the law of gravitation, and the characteristics of electricity, to say nothing of the facts given it by modern physics, astrophysics, chemistry, biology, anthropology, psychology, and the various branches of medical study.

And yet there was Christianity, a thoroughly integrated element of our civilization. Those who were loyal to the Christian movement and yet accepted these scientific elements which characterize our modern social mind needed method rather than appeal to authority or denunciation of opponents. If Christianity was to be championed it must be shown sufficient to satisfy today's intellectual and moral needs.

The first attempts at such readjustment had been largely in the field of ethics. It was urged that, even though men could not believe in the formulas of orthodoxy, they could believe in Jesus as a moral example and in the influence of Christianity as a moral power. This was one reason why younger men, whose education had been affected by the religious skepticism born of scientific training, turned to what was called the social gospel. If mankind was engaged in creating a Kingdom of God, theology was of secondary importance. The main thing was to introduce the principles of Jesus into modern life. Social reform seemed much more practicable than the solution of religious doubts. Since religion was thus primarily of the nature of morals, it could be left to religious education and the Sunday school. We were engaged in making a new world.

It was a thrilling hope.

And then came the war. The power of Christianity to prevent violence was seen to be negligible. The

Kingdom of God disappeared in the smoke and poison gas and treaties of a civilization that was anything but swayed by the principles of Jesus. The catastrophe had no theological bearing for orthodoxy, because orthodoxy had embodied in itself the very political principles which had led to the war, and its God had justified the wars of Canaan. But for those of us who were attempting to apply Christianity to our modern world, the repercussion was disillusioning.

Was there, then, nothing in the social process that could justify the belief that principles which Jesus had enunciated and which the Church had always though imperfectly embodied in its doctrine could survive as ground for religious confidence in social disorder? As I look back upon those years, it seems clear that the disillusionment barely missed becoming a religious tragedy. If Christianity were not to disappear there must be that in the social process which, conditioning and shaping the doctrines of the Christian movement, was independent of time and change. It became fashionable, despite obvious facts, to disparage the social gospel and to turn from moral endeavor to worship and mysticism. Intellectual elements in religion were slighted.

It was commonly said that the nineteenth century had taken a complacent view of life because of its belief in evolution; that it had believed that all things were coming out right and all that was needed was to trust nature. I doubt the accuracy of any such portrayal. Evolution did furnish a ground for confidence, but the pre-war leaders of religion were anything but complacent or reliant upon impersonal process. The social gospel itself is an indication of their attitude. But confidence was undoubtedly jarred. Human nature did not seem so reliable as we had believed it to be, and the relation of God to the world was no longer a matter of mere metaphysics. Ethical optimism needed support. A theology to be of any significance had to be squared with the condition which threatened the loss of belief in the worth of anything except forces which we had hoped that we were outgrowing.

It was natural, therefore, to reexamine history in the large to see whether there was any basis for believing that the ethical and religious emphasis of Christianity was in accordance with human nature. From my point of view such an examination was of course inevitable. If Christianity were a phase of a social process, then there must be in that process that which warranted the practicability of Christian faith and the organization of Christian thought. The Noble Lectures which I gave at Harvard on *The Spiritual Interpretation of History* were the outcome of this need of examining history to see whether there was within it any spiritual quality which could justify a functional theology and a belief in religion as a legitimate element of our social life.

In such a study one could not begin with theological assumptions. As objectively as possible, it was necessary to trace the historical processes to see in what direction human society had in the large actually moved. The result, so far as I was concerned, was a corroboration of a basic religious attitude. For there are discoverable in human history tendencies which led people away from animal survival, both individual and social, into a larger recognition of the values of human personality.

A more detailed study, perhaps unfortunately under the influence of the war tension, I tried to make in a book on *Patriotism and Religion*, and more objectively in a series of lectures given at Wesleyan University on *The Validity of American Ideals*. The result of such study was a new confidence in the presence of a process in history toward personal and spiritual values and the consequent legitimacy of attempts to organize a religion. Orthodox theology had failed as a foundation

for modern morality, but those attitudes and that religious trust which it had sought to justify in days of
creative tension, might be discovered and examined.
The real problem was still one of method. History
and social psychology must furnish it.

The war illustrated on a grand scale the processes by
which belief is socialized. As executive secretary of the
War Savings of Illinois, I was brought into immediate
contact with the processes by which social attitudes were
aroused and then rationalized. War-time propaganda
was not merely a method of arousing passion. It undertook also to give intellectual basis and justification to the
passion. A nationalistic creed grew up which is still
operative. National groups became self-conscious and
developed all forms of coercive measures for maintaining political conformity. Beliefs about the enemy, the
ascription of motives to the Allies and ourselves, the
idealistic justification of the war as one to end war, and
make the world safe for democracy, all were organized
and socialized in the same way that the Church had
developed its authoritative formulas and intellectual
tests through synods, councils, parties and preaching.

Indeed, at certain periods the methods adopted for
the organization of orthodox dogma were even more
brutal than those deemed legitimate in the midst of
the war. My participation in the production of an
orthodox nationalism confirmed my conviction that in
dealing with religious attitudes, organizations, and
group beliefs the theologian must recognize doctrines
as the expression of the group mind of the Church
which in turn is a phase of the group life of a society.
This fact I found illustrated in the differentiation of
Protestant groups. I discussed it at some length in a
series of studies as Editor of Volume III of the *Outline of Christianity*.

The tension caused by the war psychology reappeared in the religious life. It became clear that in our day, as in the past, men would not be content to act without some form of intellectual justification for their religious faith. The shock to our moral sensibilities given by the war brought the question of the truth of Christianity immediately to the fore. The struggle that resulted was two-sided. The champions of the inherited theological *status quo* were against all demands at modification that did not start with the doctrine of inspiration, while those who were ready to take Christianity on its own merits found themselves challenged by other representatives of modernity to justify their attitude by methods which were scientific.

There was really no evading the issue. The choice was between an authoritative and an experimental theology as a means of expressing and rationalizing the Christian religious attitude. The scientific methods would have to be used for constructive purposes by those who had so far committed themselves to them as to break down the traditional authority of the Scriptures. Thus, on the one side was a struggle between a method of finding truth, and on the other side between interpretations of facts gained by the same method. The situation demanded constructive rather than critical thought. Ultimately this amounted to a question as to a method of treating the inherited beliefs of the Christian movement; *i.e.*, of history.

The effort of Ritschlianism to find a basis for religious assurance in judgments of value was a distinct contribution to the revaluation of the inherited past, but, paradoxical as it sounds when one recalls the historical work of the Ritschlian school, it was swayed by theological pre-suppositions to the effect that there was an essential Christianity which had been modified into something other than itself. This was equivalent to saying that there is an essence of Christianity independent of Christians. In other words, Ritschlianism made theology a philosophy that was not interested in metaphysics or society.

My studies had convinced me that Christianity was the religion of people who called themselves Christians; that is to say, who believed themselves loyal to Jesus Christ, but that there was no static body of truth which was a continuum to be accepted or rejected or modified. Christianity, like all religions, was a form of rationalized behavior both individual and social. Such a position was open to criticism not only from orthodoxy but from the natural and social sciences. It was necessary to discover not only how the Christian movement could be historically evaluated, but to estimate the legitimacy of the attitudes and beliefs which had found expression in authoritative doctrines.

I had already published an outline of the development of Christian dogma as the religion had been shaped by social processes in the *Biblical World* in 1915. In 1924 I published *The Faith of Modernism,* in which I endeavored to set forth constructively the theological results of the method. Such a study showed that men were Christians not when they held to a certain body of doctrines, but when their common effort for social life was controlled by the attitudes and convictions which, however expressed in doctrines or in life, had been the possession of a continuous Christian community.

This marked a distinct development of the position taken in *The Gospel and the Modern Man.* It made the real issue the question how such attitudes and convictions could be discovered and whether they were in accordance with reality given us by our knowledge of the universe. Central in such a problem was the question whether the word God stood for anything more than personified social values. This question was answered in the negative both by a body of intellectuals who described themselves as humanists and a much larger body of scientific investigators who held to a mechanistic interpretation of life.

Here was a new frontier which not only demanded defense, but which it was possible to advance. The opposition presented by the natural sciences could be met only by distinguishing the facts which their methods gave from philosophical interpretation. This was not difficult, since the dogmatism of the antitheistic scientist showed a lack of philosophical and historical training in the field of religion.

In 1929 I published *The Contributions of Science to Religion,* in which thirteen scientists of the first rank in America epitomized their factual results, while I discussed the legitimacy of the religious attitude in the universe of which these discoveries gave us new knowledge. This I found in these facts: The ultimate conception of science is activity which, so far as the physicist and the astronomer could tell, was uniform throughout the range of ascertainable fact. Such limitless activity was intelligible and capable of being expressed in mathematics and in those inductions called natural laws.

While it is impossible to speak of a cosmic purpose there are discernible tendencies which are akin to what in human life we call purpose. From one such tendency human personalities have been evolved. It would seem, therefore, that by the very nature of life the human person must live personally in the midst of environmental activities; that is, must set up dynamic situations on the level of personality. Such a view, of course, pointed toward some type of monism, but, so far as I could see, the problems involved were no more obscure *a priori* in the case of religion than in any other form of the life process.

Religions therefore could be studied by the use of social hypotheses. Their own functions could be treated as techniques for gaining help from an environment which was responsive to personal approach at least in the sense that men could attempt help-gaining cooperation with it in the level of their own personal powers. Christianity was a religion which, as a phase of a developing civilization, had utilized social experiences in making such adjustment and had rationalized its attitudes at points where tensions arose.

There was needed, therefore, a detailed study of the actual operation of the Christian movement to discover whether such an hypothesis were tenable. The chief instrument of such an evaluation of an historical religious process lay in the fact, already derived from historical study, that doctrines were social patterns, that is to say, analogies drawn from controlling social experiences and ideas which seemed to those who used them not analogies but facts. Their analogical value historical criticism would discover, but their function is plain, *i.e.*, to coordinate religious behavior and ideas with what is regarded as reality. It was necessary, therefore, to make a study of the social process of Western Europe somewhat in detail, in order to discover how social experience had been used to rationalize and formulate religious experience.

The central teaching of historical Christianity as to the dynamic adjustment between men and the personality-evolving and personally responsive elements of the environment with which they were organically united centered around the person and work of Christ. The christological doctrine of the theizing of human nature in the incarnation of the Son of God, had found expression in the belief in a virgin birth of Christ, and the consubstantiability of the Son and the Father had become dogmas necessary to believe but incapable of translation into religious experience.

In the course of the development of the Christian movement, its operating center was the death of Christ as set forth in the holy mystery of the mass and the various doctrines of the atonement. For Protestantism particularly the atonement has been the central evangelical doctrine involving the other doctrines of the person of Christ. This seemed, therefore, to be the first matter of investigation, especially since it promised particularly intelligible material for the exposition of the place of patterns in the formation of doctrine.

In 1930 I accordingly published *The Atonement and the Social Process*. In it I showed how the conception of God and His relationship with men had become increasingly juridical and political. Theology had become transcendentalized political practices. Maladjustment, that is to say, social and individual sin, was expressed in political patterns which varied according to a dominating political conception of sovereignty such as imperialism, feudalism, and nationalism. Forgiveness needed justification in the case of God precisely as in the case of a sovereign. The death of Jesus was in each case interpreted as an element in the pattern and served to give the assurance of adjustment (in theological terms forgiveness or pardon) with God. The functional significance of the death of Jesus as a means of such adjustment was therefore constant, but its use varied. When the inherited formulas were seen to be patterns, atonement as such was untenable. Sovereignty with its juridical corollaries was no complete concept of deity and there was no need of justifying the act of a sovereign.

There was left the determination only of the patterns which would make it helpful to men of our day in establishing the adjustment of themselves with God. Such patterns would be drawn from the creative ideology of our modern world. This would be derived mostly from the relation of the individual to society and of the living organism to its environment. Any theological use of Jesus' death would therefore not be juridical or political but revelatory of the power both over sin and death of a life perfectly adjusted to God.

Such a conclusion carries Christianity away from belief in doctrines into the field of religion itself; *i.e.*, of human behavior enriched and directed by normal relations with God. But the question as to just what is meant by God still had to be answered. This I attempted in the volume, *The Growth of the Idea of God,* in 1931. Again, by a study of patterns, it could be seen that the word God had never had a consistently identical content but had been shaped by the social experience. In it, however, there was always the conviction that there were elements in the environment with which men could become personally adjusted in the interests of gaining help or satisfaction for their developing needs.

Here the constructive step consisted in raising the question, already answered, as to whether the universe as we know it made such an attempt at personal adjustment reasonable, and of the availability of patterns drawn from contemporary intellectual controls by which the adjustment of man with cosmic activities on the personal plane could be portrayed. This introduced an epistemological question which it seemed to me could be simply answered by the recognition of the fact that in the personal relations of human beings there is always a mutual anthropomorphism. In such relations men project into the percept formed by sensations personal values similar to those which each recognized in himself. In religion the same process is utilized in cosmic relations. A conceptual theism results.

Religious or cosmic anthropomorphism is therefore of the same general order as that in society. The experience gained in a relation more subject to experimental test can be used as a means or instrument for help-gaining relations with those cosmic activities from which personality has sprung and which constitute the environment on which, in the nature of the case, men must depend. Such a relation will not be passive. Rather, as in all vital processes, there is activity on the part of each element. A dynamic situation is set up which as an element in reality cannot be ignored. God acts on man as truly as man acts with God.

Such a method gives to theology a basis which is not that of authority, but of experience. For its direction it must utilize the new data which the various sciences place at our disposal. Society is an element in the total, but since it is composed of persons, it is of cosmic origin and in cosmic relations. Therein lies the basis of morality. The proper way of life is set by human practices only as they are in accordance with the cosmic process which has within it elements making toward personal values. The way of such process is one of coordination or integration, both in the organization of matter through chemical compounds, life through the blending of such compounds into a vital mechanism, and also in the coordination and integration of human persons.

In humanity such integration must be on the level of personality. That is to say, only as human institutions and human relations are dominated by personal values, not only of oneself but of others, is there help-gaining adjustment with the creative cosmic activities. Such a fact gives rise to an imperative will to be expressed in accordance with the anthropomorphic pattern in which men think of such environing activities, that is with God. If He is thought of as a sovereign, maladjustment will be thought of in the patterns of orthodoxy as a violation of His will and His laws. If, however, the pattern is that of the organism in its environment or the individual in the group, it will not be thought of as a violation of statute, but as a failure to appropriate environmental activities.

The old theological conception of sin therefore reappears, no longer as an analogy but as a factual malad-justment due to the atavistic pull of inherited but out-grown goods. That is to say, the recognition that others are to be treated as persons; *i.e.*, as ends rather than as means for the satisfaction of individual needs and desires, is conformity with the cosmic process on the level of personality. It is the business of religion to enforce this fact and this adjustment.

Such an imperative becomes a criterion for the esti-mate of all social relations, economic, political and international. Science must implement this motivation, but the proper adjustment with creative forces will give the ability to adopt such methods as expert knowledge shows to be most conducive to the development of per-sonal values. For, as the individual through prayer and altruism, and as society through the implementing of attitudes by institutions, come into proper relations with the environment of the personality-producing activities of the universe, they share in the power of the cosmic process. Morality, therefore, is more than convention, just as religion is more than beliefs or rites. It is the carrying on of the evolutionary cosmic process from which personality has come.

The outcome of such a method is a simplification of theology. At first glance it may appear iconoclastic, but actually it is constructive, for it is engaged in re-asserting in our modern world the permanent values of Christianity expressed in patterns. It might be argued, indeed, that the method is too conservative; that the real student of religion should be noncommittal, even indifferent, to the religion he is studying. My reply would be that the theologian is the representative of a group; not simply an investigator. He can no more detach himself from the Christian movement than the lawyer can detach himself from the state in which he practices law. Ideally both the theologian and the lawyer believe that the current of social interests in the midst of which he lives are not all that he could wish, and that they can be improved. But realistically, neither can neglect concrete situations. Each has a social order on his hands, and each has a group which has its own history and its own directions. The theologian, like the lawyer, must interpret and improve, but he does not originate a movement within the limits of which, by his geographic situation as well as for many other reasons, he must work.

Nor is the theologian's interest primarily that of the apologist. He is not trying to defend but to discover the values of the religious-social process of Christianity and, so far as his investigations warrant, he must test and, if the decision is warranted, use inherited values in meeting the needs of his own day. Many questions he will leave to the psychologist, but he will not forget that religion is not a matter of speculation and abstraction, or metaphysics, or even of science, but a form of behavior subject to the concrete operation of many forces, chief among which would be the universe, heredity, and society.

When once theological formulas are seen to be patterns, the importance of most theological discussion disappears. The constructive process becomes realistic. The Christian religion, as a technique of help-gaining relation with God, seeks intellectual legitimization that will be repeatedly renewed as the intellectual climate changes. The thrust is not toward truth but toward the good life in which the worth of others as persons is fully recognized. When once the fact is recognized that the Bible is a collection of literature representing different stages in the development of a religious movement, it can be treated as what it is really worth. If the criterion be that of personal adjustment, there is no call to accept the Bible literally as infallible. It can be judged as any other literature, and it can make its contributions to our own religious thinking just as far as it is material capable of being used in our religious living. Its value as material for the reconstruction of a modern theology is as historical material subject to criticism and valuation. The stories of miracles get value as forms in which faith and appreciation of the past are expressed, and have no more claim to acceptance than similar stories found in any literature.

The bearing of such a method upon Christology has already been suggested. Jesus has a central position in the movement which He inaugurated, but as a guide and inspiration to religious and moral living rather than as a psychological problem, a sacrifice or an endurer of punishment. These latter conceptions of His work were corollaries of the political pattern which has been discarded. Justification by faith, since it is an element of the same juridical and political pattern, also passes from consideration, and in its place comes faith—a readiness to make the example and central teaching of Jesus regulative in one's moral life. With the further conviction that so to act produces in a different situation and with different rationalization the same attitudes of service and religious trust which dominated Jesus. Thus His experience rather than beliefs about His person acquires a revelatory value which becomes a supreme moral ideal. Such a faith implies metaphysical and other elements, but the supreme test is moral.

A theology will recognize that the moral change involved in the Catholic doctrine of justification and the Protestant doctrine of sanctification is due to a realistic relation with God. Such transformation, by virtue of a proper adjustment of the active soul with God is the heart of the Christian religion. Such religious experience demands the aid of psychologists and other experts, and is not altogether connected with formal beliefs. The test is real rather than formal—the increase of personal significance and social cooperation rather than acceptance of unintelligible formulas.

Finally, the outcome of this adjustment which has been accomplished by loyalty to Jesus as the revealer of life adjusted both to society and to God may be expected to survive the shock of chemical and biological changes which we call death. The conception of cosmic reality of matter is suggestive of new confidence in survival of individuals after death. But with such intimations of immortality the theologian would naturally stop. He gets little or no express knowledge from the accounts of the resurrection of Jesus that would make belief more distinct. The eschatology of orthodoxy is quite out of the question for one who knows the origin of this picture and the scientific presuppositions which an ascending and descending Christ involve. Heaven and hell can have no geographical reality in the mind of one who has any knowledge of the universe such as that given by modern astronomy. And similarly, there can be no theological discussion of such doctrines as predestination or election, which are obviously *ex post facto* use of the sovereignty pattern to rationalize the experiences and hopes of Christians. In their place comes the exposition of the implications of the conception of vital and dynamic adjustment of the organism to the environment on which it is dependent.

Such an historical theological method starts with the study of religion as actual human behavior and traces the development of mankind's explanation and justification of it by religious hypothesis and doctrine, and arrives at two conclusions: first, a religion that does not eventuate in a morality is not in accordance with the historical movement of Christianity. Second, a theology that starts from an unknown God and works toward humanity through some form of supernaturalism is an inconclusive method of setting forth the experiential relationship of man and God. Such a relationship, of course, implies that personality-producing activities were antecedent to humanity, and condition human experience, but the vital question concerns the proper technique for developing an ever increasingly dynamic and influential adjustment to the environing activity of God. Such a technique is the gift of an expanding science, for only as we know the general laws of personal adjustment can we properly and effectively make such adjustment.

As I look back over this theological Odyssey, it seems to me that one of the controlling elements of my thought has been the conception of the present as including the past. So long as one undertakes, therefore, to live in the present he must in some way recognize the present-past. There are at least two methods of appreciating and if possible directing this present into the future. The one is that of philosophy which seeks to get absolute and universal truth. The other is that of historical evaluation, which in the field of religion endeavors to carry forward the heritage of experience. Every religion is a more or less effective technique for the setting up of mutually dynamic relationships between man and God. In the case of the Christian religion this technique centers around Jesus. His way of such relationship—as we say theologically, of salvation—is simplicity itself—to love and serve one's fellowmen is to cooperate with and be aided by God.

Doctrines are, therefore, of value in the same proportion that they aid one in showing the intellectual legitimacy of such relationship. We cannot dissect human personality. A man must be religious intellectually as well as vitally. The real question as to doctrines is, therefore, not whether they are scientifically accurate, but whether they help men believe that religious faith is at one with other beliefs about which there is no question. Only thus can the real function of a doctrine be fulfilled. Neither the doctrine nor the church that made the doctrine is an end in itself. It is only when the individual feels his life renewed by his relationship with his fellows and his God that he is consciously religious. To possess an intellectually satisfactory doctrine does not prevent the use of analogical terms and dramatic concepts which assist him to express the emotion of the attitude justified.

As we live socially in the midst of anthropomorphic adventures, so do we live religiously. As we do not analyze the terms with which we express our attitudes in friendship, however ready we may be to defend the legitimacy of friendship on the basis of psychology and epistemology, so in religion, while our emotional expression must not violate our intellectual probity, it is not in intellectual shackles. I trust God not as a formula, but as I would trust a person. But in the formula by which I justify such a faith I find inspiration and a basis for courage to do what I can to serve my day and generation. For it is another way of saying that I believe that Jesus Christ has shown the way to the Father.

PRINCIPAL PUBLICATIONS

Books:

Select Mediæval Documents. New York, Silver, Burdette & Co., 1891, 1900.

The Social Teaching of Jesus. New York, The Macmillan Company, 1897.

A History of New Testament Times in Palestine. New York, The Macmillan Company, 1899. Revised and Enlarged Edition, 1933.

Constructive Studies in the Life of Christ (with E. D. Burton). Chicago, University of Chicago Press, 1901. Revised Edition, 1927.

The French Revolution—A Sketch. New York, Longmans, Green & Co., 1901.

Principles and Ideals for the Sunday School (with E. D. Burton). Chicago, University of Chicago Press, 1903.

The Messianic Hope in the New Testament. Chicago, University of Chicago Press, 1905.

The Church and the Changing Order. New York, The Macmillan Company, 1907.

The Gospel and the Modern Man. New York, The Macmillan Company, 1907.

The Social Gospel. Philadelphia, American Baptist Publication Society, 1909.

Scientific Management in the Churches. Chicago, University of Chicago Press, 1911.

The Making of Tomorrow. New York, Abingdon Press, 1913.

The Individual and the Social Gospel. New York, Missionary Education Movement, 1914.

The Spiritual Interpretation of History. Cambridge, Harvard University Press, 1916.

Patriotism and Religion. New York, The Macmillan Company, 1918.

Dictionary of Religion and Ethics (with G. B. Smith). New York, The Macmillan Company, 1921.

The Validity of American Ideals. New York, Abingdon Press, 1922.

The French Revolution (1789-1815). New York, Longmans, Green & Co., 1923.

The Contributions of Science to Religion (with the cooperation of various scientists). New York, D. Appleton and Co., 1924.

The Faith of Modernism. New York, The Macmillan Company, 1924.

Outline of Christianity, Volume III (with others). New York, Dodd, Mead & Co., 1926.

The Student's Gospels. Chicago, University of Chicago Press, 1927.

Jesus on Social Institutions. New York, The Macmillan Company, 1928.

The Atonement and the Social Process. New York, The Macmillan Company, 1930.

The Growth of the Idea of God. New York, The Macmillan Company, 1931.

Editor:
New Testament Handbooks. The Macmillan Company.
The Bible for Home and School. The Macmillan Company.
Social Betterment Series. D. Appleton and Company.
Woman's Citizen's Library Series. 12 Vols. Chicago, Civics Society, 1913-14.

Associate Editor:
Dictionary of the Bible. New York, Charles Scribner's Sons.
Constructive Series of the University of Chicago. Chicago, University of Chicago Press.

Magazines and Periodicals:

Editor:
The World Today, 1903-11.
The Biblical World, 1913-20.

Contributing Editor:
The Constructive Quarterly.
The Independent.
American Journal of Theology.

Articles in:
The Biblical World, The Journal of Sociology, American Journal of Theology, The Journal of Religion, The Forum, Religious Education, The Christian Century, The Baptist, The Methodist Quarterly, Current History, The New York Times, The Journal of Political Economy, The World Today, The Constructive Quarterly, The Independent, etc.

TOWARD A BIBLICAL THEOLOGY FOR THE PRESENT

By FRANK CHAMBERLIN PORTER

(b. January 5, 1859, Beloit, Wisconsin)

Winkley Professor (emeritus) of Biblical Theology in
Yale University
New Haven, Connecticut

TOWARD A BIBLICAL THEOLOGY FOR THE PRESENT

By FRANK CHAMBERLIN PORTER

BIBLICAL THEOLOGY was at first a part of doctrinal theology, indeed its chief source and its decisive demonstration. But it was soon discovered that the Bible contains many theologies, and that the result of unprejudiced and intelligent study was a history of religion rather than a proof of doctrines. The word historical became the accepted definition of the aim and method of Biblical Theology. To speak, then, of a Biblical Theology for the Present may seem to involve a surrender of the hardly won freedom of Biblical Theology from dogmatic prejudice. Does not Dr. Flint's definition hold good that Theology seeks what is true, Biblical Theology only what is truly in the Bible, and if so is it not dangerous to attempt to pass from one to the other? Does the study of the Bible, when it has once become historical, open any avenue whatever toward a theology which can be true for us? The modern historical student of the Bible is suspicious of any attempt to find a theology in the ancient Scriptures of the Christian religion. The historical sin of which he is most of all fearful of being guilty is modernizing.

That there are beginnings of a Christian theology, or rather of various theologies, in the New Testament is of course true; and the historian has his own responsibility to describe and explain in his own way these theological beginnings as historical facts, and to trace their influence. For his ultimate interest, however, and

especially for his supreme problem, the recovery of the
Jesus of history, these early theologies, which are chiefly
Christologies, take on the appearance of obstacles in his
way.   We who are students of the history of religion
naturally like to claim the word scientific as character-
izing the method and purpose of our studies.   If by
scientific we mean that we are trying to recover facts,
to see them as they were, and to understand and explain
them by putting them in their place in the course of
human history, then our claim to the word would seem
to be justified.   Reality, objectivity in that sense, is the
aim and shapes the method of the study of history as
well as that of nature.   And it is when the historian
defines his task in this way that he realizes that theologies, both those that his sources contain and those that
he himself more or less consciously holds, constitute the
greatest of his obstacles and dangers.

In the New Testament, not only in Paul but in the
Gospels, and not only in the Fourth, but in the Synop-
tists, and even in their oldest discernible sources,
Christologies have influenced the accounts of Jesus, so
that the historian whose chief aim is to recover and
understand the Jesus of history finds his way everywhere obscured and made difficult by these various beliefs of his disciples about him.   The Biblical theologian
has of course his positive duty toward the Christologies
also and must explain their sources, their interrelations,
and their developments; for they are facts of the highest significance in the religious history of man.   But the
question of their truth is one that the historian regards
as outside of his field.   His task is to find not what is
true, but what is truly in the Bible; and not only what
is truly in the Bible, but what was actual in history,
and above all what Jesus actually did and said and
meant.

The case of the Biblical theologian is however not

so simple as even this definition of his task would suggest. These beliefs of the disciples, of Peter and the
other immediate followers of Jesus, and also of Paul
and the writers of Hebrews, of Revelation, of the
Johannine books, are not only obstacles to be removed
in order to approach Jesus as He really was; they were
also actual effects of Jesus Himself, efforts to express
and explain the impression He actually made, witnesses
therefore to His greatness and even to certain qualities
of His personality, even when their terms and the world
of ideas in which they have their place were not those
of Jesus Himself, still less those of our own age.

They have therefore not only to be recognized so
as to be set aside in order that Jesus Himself may stand
before us as He was, but they have also to be used by
the serious historian as helps to a deeper understanding
of Him. And that in two ways. He must have been
of such a nature, He must have made so powerful an
impression and produced such great effects, that interpretations of Him such as those that we find in the New
Testament, incredibly high and great as they are, could
have been made. But something more than that has
to be said. We should expect to find that Jesus Himself, the historical Jesus whom the Gospels do allow
those who read them and reread them to see and feel,
had a certain measure of control over the Christologies,
foreign though these may have been to His historical
actuality.

Obstacles they no doubt are in an important sense
between us and Jesus Himself; yet in their earliest
Christian form they had been in some measure, sometimes more and sometimes less, refashioned by His
influence, conformed somewhat to Him, so that they
bear their witness, if we are able to detect and estimate
it, to Jesus Himself. No doubt our chief impression is
that Jesus has been interpreted by the Christologies in

such a way that they have to a dangerous degree tended to displace Him. But it must always have been true from the beginning that these christological terms, Messiah, Son of God, Son of Man, Lord, Wisdom, Logos, were changed when they were identified with one who had been a man among men, and had been crucified. In some measure He interpreted them, He took their place, though there was always the danger that they would take His. Much depends on this distinction. The ideal, both historian and man of religion would say, is that He, the man Jesus Himself, should do the interpreting, so that He would remain when the time came that the terms that had helped men to realize and express His nature and His greatness had ceased to have value and reality.

Modernizing is a word which the historian uses only in criticism of the work of others. It is that which the historian above all ought not to do. But I have come to believe that the distinction between right and wrong historical procedures cannot be so easily defined. When the object of our knowledge is a person, then personal ways of knowing assert their right and prove their necessity. Spiritual realities can be only spiritually discerned. In that sense the word objective which historians value proves inadequate. There is indeed a subjectivity which means doctrinal prejudice and has no historical rights; but when the object of one's study is the understanding of a person we must have courage to assert that there is a subjective way toward reaching an objective goal. There is a modernizing that cannot be escaped and that need not be feared. Another impression which has become to me stronger with the passing years is that no modern theology is likely to meet the need of our own or of any new age which cannot find its roots and its justification in the New Testament. Of both of these convictions there will be more to say in what follows.

Having thus suggested some of the problems involved in any movement toward a Biblical Theology for the Present, I must now attempt to explain my own attitude and the outcome of my reflections in the form which this volume calls for, that at least in part of autobiography.

As I look back at the religion of my early years I now think that I must have felt in my youth an inner aversion to some of the formulas of religious faith, some of the ways in which the religious experience was cultivated, and some of the phrases and actions in which it was expected to express and to impart itself. Not that I then doubted their value and necessity, but that, accepting them and pursuing them as best I could, I did not succeed in finding any satisfaction or freedom or joy in them. I was, I think, at first unconsciously, seeking for a religion that should be deep and real but yet rational and natural. I had the great advantage of having constantly before me at home a religious life and spirit marked by a rare wholesomeness and genuineness, without dogmatism or formalism, deeply emotional but restrained, and always with the soul of sincerity and humility. When later on I dedicated my book on *The Messages of the Apocalyptical Writers*, those representative cultivators of a completely otherworldly and supernaturalistic religion, to "my father, one of those who see in daily life and common things a revelation of God," it was in recognition of the fact that the Christian religion in its simplicity and purity is human and natural. "The natural truth of the Christian religion" was that which appealed to me from the beginning, and I have never ceased to look for the supernatural within the natural rather than in any physical sense separate from it.

But the Bible contains much that is supernatural in a sense that cannot well be naturalized. How then could the Bible be the authoritative teacher of religion to one who was looking for a religion which could be verified in man's own nature and experience?   Toward the end of my college course I became acquainted with the work of Wellhausen, at first through Robertson Smith.   I owed much also to a skilful and convincing exposition of this new view of Old Testament literature and history in the *Princeton Review* by Henry Preserved Smith.   This was an experience of great importance.   I saw in a peculiarly brilliant example that historical criticism, the analysis of sources, the understanding of backgrounds, the reconstruction of movements which the later theology of Judaism had obscured, could produce results that were not only of the greatest interest to the historical student, but also of the greatest value to one who would understand what religion is.

Two new facts came into view.   The first was the fact that behind the Old Testament literature, revealed by that literature when its parts were put in their proper places and relationships to one another, there was a great religious development from simple and crude beginnings to very high spiritual levels; not a movement always forward and upward, but a living historical movement, of which the high points were reached not in the beginning, once for all, by a wholly supernatural revelation, but gradually, as human achievements, the divine being within the human, not coming upon it from without.   The second fact was that the highest points in that history were great persons, the prophets; that the greatest of these, Amos, Hosea, Isaiah, Jeremiah, were the creators of that ethical monotheism of which the Old Testament canon was the final textbook, and which was the inheritance of Christianity. The prophets themselves were the greatest religious facts of this history.   The greatest parts of the literature were written or spoken by them; and the highest thoughts about the nature of God and of His demands, the most ethical and spiritual interpretations of religion, were theirs.

There were declines as well as advances, and the Judaism which selected and arranged and canonized the Old Testament did not always value the highest things most, but gave the first place to some of the earlier ideas and usages of Israel's religion, which the prophets had condemned, keeping nevertheless also the prophets' condemnations, which would inevitably be from time to time the inspiring force of reformations and still further movements forward.

As we look back at the Old Testament as a whole in the light of what historical criticism reveals, we see that three things appear on the surface to be the matters of principal importance, with the most obvious and emphatic claim to be acts of God and revelations of His nature and purposes: the fact of Israel, the chosen and peculiar people of God; the fact of the temple, its priests and its ritual of sacrifice, purification, festival; the fact of the Law.

But over against these great and characteristic facts in the history of Israel's religion and in its outcome, there are in the Old Testament directly opposing facts. Over against Israel's exclusive claim there are expressions of belief in a God of all nations, in a religion universal not national, a purpose of God which includes all men. In contrast to the religion of priestly rites, there are declarations that God requires none of these things, but only to do right, to love kindness, and to walk humbly with Him. Even the law is criticized, though it was peculiarly the religion of Judaism, the final and only revelation of God. Jeremiah looks forward to a time when the law will be written in the heart of every man, and every man from the least to the greatest will know God for himself; a time when religion will consist in the experience, through the spirit of God, of a new heart, a new moral nature, to which righteousness will be possible and natural, and independent of the definitions of the law with its promises and threats.

This universal, ethical, and spiritual religion was the discovery of the great prophets, and it is the greater thing in the Old Testament; or rather that which is greatest is the prophets themselves. Great men of religion are the best that the Old Testament gives. They were radical critics of conventional religion, and the religion they preached over against that of the professional religious officials and of the people as a whole was a religion of reason, of conscience, of inwardness, of personality. This discovery of the chief significance of the great revolutionaries, the radicals of Israel's history, the discovery that the religion of the Old Testament when it is rightly recovered, and the obscuring veils of the later Jewish theology are pushed aside, is the religion of great men of God, was to me a source of deep satisfaction; though the discovery of what this significance of the prophet would mean when applied to the New Testament and the nature of Christianity became only slowly possible.

I came upon a definition of prophecy in Tolstoy's essay on Non-Acting which has always seemed to me illuminating. "First, it runs quite counter to the general disposition of the people among whom it makes itself heard; secondly, those who hear it feel its truth, they know not why; and thirdly, and chiefly, it moves men to the realization of what it foretells." This puts in concise and striking form what had seemed to me to follow from the historical study of the supreme place of prophecy in the Old Testament religion. Not only were the greatest men of that classic history of religion the most radical and revolutionary, but there was something in them that convinced men of the truth of what they said, and something in them that gave their words power to bring things to pass, to make themselves come true.

What was the secret of this quality?   The *word* was the prophet's tool, the means of his self-expression and of his influence (Jer. 18:18).   The prophets' words are words of passion, not the words of wise men, sober reflections on universal human experience; they are words of beauty and of power as well as of truth.   The secret of the words of the prophets, which carried conviction even to those to whom they were strange and unwelcome, lay in the depths of their personalities. The whole self of a prophet uttered itself in his words. Through his words we understand himself, and again through himself we understand more truly and deeply his words.

We find, then, by the help of historical studies that the prophets are the most important facts in the Old Testament literature and history; this means that the religion of the prophets is greater than the prevailing religion of their times, which they condemned.   Understood according to the prophets, the religion of the Old Testament is not national and exclusive, but universal in range, a religion meant and destined for all men; it is not a religion of priestly rites, but a religion of righteousness and mercy; not a religion of law but of inwardness, freedom, spirituality.   Both religions are in the Old Testament.   Judaism, as the canon itself shows, chose the first of the two.   Christianity chose the second.   Historical criticism justifies the second choice.   Newness, originality, distinction, belong to the prophets and their work, rather than to the religion of the one nation, the one temple, the one book.

It is true also that Judaism itself has often recognized that the prophets are its greatest possession. "The nature of religion can be best discovered in the religious genius, just as the nature of art is grasped in the great artists and their work. If we would comprehend Judaism we must therefore learn to understand its prophets. . . . They created the history of Israel" (Leo Baeck). A Jew can say this; and it is also true that Christians have made the other choice and conceived of Christianity as the religion of a chosen few, as a religion of institutions and sacraments, as a religion of authority, which gives to that which must be believed the same place that Judaism gave to that which must be done.

Is there, then, in the New Testament also a distinction to be recognized and a choice to be made between two sorts of religion? No doubt when we turn from the Old Testament to the New the first thing that impresses us is that between the two religions in the Old Testament Jesus chose the prophetic. It was a new prophet of the old order whom Jesus recognized as the representative and champion of the Judaism that He Himself approved. Moreover, Jesus regarded Himself as a prophet, and in the prophetic spirit He denounced the religion of the priests, the scribes and the Pharisees. That religion in the Old Testament which as historians we find most important because of its greater originality and its creative power Jesus chose because He saw its higher value, because of the universality of its human appeal, because of its inwardness and its stress on righteousness toward men as the best service of God. But to recognize that, of the two religions which the Old Testament contains, Jesus definitely chose that which to us also is of the greatest value and the most abiding truth does not answer all of the questions that face us when we turn from the distinction between things greater and less in the Old Testament to the use of the same distinction in the New.

The New Testament is not only and altogether prophetic in character, and the question naturally arises,

and once seriously asked becomes pressing, whether we
have not only to recognize that the prophetic religion
of the Old Testament was that which Jesus approved
and carried up to new heights, but also that there are
two religions in the New Testament also, two Christianities, as the Old Testament contains two Judaisms,
and that very much indeed depends on how we make the
distinction and on which we choose. Both are truly in
the New Testament, but which is true? Does the historian himself help us to recognize these two religions
and to decide which is greater, which has the better
right to be called the religion of the New Testament?
Historical studies have distinctly helped in these ways
in regard to the Old Testament; it is reasonable to
suppose that they will help also in the New. Not indeed that it is to the historian as such a question of
greater and less present truth and value. To him it is
rather a question of greater and less originality and
significance in the history of religion. Yet the greater
historical importance and the greater religious value are
not unrelated to each other. Both have to do in their
real nature with the greatness of personalities, with the
significance of prophets.

A result of the historical study of the Old Testament
was to show that freedom from tradition, that liberal,
critical, forward-looking men and movements, are the
greatest things that it contains. What distinction then
have we the historical right and duty to make in our
reading of the New Testament, and how does the making of the distinction bear on the question of value and
truth for us? Does it open a way toward a New Testament theology for the present? Have we a right to
desire and even expect to find that present liberal and
progressive thinking may be more helped, may even
find a firmer basis and make a stronger appeal if they
can make positive connection with the liberalism, the

radicalism, the spirituality, of the Bible itself, of the prophets, of Jesus, of Paul?

The idea that liberal, progressive, ethical, spiritual religion can be found in the Bible with equal or even with greater right than can the exclusiveness, the institutionalism, the dogmatism, of much traditional Christianity was to me from the beginning a liberating and inspiring conception. A liberalism which simply breaks away not only from tradition but from the Bible also I felt would be likely to find itself without religious motive, without that sense of the Other-than-Man, that supernatural, without which religion cannot exist, and for the lack of which liberal Protestantism is being now so generally condemned. With the problem in mind, what distinctions it is historically right to make in the New Testament between things greater and less, and the further question what the recognition of these things may signify in our present religious thinking, and, in order to approach an answer to these questions, let me now return to that which this article should primarily offer, some account of the course of my own thinking and the influences that I have found helpful at this most critical point in the work of the New Testament theologian.

I began my theological studies with the conception, which for me was chiefly due to Wellhausen and his followers, that historical criticism was not only inevitable for the modern student, but that it had proved in the case of the Old Testament the way toward the finding of the real course of religious development, and the understanding of the great men who inspired and determined that development, creative personalities whom time cannot rob of their power to inspire and their right to guide. It seemed to me a matter of the greatest importance to discover what similar studies in the New Testament might reveal, and whether the rationality and freedom which seemed to me necessary could find a like justification when applied to the new Christian Testament.

My first year of theology in the Chicago Theological Seminary was the first year of Professor Hugh Scott's teaching there. His chair was Church History, but he gave to the entering class a course which proved of unexpectedly great influence on my own future studies. Perhaps he was the first in America to give an entire course of lectures on the Contemporary History of the New Testament, the Judaism of the time of Christ. That was in 1881. Schürer's book on *Neutestamentliche Zeitgeschichte* was published in 1873. The second edition, much enlarged, with the new title, *Geschichte des jüdischen Volkes im Zeitalter Jesu Christi*, appeared in 1886 and 1890. My chief interest being the approach to the New Testament in the light of the Old as newly understood, I was naturally attracted to this new way of attempting the transition from Old Testament to New.

I finished my B.D. course at Yale, writing my graduating thesis on the history of the Synoptic problem; and then was encouraged to stay on for further studies in the Judaism of New Testament times. My Ph.D. thesis was on the beliefs of the Judaism of that period about Life after Death. For encouragement and guidance in these studies I was most indebted to Professor Russell, whom I afterward succeeded in the chair of Biblical Theology when he became Professor of Philosophy in Williams College. At that time it was still possible at Yale to add a minor to one's major subject for the Doctor's degree; and I have always counted it a great advantage that I read Kant, Schopenhauer, and Lotze in the classes of Professor Ladd. History and philosophy need each other, and I cannot but think that the narrowness of the way that now leads to a Doctor's degree accounts for the ease with which some historical writing passes by the more fundamental problems which are involved especially in every history of thought, and in every historical study of great men and their works.

Lotze in the Preface to the *Microcosmos*, after speaking of the mechanical view of nature, the right of which he vigorously defends, and of that other aspect of reality, which he says was equally near to his heart, adds that the mediation between these two, the mechanical and the spiritual, is to be found "not indeed in admitting now a fragment of the one view and now a fragment of the other, but in showing how absolutely universal is the extent, and at the same time how completely subordinate is the significance, of the mission which mechanism has to fulfil in the structure of the world." Applying this sentence to the Bible I found it so suggestive that it must have a place in any account of my mental history. Even now, in view of some recent movements, I find it still necessary to say that there are no parts of the Bible, no events, no persons, that are outside of the field of historical criticism, but that there are realities in this literature which can only be grasped in another way, and that these are the greater in value. Absolutely universal is the extent, yet completely subordinate is the significance, of the mission which historical criticism has to fulfil in the interpretation of the Bible. It was at first necessary for my own good to emphasize and to justify the second half of this sentence, but now the first half needs emphasis and demonstration âgain, for there are those who think that the only way to preserve the two kinds of reality which the Bible contains, and the two ways of grasping them, is by limiting the range of historical criticism to the word of man, and denying its right to deal with the word of God.

That there is an important difference between Lotze's sentence and my paraphrase and application of it I freely confess; but the effort to select on whatever principle the particular things in the New Testament which Church, creeds, and dogmas have chosen as divine revelation—the nature of Christ, the significance of His death, the expectation of the world to come—and to affirm of these things alone that historical science can have nothing to say in explanation of their origin and meaning, and in estimation of their significance, is to make a distinction which it is contrary to the nature of science to allow. Everywhere in the Bible historical science can and must look for its own explanations; but religion also can go freely where it will and find the truth and the life, the value and the joy, that are there for one who has the eye to see and the heart to feel.

There stands out in my memory a little book by Rhondda Williams called, *Shall We Understand the Bible?* His answer to the question is yes, but only by the method by which we understand other books of the past. Understanding means to us scientific knowledge and explanation. Only by historical, critical studies can the Bible be understood. I gave a hearty assent to the argument, but felt that another question, which perhaps I took from Matthew Arnold, should also be asked: Shall we enjoy the Bible? and that the answer to that question also is yes, but only in the same way as that which leads us to experience joy in other literatures which have the quality of greatness. I should now be inclined to criticize Mr. Williams's answer to his own question, and to claim that not only joy but understanding requires not only the knowledge that historical science alone can give, but also that which sympathy and insight yield, so that to understand and to enjoy are not two entirely distinct results of two separate operations of the mind.

Different as are the two ways of reading great books, the historical and the literary, they should not be kept apart. Reitzenstein is right in saying that the knowledge of personalities is the chief end of historical study; and that personalities are to be known both from their surroundings and from themselves. To know a great man of the past from himself is to come into immediate contact with him through the works or the words in which he expressed himself and gave himself to the world. But this anticipates a later stage of my effort to make the right distinction in the study of the Bible between what historical methods can do and what they cannot.

When I began to teach I found myself obliged to work backward from the period between the Testaments into the Old Testament, and also forward into the New, for my field was Biblical Theology and covered both Testaments, with courses also always in the period intervening. No scholar would choose so large a responsibility with the impossibility of properly specializing in all parts of his field. Yet there were advantages. I am sure that it is well to go back and forth between the Old Testament prophets and the teachings of Jesus and of Paul. Someone has said that the historical study of the New Testament means the reading of it in the light of Josephus. Ritschl emphasized the Old Testament as the right approach, the one key needed for the unlocking of New Testament meanings. If a choice between these two approaches were necessary my own decision would be for the Old Testament. That was the sacred Scriptures of the Judaism of Jesus' time, of Jesus Himself, and of Christianity in its beginnings. The New Testament was for the Christian religion the needed supplement, the authentic interpretation of the Old, as for the Jewish church the Talmud was nothing but the same Scriptures expounded and applied.

In my first special field of study, the Jewish literature and the various movements within Judaism during the two or three centuries in the midst of which Chris-

tianity arose, I had occasion to give special attention
for some time to the apocalyptical literature, studying
the secret of the power of this type of prophecy, strange
as it is to us, and inevitable as is our judgment that it is
inferior to the words of the great prophets of the earlier
period. It is taken for granted by many New Testament scholars now that the historian can be known to
be such by his assent to this dogma of criticism, that
eschatology of the apocalyptic type was the fundamental characteristic of the Judaism of Jesus. The natural
inference is that, since the apocalyptic view of the world
is impossible for us and cannot possibly be fitted into
the world as we know it, therefore every effort toward
finding a theology for our age in the New Testament
is excluded.

I have long felt that to make this opinion a mere
matter of choice for or against, a question requiring a
simple yes or no for an answer, is a mistake. It is a
far more complex question. In one way or another
hope for the future, trust in the final triumph of good,
enters into all religious faith. In one way or another
the conception of history as a plan of God, and of man's
calling as the fulfilling by each of his assigned place
and responsibility in the realization of that plan, his
working together with God, is an essential part of every
vital religious experience. But in what way? To
answer that becomes more difficult the greater the man
whom we are seeking to understand. In the case of
Jesus and also in the case of Paul we have in this matter
no simple question that can be answered by yes or no.
It is a problem for the most careful weighing and discernment. The same language does not mean the same
thing when used by ordinary and by extraordinary persons, nor does it always continue to mean what it meant
when it was first shaped.

An event of much significance in the development of
my own thinking was my undertaking many years ago

to write one of the volumes in a series on Modern Theology, my subject being "The Word of God and the Spirit of God." I gave the book the title *The Bible and the Religion of the Spirit.* It was finished, but remains in manuscript, for I did not find myself willing to let it go. If I should publish it at last it would have to be largely, though I do not know just how largely, new. But the study and reflection that entered into the writing and that followed after it have had their important effects on my teaching and on other writings. At some time during the period when this work was on my hands I became strongly impressed with the conviction that the real values of the Bible could be gained only by an approach that is literary rather than chiefly historical in character, by appreciation more than by criticism. Much of the Bible, Old Testament and New, has the character of poetry, and much that is not fully poetic in form is yet inspired by deep emotion and has the quality of beauty and of greatness as literature. I found it rewarding to approach the Bible with the assumption that it is great literature, that it is to be enjoyed and not only understood, or rather that it cannot be really understood unless one adds to a knowledge of outward facts, which may help us to see each book in its original place and immediate purpose, a sympathetic insight into the mind and soul of its author, an understanding which should be less a knowledge of things than a knowledge of persons by a person.

The historical facts which lie behind the Old Testament books are partly concealed by certain ideas as to their causes and effects and by certain feelings as to their value. The work of the modern historian consists in an important degree in removing these upper surfaces of the Biblical records and uncovering the facts beneath. The historical critic is not unlikely to pursue such analyses under the impression that all that in the records which stands between him and the facts is of the nature of an obstacle, and requires simply to be recognized and set aside. The records are imperfect and require critical handling because of a subjective element in them, whether more theoretical or more emotional in character; we might say whether more theological or more religious. But this modern prejudice rests on the assumption that the Biblical writings have chiefly the character of historical documents. If they should prove to have chiefly the character of literature our judgment as to the relative value of the original facts and their subjective appropriation, their transfiguration through religious feeling and imagination, may be reversed.

The sense of God which the prophets brought to the interpretation of the facts of Israel's history expresses itself in passionate and beautiful words; and only by the beauty and the passion of the words does it impart itself to us. It is important to unearth interesting and significant facts in ancient records, which are obscured through primitive ignorance or later dogmatism; but it is a totally different matter to seek for the underlying facts which in a great poem are illumined by thought and imagination, and made to picture in forms of beauty great human and divine truths. In the first instance the student is making his way from less to greater values, but in the second from greater to less.

The question which of these two things historical criticism undertakes in the Bible should depend on the question what sort of book the Bible is, or rather with what sort of book within the Bible the historian chooses to deal. It is not correct to treat our problem of the historical and the theological, or the historical and the religious, elements in the Bible as if the Bible were the *one book* which Jewish dogma affirmed it to be. In reality we may say that there are parts of the Bible, such as the Psalms, of which the religious value is hardly touched by critical historical studies. There are parts of which the religious value may almost entirely vanish in the light of the historian's work. Again there are parts of which historical study positively adds to the religious value, as the historian's recovery of the great prophets certainly does. And I venture to say that there are also cases where the religious use positively helps the historical. This would be the case where the problem is that of understanding great men of religion; since such understanding is possible only through sympathy and a certain likeness.

The Bible is far more largely a book of poetic character than is indicated in the Revised Version. Large parts of the books of the prophets should be printed in poetic form no less than the Psalms and the Wisdom Books. The Bible as a whole is great literature, and a study of the nature of greatness in books, of the nature of poetic genius and its creations, is at least as necessary for the real understanding of the book as is the training of the historical critic. A great book is the creation and the self-disclosure of a great man, one who, though a man of his time, has a universal humanity. He belongs to all times, and his book contains eternal truth rather than particular facts. If his genius, his greatness, is in the sphere of religion his book will reveal God to men and men to themselves. The Biblical critic may well take to heart this sentence of Goethe: "A book which has had a great effect can in reality no longer be judged. Criticism is in general a mere habit of modern men. What will that mean? Let one read a book, and let it have its influence upon him; let him give himself up to this influence; then he will come to the correct judgment in regard to it."

I can here hardly do more than suggest the influences in this direction to which I found myself deeply indebted. First of all it is Aristotle's *Poetics* through which one must approach the study of the relation of poetic truth to historic fact in literature. He teaches us that it is poetry which, looking at human life as it appears, sees universal truth in it, not as philosophy discovers it by pure thought and attempts to express it in literal and so necessarily abstract terms. The poet sees universal truth only in concrete manifestations, in the actual facts of human life. He looks at the facts apart from all that is accidental in them, all that keeps them from being what they ought to be and tend to become, and he describes them so as to make this purpose and tendency clear. The poet's description of the universal is a description of things as they are, but he re-creates them and makes the impress of the ideal upon them clearer than it is in nature. He idealizes the facts as the historian cannot do, yet poetry is a higher thing than history, as the universal is higher than the particular and the rational than the accidental. Even unhistorical elements are not inconsistent with poetic truth; and on the other hand if the poet describes an historical event, he will still be a poet, a creator, through the choice and form which his feeling dictates, through which the feeling imparts itself to the reader.

Poetry as Aristotle conceives it is closely allied to religion. It is a relationship that has often been pointed out, but of it theology has not taken too serious account. Religious faith, like poetry, seeks the universal not the particular, but finds the universal in particular things in nature and in human life, sometimes in extraordinary but often in common things, and it expresses the universal not in abstract terms but in concrete imagery. Things not as they are but as they ought to be and are to be are as characteristically the concern of religion as of poetry. Both poet and man of religion seek to pass through the seen to the unseen, and yet to hold to the seen as the image and language of the unseen. The native language of religion as of poetry is metaphor and parable. The Biblical writers of history are always looking at truths within the facts they narrate, at the eternal within the local and individual. Things outward were to them also the imperfect shadowing forth of things invisible.

Another book to which I am in debt is the famous treatise, Longinus *On the Sublime*. His distinction of the two normal effects of great literature on the mind is illuminating. Sublimity is due first to weighty thought, and then to intense passion. The greatness of thought reveals the presence of a great mind, and the proper response to greatness is admiration, reverence. But it is characteristic of great literature to uplift those whom it first humbles. The greatest writers carry us on to their own faiths and ideals, not by the convincing force of their logic but by the passion that fires them, not by the reasons for their faith but by its strength. Our souls are somehow naturally exalted by the true sublime, and are filled with joy and exultation as if themselves had produced what they hear. The great writer has the power to lift us up to his own level, to give us the sense of sharing his thought, of thinking with him, so that his words seem to us a revelation of our own minds. This is due in part to the universal human truth of what he says; yet thought without passion does not produce this wonderful effect. An inexhaustible suggestiveness also belongs to all truly great writing. It disposes the mind to high thoughts beyond what is actually said. Through a great book the thoughts and feelings of a great mind become in a marvelous way our own. The book does not exercise an outward authority over us, but it has a mysterious power to become an inner authority, to make us hear the voice of our own reason and conscience. It does not disclose mysteries hidden from the common eye, but makes us conscious of the greatest truths that belong to us as men. To the great thought of a great book our response should be reverent wonder. Admiration for greatness is man's noblest quality. But the

passion which inspires great writing also transports us
so that we feel its thoughts to be our own.   The union
of these two opposite tempers, wonder and transport,
is the secret of the right reading of great books.

It would be hard to find a discussion of the doctrine
of Sacred Scripture by a theologian which contains as
much value for our present purpose as is offered by this
old Greek rhetorician.   I must leave to the reader's
own reflections the effects of carrying over to our reading of the Bible conceptions such as these of the nature
of greatness in literature, and of the relation in great
literature between fact and truth.   That the authority
that a book may rightly have over us is inward not outward in character; that the greatness of the book is to
be found in its power, not in its inerrancy; that the
secret of its power lies in the greatness of the writer's
thought and the intensity of his feeling, in his own
greatness of nature; that it is these great spiritual qualities, and not any artfulness or adeptness in style, still
less any power not his own, that determine the choice
and fit ordering of beautiful words, and in a mysterious
way create in them a body in which the soul lives on
and works effectively; that the great book does not
persuade but transports, does not inform but inspires;
that our proper response to the book is therefore exultation of spirit and quickening of thought, but at the
same time wonder and awe as in the presence of the
divine; that we are to go beyond the book by the impetus
which the book itself gives, and are always to return to
the book again for fresh impulse—these are wholesome
and helpful truths for those who wish to interpret real
experiences and to recognize real values in the reading
of the Bible.

Among more recent reflections on the nature of the
poet's creation, and especially on the relation between
fact and truth in poetic literature, I know no words
better than those of Wordsworth.   The influence of

some of the sentences in his Prefaces to the *Lyrical Ballads* on my thinking has been so great that I must quote them here, familiar though they are, though I must again leave it to the reader to make the inferences that they suggest when applied to the Biblical literature. Like Aristotle, Wordsworth defines poetry not by its contrast to prose, but by its distinction from matter of fact, or from science. "Aristotle, I have been told, has said that poetry is the most philosophic of all writing; it is so; its object is truth, not individual and local, but general, and operative; not standing on external testimony, but carried alive into the heart by passion; truth which is its own testimony, which gives competence and confidence to the tribunal to which it appeals, and receives them from the same tribunal."

The pursuit of science and history, he says, is necessarily the lonely and isolating occupation of the student, it is a wisdom not for babes but for the wise and understanding; but poetry speaks the thought and feelings that are common to all men; so that while science cannot but divide, poetry binds men together by passion and knowledge, carrying everywhere relationship and love.

The application of such thoughts to the nature and power of the Biblical literature is too evident to require unfolding here, and too far-reaching to follow out within our present limits. It is chiefly with poetic truth rather than with matter of fact, or science, that the Biblical writers are concerned. And it is truth of the kind that cannot in the nature of the case stand upon external testimony; truth that requires imagination to grasp, as it requires emotion to express; truth that must transport us by its beauty, and must reveal itself to us in the end as in reality our own. By the word poetic as applied to the Bible I mean to describe that quality in it which to the seeking and responsive soul makes

even records of historical facts a means of access to the
eternal and present fact of God.

In what lies the undoubted power of the Bible to
move the heart of man, to stir his conscience, to give
him a sense of the world unseen? The historian does
not feel called upon to answer the question, or even
to reckon with the power. The old dogmas did try
to answer it, but often in ways which the historical
student can only criticize and reject for his own reasons,
because he has his own account to give of the origin and
the nature of the dogmas. It is for the answer to this
question that we must turn to the character of the Bible
as literature, to its poetic quality. If it is the greatness
of the Bible that it touches the deeper places of our
inner life, that it stirs us to right action, impels us to
sacrifice, strengthens us to bear and resist evil, imparts
joy, makes us conscious of living in the unseen world
and for eternal ends, then its greatness is in its truths
not in its facts, in its literary—one needs to say its
spiritual—quality, the quality which it has because it is
due to the great thoughts and feelings of great men
of religion. It is their greatness that their words enable
us to share. It is a greatness in our own nature as
human beings of which they make us conscious, which
they impart to us or reveal in us as a native possession
of our own, a real part of ourselves.

In his *Einleitung in die Psalmen*, Gunkel criticizes
Mowinckel for two underlying faults, for underestimat-
ing the spiritual high level of the psalmists, and for
understanding Israel's spiritual life in general, and that
of the psalmists in particular, in too primitive a fashion.
Both criticisms apply to much modern Biblical interpretation. The spiritual level is not high enough, and
primitive conceptions are given too great importance.
Everywhere the discovery of the primitive, and emphasis on the wide chasm that separates primitive ideas

of religion and morals from our own, threaten to claim
the first and chief place in historical studies. In fact
the primitive meaning of words and phrases seldom
remains unmodified in their use by later writers.
Religious language is traditional and has an emotional
value because religious thoughts and feelings have so
long gathered about it and have been called forth by it.
But the literal and physical meanings are left far behind. The language becomes poetic, symbolic. It is
especially true of great and original men, men who
have religious experiences of their own, that the old
words and formulas which must still be used have new
and more inward and spiritual meanings. There is of
course a value in discovering beginnings, but there is
also a danger in assuming primitive meanings and missing higher values; and it is one to which modern
historical science is peculiarly exposed.

Among those who have applied the training and insight of the man of letters to the understanding of the
Bible a high place belongs to Coleridge and especially
to his Letters on the Inspiration of the Scriptures, the
Confessions of an Inquiring Spirit. No one can have
passed through the experiences I am describing without
acknowledging his debt to Coleridge. Reading the
Bible as he would read any other book he met in it, he
says, "everywhere more or less copious sources of truth,
and power, and purifying impulses"; there were "words
for my inmost thoughts, songs for my joy, utterances
for my hidden griefs, and pleadings for my shame and
my feebleness." "In the Bible there is more that *finds*
me than I have experienced in all other books put together. . . . The words of the Bible find me at greater
depths of my being; and whatever finds me brings
with it an irresistible evidence of its having proceeded
from the Holy Spirit." He would convince himself
and others that "Bible and Christianity are their own
evidence." "The truth revealed through Christ has

its evidence in itself, and the proof of its divine authority in its fitness to our nature and deeds." But "to
make the Bible the subject of a special article of faith,
I hold an unnecessary and useless abstraction."

Eloquent and passionate is Coleridge's argument for
the reading of the Bible as we read other books, and
finding in it what corresponds to the divine spirit working in our own thoughts and emotions and aspirations.
We find there "a correspondent for every movement
for the Better felt in our own hearts." The greatness
of the Bible is the greatness of its expression of the
highest needs and ideals of human nature. Its value
is the assurance it gives that "the hopes and fears, the
thoughts and yearnings, that proceed from, or tend to,
a right spirit in us, are not dreams or fleeting singulari-
ties." But we must be free to read it for what we need
and what we like, for what finds us at the greater depths
of our being; and this means that the Christian faith
does not need and cannot allow a doctrine of Sacred
Scripture. It needs only the book itself and no declaration of its divine authority, its unhuman infallibility.

Among those who have approached the Bible by this
way one must not fail to mention Matthew Arnold and
his attempt "to give a new life to religion by giving a
new sense to the words of the Bible." As Coleridge
declared that the truth revealed through Christ has its
evidence in itself, and the proof of its divineness in its
fitness to our nature and needs, so Arnold's assumption
in his reading of the Bible is "the natural truth of the
Christian religion." The abiding value of the Old
Testament, that for which we shall always need the
book, he defines as the passion of Israel's conviction that
the power not ourselves makes for righteousness, and
that to righteousness belongs blessedness. The value of
the New Testament is Jesus' new conception of what
righteousness is, His method and His secret, the method
of inwardness, and the secret of self-renouncement;

and we shall always need the New Testament because of the presence in it of Jesus Himself, the mildness and sweet reasonableness of Jesus, by which His method and His secret are controlled and interpreted. Who can say that the training and genius of the literary critic, poet as well, have not here helped to open our eyes to things that may fairly claim to be the supreme and permanent treasure which we possess in our sacred Scriptures?

We have found that the critical historical study of the Old Testament helps us to distinguish in it things less and things greater in value, and that the character of much of the Bible as great literature, as essentially poetic, not only confirms the historian's decision as to what is greater and what less, but brings an appreciation of greatness where it is often overlooked by those who read only for facts of the past, and fear the recognition of truths for the present. Let us now return to that which is our main problem, the defining of the right distinction within the New Testament, and the making of the right choice, the finding of value and truth where they are in reality present. In the Old Testament we found, contrary to first impressions, that the greater things were not Israel as God's loved and peculiar people, but universality, inclusiveness, as the real nature and the purposed destiny of Israel's religion; not the temple and priestly rites, but righteousness and mercy as that which God requires of man; not the law but an inward and spiritual knowledge of His will, the knowledge which every man may have for himself, and the freedom and moral power through which the doing of righteousness becomes the inevitable and joyful expression of man's own nature. We have seen that Jesus chose the second of these alternatives as the greater of the two religions which the Old Testament contains, but that we cannot say that the New Testament as a whole is according to Jesus in the consistently prophetic

and spiritual character of its religion. Our present
question therefore is whether within the New Testament also a similar distinction is to be recognized and
a similar choice made. Are there two religions, two
Christianities, in the New Testament? I believe that
there are, and that the parallelism is significant. In
the New Testament as in the Old there are things that
seem greater but prove less, whether judged by their
historical newness and originality, or by their abiding
religious truth and power.

That in the New Testament which corresponds to
Israel in the Old is Jesus Christ, the peculiar Son of
God and the destined heir of the Kingdom of God. But
there is also in the New Testament that which con-
tradicts the separateness of Christ and makes Him the
first of many brethren. In a degree which it is not easy
for us fully to recognize, the qualities and prerogatives
of Jesus are such that His disciples can and must share
them. Newer, stranger, and greater than the sole sonship of Jesus is the sonship which He reveals and creates
as God's gift to man.

To the Old Testament conception of Israel belonged
the expectation that God's rule over the world would
be Israel's rule over all other nations. In the form of
the apocalyptic eschatology the expectation of the coming reign of God has an important place in the New
Testament also. But there are in reality two eschatolo-
gies, two doctrines of the world to come, in the New
Testament. One is the common Jewish expectation of
the coming of the heavenly Messiah as judge, with the
single change that the coming judge and king is known
to be Jesus. To Him and to those who are His, ruler-
ship will belong when the Kingdom of God appears.
In this eschatology Jesus Himself is interpreted, it is
hardly too much to say displaced, by the heavenly son
of man, the coming judge of the world, of certain
Jewish hopes. But there is another conception of the

226 CONTEMPORARY AMERICAN THEOLOGY

world to come, one in which Jesus Himself is decisive and has effected a complete transformation. The new age began with His earthly life, death, and resurrection. The coming of God and His decisive act was past and the new age was present. Jesus Himself gave it its new character. Because it was present, and consisted in Christ and in the Christlikeness of Christians, it could not be chiefly supernaturalistic in the material sense, as were the Jewish and the Jewish Christian hopes.

Paul's new world was one in which men had died with Christ and risen with Him to newness of life. It was a new world in the sense that men no longer lived to themselves, no longer sought their own. Christians were already a new creation, and wherever there were Christians the new world was already present. When men were in Christ the old distinction between Jew and Gentile was at an end. No separations, no exclusiveness, remained natural or possible. Men had a new knowledge of one another, an attitude and disposition in which selfishness, envy, greed, fear, hatred, had no place. Men lived in oneness of spirit. This oneness, of which Christ was the creator, was the newest characteristic of the new world in contrast to the old.

This new conception of the world to come in the New Testament is not to be paralleled and explained by the study of backgrounds and surroundings. It is an eschatology not derived from Judaism, for the decisive thing about it was that it had already come in Jesus, and that it consisted in the transforming power of Him in the lives of His followers. The new world had begun although all things remained outwardly as before. The nature of its newness is not material but spiritual. A new outer world will indeed come, but as the natural result of the inward newness. This meant a new responsibility; the conception of a reign of God for which believers in it must not merely hope and wait as for a pure act of God, but for which they must labor.

The new thing in this whole region was altogether the creation of Jesus Himself, and the new was greater than the old. The greater thing was not that which shaped men's beliefs and expectations about Jesus, but that which Jesus Himself shaped and created, that which He was, that which He enabled His disciples to become.

Corresponding to the temple and its priests and ritual in the Old Testament is the New Testament conception of the death of Christ as a sacrifice for sin, a deed of God once for all for us and our salvation. But by the side of this the death of Christ appears as in some way symbol or type or cause of that death to sin which is the moral task of all men, and also of the sufferings of men for their fellowmen, accepted and rejoiced in as, like Christ's, an expression of love and an instrument of love's redeeming self-sacrifice. Not the acceptance of the dogma that Christ died for us, but the ethical appropriation of His death, the will to make it our own, not an understanding of the mysterious meaning of His sufferings and death, an assent to their significance for God's forgiveness of sin, but a knowing of the fellowship of His sufferings, a becoming conformed to His death, is the greater thing.

Christianity is a religion, and to a religion nothing rightly belongs which cannot be made our own by inner experience through moral effort. This only is the real meaning of faith. Nothing can enter into a religion as a mere fact of the past, for every such fact is a matter for history to determine. Neither can speculative theories about facts be matters of faith; since all such matters are for philosophy to test and prove. All that is given us in Christ and the Christian redemption we must also strive after and grasp for ourselves. It is true even of the death of Christ that what God does for us we must do for ourselves, and also that what God does for us we must do for others. All this, of course, I am saying not as an opinion of my own, but in the language of Paul. It is one of the two religions which the New Testament contains. It is the one which goes back through Paul to Jesus himself. And it is the greater thing in the New Testament.

To the law in the religion of the Old Testament the parallel in the New Testament is to be found in the beginning of doctrine. There is truth in what Jewish scholars often say, that the Jewish church chose a law of conduct, *halacha*, a way of life; while the Christian Church chose a law of belief, doctrines, consent to which was the condition of salvation. Its beginnings are in the New Testament. But there is something else in the New Testament which is greater, more distinctive, more really new, far more the creation of Jesus Himself. It is what Paul calls the law of the spirit of life in Christ Jesus, which was not really law at all but the end of law. Doctrines even about Christ are not the greater thing in the New Testament. Greater is the spirit of Christ in the disciple, Christ Himself in men, men in Christ and as Christ.

Christians are the newest and greatest expressions of what Christ was; Christologies, formulas as to His nature and work, are less great and less new. They have their roots in various older and current conceptions of agents or intermediaries between God and the world and between men and God. The new was also the more difficult conception. To become like Christ, to deny oneself, to love one's enemies, was far harder than to obey the laws of Moses; it was harder also than to give believing assent to any, however great, affirmations about Christ. It is harder to take up our own cross than to trust in the adequacy of Christ's; harder to fill up what was lacking in His sufferings through our sharing them than to believe that His were sufficient.

It will not have escaped attention that the new and the greater things in the New Testament are almost inevitably described in the language of Paul. It is my conviction that Paul is our greatest leader and guide in our movement toward a Biblical theology for the present. I am a liberal, a modernist, and am not at all deterred from the use of these terms, although it is popular now to deride and reject them. I am not among those who think that the course of theology from Schleiermacher, through Ritschl and Herrmann, to Harnack, and to Troeltsch is now to be set aside, and that we are to begin again with Luther or with Calvin. But I do wish to carry my liberalism, my modernism, in fact still further back.

The Bible itself is a liberal, a radical, book of religion. The greater things in the Old Testament and in the New are those that have the prophetic quality as Tolstoy described them: prophets are opposed to the common disposition, to traditional and current religious ideas and practices; they convince us not by argument but by the strength and passion of their own convictions, by the power of their personalities; and their words have power to bring what they say to pass. The prophets speak in their own time; their words are inseparable from the human life about them. They do not attempt to utter truths eternal and timeless, but to interpret the meaning of events of the present and their place in the plan of God. Yet their words, conditioned though they are by time and place, have a universal quality. It is conspicuously true of the words of Jesus that they have this timeless element, that they are words of universal and abiding truth, although they are so fully words of His own time, shaped by immediate events and directed to those who heard them. This is also true, in a degree which is not always acknowledged, of the words of Paul. There is no revolutionary or truly spiritualizing movement in the history of Christian thought that does not in some way appeal to Paul and start from him.

When I began to lecture on New Testament Theology my notion was the usual one that Paul was responsible for the departure of Christianity from the religion of Jesus, and for the substitution of theology for the God of Jesus' faith, and of Christology for Jesus Himself as the object of belief. I assumed, that is, that Paul was chiefly responsible for the substitution of the less for the greater religion of the New Testament, of the religion about Jesus for the religion of Jesus. I studied Paul, therefore, in order to find the explanation of his departure from Jesus and his creation of a religion about Him, and I was surprised to find that Jesus Himself was far more the dominating factor in Paul's Christianity than were any doctrines about His nature or about the significance of His death.

Most of the evidence for which I was looking that Paul was the creator of the "higher Christology," the doctrine of the pre-existence of Christ and His agency in the creation of the world, or the doctrine that His earthly life was not really human, but the incarnation of a divine being, was quite lacking. It came to me— this is now forty years ago—as an exciting discovery that Paul was not the author of this substitution of a heavenly and divine being, whether angel or Logos, this eternal Son of God, for the Jesus of history. He alludes to such Christologies a few times, but never as if the doctrine were his own, never with any explanation or defense; indeed always with warnings against the tendency of Christologies, and the acceptance of them as true, to take the place of that temper, that spirit of humility and of consideration for others, which was the character of the Jesus of history, and therefore should be and must naturally be that which distinguishes His disciples and makes new men of them.

The Christian was not one who believed that Jesus was the incarnation of the Logos through whom all things were made, but one who lived no longer to himself, who sought not his own, in whom the love of Christ, which was the love of God in Christ, was the ruling spirit. He was indeed one who had a new knowledge of Christ, but one also who had a like new knowledge of all men; who knew Christ and who knew all men no longer according to the flesh but according to the spirit. I found Paul to be one to whom the greatest value and the highest reality was the personality of Jesus; one whose own new personality was the work of Christ in him, his life in Christ, and was therefore itself his supreme witness to what Christ Himself was.

I found that Paul's letters were chiefly, and in a degree hard to equal in the literature of the world, disclosures of his personality, of that new man which Christ had made him to be, after His own likeness. This meant that Paul himself was one whom we must personally know if we would know what his Christian religion was and even what the historical Jesus was. I found also that what he says about Christ is the sort of truth that does not stand on argument, but is carried alive into the heart by passion, truth which is its own witness. The best result of the study of Paul, and most in accordance with the nature of his writings and with his own nature as one who had the mind of Christ, would be that we who read him should get from him the same spirit, and in some true sense should be here and now what he was then, and do now what he then did. This would only mean that it is our task to carry forward as it were with Christ and even for Christ and in His place Christ's own ministry of love to men.

This does not sound much like an historical undertaking; and for me it had to find its place and prove its right, along with that historical understanding which is so especially necessary in the case of one who was so fully as Paul was, a man of his time and place. Some of the results of such efforts to understand Paul both from his surroundings and from himself, but more from himself than from his times, are to be found in my book, *The Mind of Christ in Paul*. The secondary title, "Light from Paul on Present Problems of Christian Thinking," suggests that in this book I make the dangerous attempt to move toward a Biblical theology for the present, the attempt to discover not only what is truly in Paul, but what is true. In any such attempt one is no doubt in danger of modernizing in the sense in which that word is highly offensive to the modern historian; and he is certain to be accused of committing that serious historical offense even when he feels that he is fully aware of the danger and is not guilty of the crime. For our present purpose it will be necessary to consider briefly what the understanding of a man like Paul involves, and I may add, of one like Jesus, and how the reading of Paul's letters and of the Gospels as historical documents of a time and place far away from us, leaves room for, and even requires also the reading of them as great literatures of religion, with the wonder and also the transport that belong to the reading of what was written with passion, and has much of the inner quality, even though seldom the form, of poetry.

In what sense can a modern man in an age of science, when history also would be scientific, expect to make his own and bring back with him to the present what he finds written in these ancient books? Can he and should he in any real sense undertake to do now what Paul did then, and if he should, then in just what sense? It is natural for the historian to say that he must become as it were a man of the time that he is studying, and must not look at the men of that time as if they were like us. He must drop his prejudices and presuppositions, in a sense forget his knowledge, that he may face the facts of the past with pure objectivity. He must seek to see the facts as they were and must avoid the temptation to apply our thoughts and feelings to Paul's age, or his thoughts and feelings to ours. Only by becoming as men of that time can we understand the men and events of the time.

Now, reasonable as this demand may appear, it does not as a matter of fact describe the attitude or method of any historian. Every historian does, of course, in reality bring himself with him in his effort to become at home in the past; he does, without embarrassment or apology, use his own mind with all its modern information and training for the interpretation of the events and persons that he would understand. He does not, in fact, even attempt to forget his own knowledge, but rather to make use of it in order to explain the human beings and movements of the past; and he explains them in ways and by means that would be in part wholly strange and even incomprehensible to the persons to whom he applies them. He will indeed try to see and hear as if he were a man of that time, but he will explain as a man of our time. He will, for example, see a miracle as the men of that time saw it, but he will explain the miracle, and also the belief in it, in the way in which our own age understands and explains unusual events and the past ideas of men in regard to them.

Again, the conception of development as applied to religion is, to quote Professor G. F. Moore, "eminently modern"; if it could have been explained to the Jews of Jesus' time "it would have seemed to them a contradiction of the very idea of religion." Yet no historian hesitates to use this very modern conception for the interpretation of an ancient history. Beside this inevitable modernizing of the past by every modern historian there is the very different sort of modernizing, equally inevitable, which belongs to the reading of a great literature of the past for the sake of its greatness, for enjoyment and for use. For this also, but in a different way, we bring ourselves with us, we find ourselves in what we read, and make it truly our own. But for this end we must seek and expect to learn from the ancient book, not to impose our learning upon it.

The man of religion wants not only to understand in the sense of science but to learn from the great men of the past, in order that he may make their insights and convictions and experiences his own. One of the greatest modern composers taught musical composition with no text-book, requiring his pupils only to study with painstaking detail the works of Palestrina, Orlando di Lasso, Bach, Beethoven, so as to see how a great musician works, what his method and what his results. In the end, after the student has learned what music is from those who by common consent were great creators of great music, he is to compose freely, with no constraining rules, but only with great examples, under the inspiration of great musicians who have entered into his mind and become a part of himself. His music is to be no echo or imitation. Only in spirit not in letter are the great men of the past to control him. He is to do in the present and for it what Bach did in and for his time, what we may say Bach would be doing if he were living now, what indeed he is doing through the minds of those who have made his work their own.

This way of knowing a great man of the past is highly subjective, and the more truly and deeply subjective it is the better. Yet the Bach whom we are coming to know is the real Bach, and the subjective way of approach and understanding is the best and really the only way in which the real person and his work as a fact in history can be understood. It is an objective goal which can be reached only by a subjective way. This means that history is not like physical science. It is ultimately a knowledge of persons by persons. A knowledge in which love, sympathy and likeness are not only justifiable but indispensable. There can be no real knowledge without them. The man who has begun to do his master's work understands the master better than he did when he was only learning from him.

It is quite in this way that I think of the man of religion as undertaking to do in our time what Paul, what Jesus, did in their time. It is possible only to one who has made himself familiar with them as they were in their time. But the familiarity is not of the kind that requires learning, or that learning by itself can supply. The question how they would think and what they would do if they were men of our time will be rightly answered by us only if we are as free and as fully ourselves as they were, these selves of ours being, however, in a true sense that which they have made us. It may, of course, be objected that this defines the task of religion itself, not the task of the history of religion; that considered as history it is a wholly unjustifiable modernizing of a science which ought to be pursued in complete objectivity with the sole aim of recovering the facts as they were. To this my reply would be a confident assertion of the rights of subjectivity in historical study. It is more important for the historian to be courageously subjective than for him to be in bondage to the word scientific.

Let us remember again, with Reitzenstein, that the highest aim of the historian is to gain a knowledge of persons. This means that the knowledge he is seeking is in nature the knowledge of one person by another, not the knowledge of things. We know another person only if he knows us, and in the case of a great person we know him only as we respond to his greatness, first by recognition, reverence, joy, and then by appropriation, the sense of participation which means likeness and becomes love. Persons can be known only by this highly subjective process; and this is as true of persons of the past as of the present. We know no one as we ought to know as long as our knowledge is objective. We may by objective study know many things about other men without knowing them themselves at all.

So there is a sense in which we must take ourselves with us when we go back into the past, and a sense in which we may and ought to bring the great men of the past back with us when we return to the present; and if we grasp the sense in which this is to be done we shall understand the sense in which we can attempt to gain a Biblical Theology for the Present, and to make our way from what is truly in the Bible to what is true. There is a sense in which the Christian is to be as Christ in the new circumstances, the new human life, of our new time, a sense in which just this is what the Christian religion means; but it is not in the sense of outward imitation, or of obedience to the letter of a new law. Moreover, there is a sense in which it can be said that no one who does not undertake to do this in his own present can really understand Jesus as He was in the past; so that if to understand Jesus is the goal of the historian's task then in some real sense the tasks of the historian and of the man of religion cannot be separated from each other. It may be very important to recognize the distinction between the historical and what some call the superhistorical, I would say rather between facts and persons in the New Testament, but it may be and I deeply believe that it is nevertheless a mistake to try to keep these two things separate, and that for the simple reason that the most significant facts in the New Testament are persons.

I must end fully conscious that I have indicated only an approach toward a New Testament Theology for today. I have suggested some of the interests and influences that have led me to find the beginnings of a modern theology in the New Testament and in those parts of it which were in their time spiritual, that is inward, free, powerful and forward moving. This means that between the two religions which I find in the New Testament I have chosen for myself the religion of Jesus, not the religion about Jesus: but it does not mean that the choice of Jesus is the rejection of Paul. Our knowledge of the religion of Jesus is indeed primarily gained from the Gospels; but for the understanding of its new and distinctive character, and also of the way in which it can become a new religion in each new age and yet remain the religion of Jesus, Paul is our best interpreter, our indispensable guide.

The distinctive Christian knowledge is the knowledge of Jesus Himself, and Paul most of all teaches us what it means to know Jesus Christ. It does not mean a theology, a Christology. To know Christ means to see the beauty, the exceeding excellence of His nature, to see the glory of God in His face. This sight of the divine quality of the person Jesus Christ calls forth admiration, reverence toward one greater than ourselves, but also creates likeness in those who look upon Him (2 Cor. 3:18), and at the same time summons us to unceasing moral effort to attain that which is already ours by His gift (Phil. 3:8-14), to walk by the spirit by which we live (Gal. 5:25).

The Christian is one who knows the person Jesus Christ with this sort of knowledge. A Christian Theology should mean the thinking about God, about man, even about the world, which is natural to one who has this distinctive knowledge. One who knows Christ has a sense of what Divineness means, he shares Christ's knowledge of God. He has a new knowledge of all men, which is like his knowledge of Christ, and like Christ's knowledge of men (2 Cor. 5:16).

Christians will naturally have their thoughts also about the person Jesus Christ whom they know, and about the nature of their knowledge of Him; but the Christian's knowledge of Christ does not involve and does not require a Christology. Coleridge said that we do not need a doctrine of the Sacred Scriptures. It is the Bible itself that we need, and a doctrine about it hinders our natural use and enjoyment of it. In some such way Paul intimates that Christologies may stand in the way of our real knowledge of Jesus Himself. They become indeed too easily the cause of disputes and divisions, which should be impossible to those who know Christ, since they are contrary to His spirit, a sin against Him (1 Cor. 8).

Christologies assume that Christ is a problem needing something else for its solution, something better known and of greater importance, by which He is to be interpreted and explained. But to Paul the knowledge of Christ is the Christian's most certain possession, valued above all other things, worth the loss of all other things. His theology, his thinking, will be not his interpretation of Christ in the light of other things, but his interpretation of other things in the light of the known fact of Christ. Jesus Himself certainly did not make any solution of the problem of His nature the condition of following Him, still less could any such self-estimation have been a part of His own religion. Not any doctrine, but only the denial of self, the choice of service and of suffering for love's sake, were the conditions of discipleship.

The Christian experience and endeavor center in the likeness of the Christian to Christ; Christologies are efforts to define the difference that separates Him from us. Faith in Christ is not a belief about Him; it is consent to His ideals, taking Him as master, the vision, the choice, the love of Christ. All things are changed and become new for one who knows Jesus; and Christian thinking, Christian theology, may be defined as an effort to describe this newness which the Christian sees because of Christ. But to see God and men and the

world in the light of Jesus means to see them as He saw
them, and to see our world as He saw his.   Our religion is His religion.

What Paul says about the nature of Christian knowledge and wisdom should have produced, and should
now produce, a sort of Christian thinking very different
from that which the word Paulinism has come to signify.   If Paul was right when he contrasted Christian
wisdom with that which the first Greek Christians were
already beginning to value, then no thinking that causes
party divisions, jealousy, and strife can claim the name
Christian.   A Christian theology cannot be something
that only the learned can understand.   To Paul as to
Jesus the world's wise men were missing the wisdom—
foolishness indeed it seemed to them—which the weak
and despised possessed.

A Christian theology cannot be a knowledge of which
one is proud.   "If any one thinks that he has come to
know anything he does not yet know as knowing ought
to be."   It is a knowledge of God which depends on
God's knowing us, and is like God's knowledge of us.
"But if any one love God, such a one is known by
God" (1 Cor. 8:2-3).   It is not a knowledge which
thinks itself to be adequate and final.   "If there is
knowledge it shall pass away."   "Now we see in a
mirror, in an enigma: but then face to face: now I know
in part; but then shall I know even as also I have been
known."   Not only knowledge but even prophecy is
imperfect and will end.   But there are things that abide
—faith, hope, love—and of these the greatest is love.
So in 1 Cor. 13 Paul gives love its place not only in
Christian life but in Christian knowledge.   Love is not
only greater than knowledge, but knowledge at its
highest is love.   Only in love can men hope to see God
face to face, and only as love can our knowledge of
God aspire to be like His knowledge of us.

Here are definitions of the nature of Christian
knowledge by which I could wish my theological thinking to be controlled. As Christian knowledge at its
beginning is to know Jesus Christ—not to know about
Him—so at its goal it is not to know about God, but to
know God. It is as hard to pursue these two sorts of
knowledge together in the case of Christ and of God
as in that of our closest human friends. To know them
and to know about them have very little to do with each
other.

Looking back from the Hymn to Love to the Hymn
to Wisdom (1 Cor. 2:6-16) we cannot now be mistaken as to what Paul means by saying that we know
God because we have the spirit, the mind of God, the
mind of Christ. We cannot be misled by some of the
phrases early in the hymn into supposing that Paul
has any advanced knowledge, which he can impart only
to advanced Christians, about the mysteries of the unseen world or of the future, or of the nature of Christ
and of His incarnation, or the significance of His death.
It is not what happened to Christ, but the mind of
Christ, the love of Christ Himself, that the Christian
knows, and only the Christian, since to have that knowledge is itself to be Christian—a thing that cannot be
said of most affirmations about Christ that creeds and
theologies have made. The highest things that we can
know of Christ, indeed the only things that can in any
truly religious sense of the word be known, are the
things that we can experience as our own; and the
measure of our knowledge of Christ is the reality and
degree of our oneness with Him.

I incline then to get from Paul my theology, in the
sense in which I have one—and it is from Paul that I
get this sense. Paul seems to me to know best what
Christian knowledge is, what it means to know Christ.
One needs to go back and forth between Jesus and Paul.
Paul contributes greatly to our knowledge of the his-

torical Jesus, and Jesus controls our understanding and estimation of Paul. So Paul would have it. "Be ye imitators of me, even as I also am of Christ."

PRINCIPAL PUBLICATIONS

Books:

The Messages of the Apocalyptical Writers. New York, Charles Scribner's Sons, 1905.

The Mind of Christ in Paul: Light from Paul on Present Problems of Christian Thinking. New York, Charles Scribner's Sons, 1930.

Chapters in books:

Articles in Hasting's *Dictionary of the Bible.* "Apocrypha" I, pp. 110-123. "Book of Revelation," IV, pp. 239-266. Etc.

"The Yecer ha-ra: A Study in the Jewish Doctrine of Sin," pp. 93-156 in *Biblical and Semitic Studies.* New York, Scribner's, Yale Bi-centennial Publications, 1901.

"The Preexistence of the Soul in the Book of Wisdom and in the Rabbinical Writings" in *Old Testament and Semitic Studies in Memory of William Rainey Harper,* I, pp. 205-270. University of Chicago Press, 1908.

"The Place of the Sacred Book in the Christian Religion" in *Transactions of the Third International Congress for the History of Religions.* Oxford, 1908, II, pp. 283-290.

"The Signs of God in the Life of Man" in *Modern Sermons by World Scholars,* VII, pp. 189-208. New York, Funk and Wagnalls Co., 1909.

"The Mysticism of the Hebrew Prophets" in *At One with the Invisible,* pp. 1-36. Ed. by E. Hershey Sneath. New York, The Macmillan Company, 1921.

"The Historical and the Spiritual Understanding of the Bible" in *Education for Christian Service,* pp. 19-48. New Haven, Yale University Press, 1922.

"Paul's Belief in Life After Death" in *Religion and the Future Life,* pp. 225-258. Ed. by E. Hershey Sneath. New York, Fleming H. Revell, 1922.

Articles:

"The Liberal and the Ritschlian Theology of Germany."
Andover Review, XIX, July, 1893, pp. 440-461.

"Inquiries Concerning the Divinity of Christ." *American Journal of Theology*, VIII, 1, January, 1904, pp. 9-29.

"The Sufficiency of the Religion of Jesus." *American Journal of Theology*, XI, 1, January, 1907, pp. 74-94.

"The Bearing of Historical Studies on the Religious Use of the Bible." *Harvard Theological Review*, II, 3, July, 1909, pp. 253-276.

"Things Greater and Less in the Bible." *Yale Divinity Quarterly*, March, 1911.

"A Source Book of Judaism in New Testament Times (with reference to Charles's Apocrypha and Pseudepigrapha)." *American Journal of Theology*, XVIII, 1, January, 1914, pp. 106-118.

"The Place of Apocalyptical Conceptions in the Thought of Paul." *Journal of Biblical Literature*, XLI, 1922, pp. 183-204.

"Judaism in New Testament Times (with reference to George F. Moore's 'Judaism')." *Journal of Religion*, 1928, pp. 30-62.

"Does Paul Claim to Have Known the Historical Jesus? A Study of 2 Cor. 5:16." *Journal of Biblical Literature*, 1928, pp. 257-275.

"The Problem of Things New and Old in the Beginnings of Christianity." *Journal of Biblical Literature*, 1929, pp. 1-23.

THEOLOGY, EMPIRICAL AND CHRISTIAN

By HARRIS FRANKLIN RALL

(b. February 23, 1870, Council Bluffs, Iowa)

Professor of Systematic Theology, Garrett Biblical Institute (Graduate School of Theology affiliated with Northwestern University)

Evanston, Illinois

THEOLOGY, EMPIRICAL AND CHRISTIAN

By Harris Franklin Rall

M Y BOYHOOD home was a potent influence in my religious life. My father came to America in early youth from south Germany, though the family name derived from Italy some three hundred years ago (Rallo, Germanized as Rall), and probably, much earlier still, from Greece. From his home my father took the warm evangelical note, with a touch of mysticism, which has so often marked the piety of Würtemberg. My mother's home was in the Swiss canton of Graubünden on the upper reaches of the Hinterrhein, to which her great grandfather had removed from Neuchâtel after having adopted the evangelical faith. Her home was also marked by a simple and devout piety under the influence of a mother, who, as a young widow, brought her family to America.

My father was a minister, with little formal schooling but with a respect for scholarship and an ambition, even more marked in my mother, that his children should have what he lacked. His religious evaluations influenced me more than his theological ideas: religion as fellowship with God in vital experience, a sound ethical emphasis for which there was to be no substitute, and a deep appreciation of the Church, not as a sacrosanct institution, but as a fellowship and a living instrument which had the right to the unfailing service which both my parents gave it. With a conservative background, he had an essentially liberal spirit. He saw too clearly where the realities of religion lay to be dis-

turbed by the progress of Biblical criticism or the controversies about evolution.   His children went to state
institutions of learning at a time when pious folk talked
of them as "hotbeds of infidelity."

So it came that, when I went to the University of
Iowa as a boy of seventeen, I had some real understanding of what religion was and a deep respect for its
reality because of the genuinely devout lives of my
father and mother.   I had some general convictions,
but religion had not been identified with a dogmatic
system.   I had a respect for scholarship and no fear of
the truth, and neither my university course nor my later
work at Yale and abroad brought me any severe crisis.

My first intellectual awakening came with my undergraduate work at Iowa and especially under G. T. W.
Patrick.   What he gave me was not so much a set of
conclusions as an example of open-mindedness and of
order and lucidity in thought and expression.   From
Melville B. Anderson in a course on Shakespeare and
from reading Henry Jones on Browning, I learned to
appreciate literature as a significant dealing with the
problems of life under the forms of art.   Poet and
dramatist and novelist have remained for me a source
of help in my thinking; they, too, like the philosopher
and the theologian, should see things whole, and I have
often found their insights surpass the labored results
of logic.

Four years at Yale were divided as to their main interest between theology and philosophy.   Samuel Harris
and George B. Stevens were my chief aid in the former,
and in the latter I worked with Ladd and Duncan.   The
Divinity School at that time still moved mainly along the
old lines of lecture method and classroom recitation, with
no special provision for directing independent thought
or guiding individual investigation.   Yet we were
brought face to face with the basic problems of religion
in an atmosphere of free discussion.   The historical

criticism of the Bible was a center of interest, but even liberal thinkers had hardly begun to realize the revolutionary implications of this inclusion of religion with all its writings and doctrines and institutions under the principle of development. Though he did not discuss these more theological questions, Frank C. Porter's courses on the development of religious thought in the Old and New Testaments were especially informing and stimulating.

Theology and philosophy remained my interest during two years spent at Berlin and Halle. I wrote my doctor's dissertation at Halle for Alois Riehl, who had not yet left for Berlin. He gave me generous recognition for my work on Leibniz, chiefly, I think, because he felt I had made good my criticism of some current views as represented by Kuno Fischer and some recently propounded theses of Ludwig Stein as to Leibniz's dependence upon Spinoza. Riehl brought me face to face with the critical philosophy, but I could not accept his contention that criticism was the real work of philosophy and that beyond this we must at best content ourselves with a purely private world view, a *Taschenphilosophie* with no claim to real philosophical standing.

My chief interest, however, was in theology, and my major attention was given to this field even while I was preparing for my degree in philosophy. Ritschlianism was still in its ascendency. Theology had come to the place where changes in thought demanded not a modification of doctrines here and there, but a new orientation. Ritschl did not offer a system of doctrine; he was no *Systematiker*. He and his followers did bring into the forefront the basic questions which had to be considered before particular doctrines could be discussed. What is religion? What is the essence of the Christian religion? What of its relation to other religions? What is the nature of religious knowledge

and the ground of religious certainty?   Is there anything certain or normative for faith in the flux of history?   My personal contact with Ritschlianism as
student was with Harnack and Julius Kaftan at Berlin
and with Reischle and Loofs at Halle.   These men
were quite independent, and that was characteristic of
the Ritschlians.   Harnack had his own genius.   Kaftan,
like Herrmann, had reached his basic point of view
independently of Ritschl.

It is quite easy now to point out the errors and limitations of this movement.   Jesus was not just the ethical
and religious idealist of Harnack's picture nor did
Ritschl represent him by his purely ethical Kingdom
of God idea.   No such isolation of Christianity over
against other religions was possible as suggested by
the Ritschlians.   Ritschl had not thought through his
theory of knowledge.   No such sharp line could be
drawn between judgments of existence and judgments
of value.   "Metaphysics" was not so easily to be waved
aside.   There was much more to mysticism in religion
than the type which Ritschl so sweepingly condemned.

Yet, while I at no time accounted myself a Ritschlian,
I must acknowledge the help that it then gave me.   It
set before me the problems that I had to study.   Ritschl,
like Schleiermacher, called men to consider first of all
what religion was as a distinctive interest of man.   He
anticipated Höffding in pointing out its concern with
the values of life.   He was a pragmatist before the
pragmatists.   His followers corrected much that was
one-sided or lacking in him.   They showed that a concern for values did not exclude metaphysical reality,
but that through the realm of values one makes the
surest approach to the realm of the real.   Standing alike
against the speculative and the dogmatic, they made
plain the place of faith as personal trust and ethical
venture and its centrality in religion.

In Max Reischle, too little known and dying all too

early, I found a discriminating discussion of these matters. In Martin Kähler of Halle I came to know not
only a rare combination of saint and scholar, but an
interesting fusion of modern outlook with an appreciation of the old evangelical spirit. Himself not a
Ritschlian, he had not a little kinship with right wing
Ritschlians like his colleagues, Loofs and Reischle. I
came to see more clearly the dependence of theology
upon religion and the nature of theology, not as master
of religion but as its minister, not as drawing from independent sources of knowledge, whether in Scripture
or dogma or speculation, but as setting forth that which
is implicit in religious experience and faith.

During a further year of study at Yale after my
return from abroad, I gave a series of lectures at the
Divinity School in which I sought to make clear the
significance of Ritschlianism not so much as a system
of theology, but rather as dealing with these basic questions as to the nature of religion and the method of
theology.

To all these teachers, known in person or through
their writings, I look back with gratitude. But no one
of them ever at any time in my development gave me
a system which settled my problems, even for the time.
And I am most grateful because the greatest among
them taught me *Nullius jurare in verba magistri*.

So far this retrospect has shown two strong interests
which entered in to shape my thinking about religion.
First there was the concern with religion as a personal
matter. My interest in theology sprang first from the
meaning that religion had for me in my own life. That
had its mystical side; religion meant God, and in my
boyhood home and in my own life God was something
very real. And it had its practical side: it was through
religion that I sought the deepest satisfactions of life.
I conceived the goal of life through religion, and in the

250 CONTEMPORARY AMERICAN THEOLOGY

fellowship with God I sought the help for living my
life. This personal religious interest and the experiences that have gone with it have furnished my point
of departure for theological thinking to this day. My
theology has not been a philosophical system which left
incidental room for religious needs. Its concepts have
gained alike warmth and substance from this ongoing
life in which God has meant fellowship and help, and
in which He has given life its supreme meaning and
worth.

My second interest in religion lay in my search for
a rational world-view and philosophy of life. The
impulse to philosophize was not independent of religion, a matter of curiosity or of separate intellectual
concern. Religion itself meant to me seeing life whole,
knowing that the object of trust was real and was the
ultimate reality, and finding some meaning and purpose for the world order and human life. The rational
had for me a religious meaning. I agreed with Plato:
"The unexamined life is not worthy of a man." Religion was the summons to think as well as to live—or
rather, to think was itself an essential part of life at its
highest. Faith in God meant for me faith in a world
that had unity and order and meaning. I found a
genuine religious note in Browning's word:

> This world's no blot for us nor blank;
> It means intensely and it means good.
> To find that meaning is our meat and drink.

To these two interests, which may be called the mystical and the rational, I must add a third, the social
interest, and I realize in retrospect how much my religious thinking has been affected by this. That interest
began with my college days. In the nineties I came
into contact with that rise of social interest among certain religious leaders which Rauschenbusch has sketched
in his *Christianizing the Social Order*. I read Wash-

ington Gladden, Josiah Strong, the early writings of
George D. Herron, and later on Rauschenbusch and
the rest. I was present at one of the first conferences
held at Grinnell College by a group that called itself
"the men of the Kingdom," and read their weekly
journal, *The Kingdom.*

The Methodist Federation for Social Service, which
I joined in its first year, brought me the stimulus of
fellowship with Francis J. McConnell, Harry F. Ward,
and others. Ten years of pastorate in New Haven and
Baltimore gave abundant opportunity to express this
social interest in the pulpit and in practical relations.
That opportunity was largely increased during five
years as President of the Iliff School of Theology in
Denver, with a summons to apply religious ideals to
civic and state affairs.

From the first this social concern furnished me material for my religious thinking. This was for me religion, though I did not cast overboard my concern with
religion in other forms. Nor could I go with those
whose newly found social interest, even while they remained within the Church, led to an easy neglect of
basic problems of thought or a general contempt for
theology. It may be, as some have told us, that the
concern with theology as with ritual and architecture
means for some men simply a flight from the challenge
of social problems. But it is equally possible that men
may flee from intellectual difficulties to the eager discussion of social problems or a devotion to social service.
The remedy for an inadequate theology is not the dis-
avowal of all theology. I distinctly recall the effect
of this interest upon my religious thinking as shown
in the sermons which I preached to the churches where
I supplied while still a theological student.

The importance of this social-ethical influence in
modern theology deserves consideration. Other currents of modern thought have been carefully studied

in their bearing upon theology: historical criticism with its underlying idea of development, natural science with its asserted naturalistic implications, modern psychology in its varied and conflicting forms. But the significance for theology of the remarkable development in social life and thought has been too little regarded, though this has moved in the sphere of values which most nearly coincides with religion.

Our modern social movement may be looked at in two ways. We may look at it from without in terms of changing political and economic organization. But we may look at it also from within in terms of the new social ideals and insights. The latter is what is significant for us here. It is perhaps best expressed by the term democracy, which is increasingly being used to indicate a social faith rather than merely a form of political organization and would seem preferable to the ambiguous term humanism.

Basic for this new social faith are certain convictions: the supreme worth of human personality, personal freedom alike as a good and as a way of achievement, faith in human nature and in the forces of truth and justice and good will as compared with physical compulsion, justice as the concern of all in securing the fullest opportunity for each, human solidarity, and the obligation of cooperation in service. This higher social faith, or social conscience, is at once an expression of the influence of religion and, conversely, a development of human insight which religious thinking must take into account.

Religion, like this new democracy, is concerned with the values of life and the way in which they may be achieved. Its basic conviction is that in some way goodness and power are one. It sees in the values of life the clue to the nature of the final reality. These social insights into human values then should be of significance alike for the doctrine of God and of salvation. As regards the idea of God, this is the line that was followed by the Hebrew prophets and Jesus. With them, as with our present-day social thought, the ethical and personal were determinative.

Traditional theology was diverted from this through the influence of Greek thought, with its concern for the ultimate essence or substance, eternal, absolute, unchanging, and in the West especially by the social pattern of autocracy, which placed the king and his absolute power above all other considerations. Our theology must move forward along the line of this Hebraic emphasis. Our concept of God is more than an induction, a conclusion drawn from observation of our cosmos. It is basically a faith, faith in a trustworthy universe, above all faith that the world of values is real and is supreme. God is good, and the goodness of God is of the same kind, whatever its degree, as that which we know in our highest human experiences.

Our second great concern in religion is with the way in which the good is to be realized, and here again our social insights are determinative for theology. Our concept of God and our idea of these goods both point away from the positions of traditional theology. We cannot longer hold to the sacramentarian magic which came in with Eastern theology. That went with a God that was conceived in terms of eternal and incorruptible essence that must somehow be communicated to man and so transform in quasi-metaphysical fashion the finite and corruptible human nature.

Nor can we think of salvation in terms of sovereign power, as Augustine and Calvin set it forth, with its arbitrary decrees and irresistible grace. That which is ethical and personal can be realized only by processes that are congruous in their nature; what is more than that is magic, for the essence of magic is the effort to secure given ends by means that are unrelated in kind.

It is quite a mistake, however, to assume that this view rules out all idea of transcendence, that it leaves us with a God who is no more than the sum of man's aspirations and efforts, and a salvation that sees in man himself the only savior. This same social viewpoint, thought through, involves a real transcendence. If the personal and ethical are a casual by-product of an impersonal order, then they can have no such ultimate value and authority as our social faith assumes. If they have supreme value and authority, then they must point to the nature of ultimate reality. That means a God who, as personal and purposive and good, transcends this changing time-space world. The tragedy of non-theistic humanism is that its cosmic faith, or lack of it, denies a basis for those values which its social faith affirms and so commits it to a fundamental dualism.

The problem then for the new theism which seeks to do justice to these social insights is to work out such a conception of God, and of the relation of God and man in the process of human redemption, as shall do justice to all that we have learned from history and psychology and ethics and man's social experiences. Barthianism certainly has not found the way. We can appreciate its reaction against those modern tendencies which have put man at the center of religion instead of God, but we cannot accept its denial of significance to the historical and the human. Non-theistic humanism gives up the problem by canceling the other side. Our clue must be in our conception of God as rational and personal and ethical. If religion be a relation that is ethically conditioned, then it can be maintained only by a response that is rational, ethical, active, and free.

On the other hand, the old externalism and absolutism have gone from this conception of God, and we reach the idea of a conditioned or limited though not necessarily of a finite God. Assuming the idea of God as purposive and creative Good Will, our social insight makes plain that the ends in view condition the processes by which they are achieved. If we trust our social-ethical insights, if we use them to interpret our world, then that world must be one in which there is a measure of freedom as well as of order.

But must we not go farther than this? Life is all of one piece; you cannot separate human nature from other animate nature, nor even draw a line to divide astrophysical evolution from the later biological evolution. Should we not expect even on the lowest level that element of contingency which modern physics has suggested to us, and on each succeeding level an increasing measure of freedom as a condition of development? Have we not here one of those ultimates which we have to accept "with natural piety"?

From these pages, mostly of retrospect, I turn to the present to attempt some account of my own theology. I can best begin this by considering two matters: first, the concept of religion; second, that changed world-view which gives the setting in which we must shape our theology today. For theology always has this double reference. First, it looks within, rooting in religion as the most intimate aspect of human life, trying to interpret the world and life from this standpoint. Second, it looks without: the outer world presents the setting in which religion must work, the knowledge of which theology must take account, and the forms of thought which it must use.

1. The discussion of the nature of religion is as vigorous as ever and apparently as far from a conclusion. To me religion has a double root. The driving power is human need and man's search for satisfaction, but the distinctive element is man's awareness of a world of a higher order of meaning and power, upon which he feels himself dependent, to which he owes reverence and loyalty, in which he trusts for help. Too many definitions are at fault in what they omit. The search for satisfaction, for example, does not indicate the dif-

ferentia of religion for that search belongs to all life. To say that the religious quest is social in its efforts and ends is true; but practically all life is social even at the lowest levels, as W. M. Wheeler has pointed out, while religion is at the same time uniquely individual in bringing to man the deepest awareness of the individual self and of its significance. And if it is asserted that religion is the search for satisfaction through right adjustment to one's world, that again is to point out the obvious rather than the distinctive, for such adjustment is the condition of all life. It is rather the presence of such a higher world, or higher Being, with which the distinctive character of religion is associated. It is the faith in this that gives confidence and courage, that calls for utter devotion, and that evokes reverence and awe. It is the character of religion as thus conceived that determines the nature of theology; for theology deals with God, with this higher world of value and power in which religion believes.

2. But neither religion nor theology moves in a vacuum. Alike the experiences of religion and the forms in which its faith is expressed are in relation to man's everyday world and his total thought life. Traditional theology was shaped in forms of thought taken from the framework of a world-picture which no longer obtains. There is a new world-picture, a new way of looking at his world to which man is being led by scientific knowledge, social experiences, and moral insights. This of itself does not give us a theology, any more than did the old world-view, but our work as theologians must be done in the light of this new knowledge and with such tools as it offers us. It will affect our answer to religion's two great questions: how shall we conceive God in His relation to the world, and what are those right relations to His world by which man may gain life.

In its main significance for religious thought, this

new world-view may be summed up in the following terms: a unitary world in which there are differences; a world of order in which there is "freedom," whose order is at once a basic condition and a gradual achievement.

(1) The modern man views his world as a unity. Here is the most significant change. Traditional theology rested on a dualistic conception. The spiritual world in which it believed was a transcendent, separate sphere. Its action upon this world was direct and absolute. That involved a dualism that ran through life. There was a divine truth, given directly in revelation and having absolute authority, to be distinguished from the truth which man could gain by his own effort. There was a divine salvation, wrought by the direct deed of God; the world of man's effort and achievement, technical, cultural, ethical, was a thing apart from this, a purely human affair. So in the incarnation, there was a direct incursion from without, a divine being translated from the higher sphere; and the human nature of Christ was nominally asserted but in effect ruled out. What really signified in the world's history was a divine drama which reached down to earth at given points in deeds of creation, revelation, and redemption.

The contrast of present-day thought is apparent. There is one order which obtains in all the world. As there is one order of development in which all that is has come to be in continuous change, so there is one order of being, some kind of ultimate unity in which all is joined. There are no two worlds, standing separate and opposed; if there be a spiritual, it must be sought and known in the here and now. There are no two kinds of truth; if there be revelation, it must come as human discovery. There are not two kinds of causation, natural and supernatural; if there be a divine activity, creative and redemptive, it must be in and through this finite order that we know; it must be known by us in "natural" event and human experience. Not duality but unity, not the absolute but the relative, not the static but the changing, not external authority but human apprehension and inner conviction.

But the unity does not mean uniformity or identity. It does not mean a wiping out of differences, the reduction to a mechanistic universe, a pure naturalism. There is still the distinction of quality for which the old division of natural-supernatural stood. It is not simply that higher levels appear with differences in quality that must be recognized, as the theory of emergent evolution indicates; the whole question of a world of a higher order in terms of ideals and values and power remains as it was. The question is not that of God or no God, but of the way in which God is related to His world. Divine revelation is related to an active human apprehension. There is as much room as before for the idea of a divine self-giving, of a higher world in whose life man may share and from which man may receive.

But there is no salvation which is a mere influx from without of something foreign; this too is related to human activity and is an element in the one ongoing life. There is, of course, the danger of losing the divine through this emphasis, and that trend is illustrated by naturalistic humanism. But there is as much ground as ever for holding to that God who is more than His world, who transcends it as purpose and power and goodness, before whom we bow in reverence and awe. And there is the great gain that the divine, the higher, the spiritual, becomes not a piecemeal affair but a movement with cosmic sweep that shows us the whole creative process as part of a high purpose, while at the same time it lifts all human activity to the plane of high meaning where nothing is "common or unclean."

(2) Quite as significant is the new conception of the order of the universe and the place of freedom in that

order. The new idea is still in the making and we do not know yet where the modern conceptions will lead, but some results and some tendencies may be noted.

And first is the passing of the old absolutism for the scientist and the religionist alike. The earlier thinkers drew from science, as they supposed, the idea of a rigid absolutism in the order of nature. The world was a mechanism under a strict causal rule which determined its course from the beginning so that it could be predicted to the last event by one who knew all the facts at any given time. Not only do we realize that all the facts are not knowable and never will be, but we recognize beyond this a principle of indeterminacy, an element of contingency reaching down to the atom itself. Man has long realized, despite all theoretical objections, that his world, inner and outer, was plastic to his touch. We know now that the frame of rigid mechanical determination is broken, that not merely has there been a plastic and changing universe from the beginning but that its course was never absolutely predictable.

And the old absolutism is going in religion also. The basic idea with both was the conception of some ultimate Power as absolutely determinative, in the one case identified with a mechanically operative causal force, in the other with an absolute Sovereign creating outright by a word, ruling every event by his decree. Our better knowledge of the natural order has helped to rule out the latter, but so has also our truer insight into the supremacy of the ethical and personal in religion and into the conditions under which the ethical-personal can be realized in life.

Significant, however, is the way in which we are seeing how order and freedom must be related in our conception of the universe. For a universe of order we still have. Without it human reason itself could not have developed. The idea that chaos has somehow given birth to an all-pervading order, that reason has come to be in a world without reason, and that it can then impose its reason in turn upon an irrational world, this is incredible. Without order no reason, no intelligible world, no science, no control, no chance for man to live and rule and achieve. It is, in fact, hard to see how there could be any existence without order, for existence, like thought, involves some abiding basis for possible relation. Whatever freedom there is in the world, whatever of contingency and change, there is a certain basic order that has been from the beginning and that conditions all events.

But what seems equally clear to us is that in our world there is at the same time a developing order, an order that has to be achieved. The importance of the conditioning order is that it makes possible this developing order. We are moving toward a thoroughgoing organicistic conception of the world. From lowest to highest, being as we know it has an "organic" form. To use a term less open to criticism, and following Jan Smuts, it is a world of wholes. And the evolution, astro-physical, biological, social, by which our present world has come to be, has moved by the way of the shaping of the individual into ever larger, more complex, and more significant wholes. But this developing order has not required a suppression of individuality or of freedom. On the contrary, the element of contingency or freedom has been as necessary a condition of this development as has been the underlying cosmic order, and the developing order has meant in turn the achievement of a higher and increasing freedom.

All this does not determine our theology or establish for us a theistic conclusion. For many of us a fair interpretation would seem to point to the latter; certainly it offers conditions within which we must shape the former. It suggests a purposive and directive Spirit working creatively toward certain ends, at once the world-order which makes possible the process and the immanent power working to achieve it. At the same time there is here a situation which must profoundly modify the whole traditional conception of divine power, of what it is and how it works. If there is order in the universe it is not one that is complete at the beginning. If there is a higher power, it is not to be conceived in mechanical fashion as working in direct and compulsory fashion, but rather as an inner impulse and a directive agent, offering to the creature the opportunity of self-achievement, and necessarily showing a movement that seems tentative, experimental, infinitely slow, and attended by failures and losses.

It suggests that somehow all this is something to be accepted "with natural piety" as inherent in the nature of things, in the very being of God Himself, that these are conditions without which there could be no finite being, no world of order and beauty and life. It suggests a God who is more than the mere sum of finite things existent at any given stage, who is in a real sense a transcendent God, and yet at the same time a God who is definitely conditioned or limited, in sharp contrast with old ideas of a sheer omnipotence to which the ethical and rational were subordinated.

I have sought to sketch the background of my theology so far as I could discern the influences affecting my personal development and the general setting within which our religious thinking must be done today. I want to indicate in closing three conclusions to which I have come: theology for me must be empirical, it must be a theology of faith, and it must be Christian. What this means and how these elements belong together, I must try to make plain.

1. Theology must be empirical. Used in the broad sense that means here that it must deal with the concrete data that life brings, that it must regard truth from every source that bears upon the convictions of

religion, and that the active experiment of life is to be used alike for the testing and the gaining of truth. Empiricism is thus both an attitude and a method: the attitude of the open mind, the method of observation and experiment. There is no other way open for those who cannot accept the idea of an external revelation with dogmatic authority, or of some innate power of human reason which can attain truth by speculative processes.

There is danger, however, in the use of the term empirical in theology. The success of natural science with its empirical method has been profoundly and rightly influential here. Natural science, with its constant appeal to concrete data and its demand for continuous experiment, has seemed to point the way for all thought. Certain considerations are important here. (1) Our empiricism must be inclusive and must give special regard to those fields of experience and the requisite personal attitudes which are most significant for religion. We must give consideration to the mystic and his claims. We must consider the realm of the ethical and the social, the realm of the higher values as the place where men may have the surest experience of the Eternal. Significant here is the position of the Hebrew prophets and Jesus (interestingly reaffirmed by Gandhi in his notable autobiography and suggested by its title, *My Experiment with the Truth*), that moral loyalty and the spirit of good will are the necessary way for him who would know God and the truth. (2) We must guard against the supposition, to which our deference to natural science so easily leads us, that analysis is the one way to reality and that the minute and fragmentary is the ultimately real. We must recognize that there is another way of knowing, that is by seeing things whole, and that only thus do the high values and meanings with which religion is concerned become evident. (3) We must realize that empiricism in no field can dispense with reflection, interpretation, and rational criticism, and that these are particularly required in religion. Knowledge never walks into the passive mind or offers itself as an immediate result from detailed observation. The active mind and the insight of spirit are as necessary as the right moral attitude and activity. Empiricism then is no simple, cut-and-dried method which can be lifted out of one sphere of study and set down upon another. It is simply the open mind and the demand that our knowing be constantly guided by reference to the concrete reality which all men may experience or observe.

2. We must have a theology of faith. Theology roots in religion, and its character is determined by the basic place which faith holds in religion. The world of religion, the world of a higher and a spiritual order, is one that is held by faith and known through faith. Theology is *Glaubenslehre*, it deals with the implications and the meanings of this faith.

The varied uses and the misuse of this term make definition necessary. Faith does not mean here, to quote a standard Roman Catholic text, which represents much traditional Protestant thought, "assent on authority, the acceptance of a proposition, not because we ourselves perceive its truth, but because another person tells us that it is true." It does not mean a given body of truth, *the* faith, "the sum of truths revealed by God." Nor is it an inferior kind of knowledge, accepted in lieu of a higher certainty. It is not credulity, a jumping at conclusions where evidence is lacking. It is not wishful thinking, a projecting of our desires.

Religious faith is an attitude of confidence and loyalty, resting upon an inner conviction. In its broadest meaning, faith is the attitude of confidence with which we face life, the conviction that our world is trustworthy and meaningful. As such, faith is a prerequisite for life in all its aspects. It is as necessary for the scientist, the engineer, the man of business, for man as a "political animal" and in his social relations, as it is in religion. It is never a matter of arbitrary decision. It is called forth by the world in which man lives, and it is constantly being tested and shaped and remolded in form by man's experiences in that world. This faith is not the conclusion of a lazy credulity but an instrument for an active enterprise.

The form of faith naturally varies in different realms. In religion it is the conviction that what we know in moral ideals and values, in mystical experience, and in spiritual insight, is real, that being real it is therefore the highest, and that man may trust it and build his life upon it. It is the assurance that in all this man is in living fellowship with the Eternal. Its underlying conviction is that in some real and fundamental fashion goodness and power are one in this universe. That does not mean that rational considerations and empirical observations do not enter in. It does mean that religion is always dealing with those meanings and values and ultimate convictions which neither pure logic nor pure empiricism can establish, and that faith is not secondary and provisional here but primary and permanent. This character of religion theology must express. Its task is not to furnish for religion some more secure basis outside of religion, as, for example, in some philosophical system.

A right understanding of faith and empiricism in religion shows how each requires the other. The urgent need of empiricism in theology today may be illustrated by the doctrines of God and salvation. Faith in God is the conviction that goodness and power are one. Jesus voiced that when He said, "Our Father, who art in heaven." But the traditional doctrine of God, with its abstractions and its absolutisms of essence and power, is quite another matter. An empirical approach bids us regard God like all other being as definite and determinate in character. It calls us away from speculative conclusions about this goodness and power. Our faith is a guiding clue, not a dogmatic conclusion. We can know the goodness of God only through the highest which human life and insight show and which we experience in commerce with our world. We have no right to shape our idea of God's goodness by our desires, to make the goodness of God, for example, a soft and sentimental affair instead of that rather hard but nobly creative power which the full experience of life suggests. So we must revise our idea of the power of God through an empirical study which will show us how creative power actually works in the world of nature and human life, under what conditions and with what necessary limitations.

The doctrine of salvation needs similar restatement. The conviction of faith is that there is a higher world in which lies both our highest good and the help to its achievement, a world with which man may have fellowship and from which he may take help. But the old abstractions in which traditional theology expressed this faith are lifeless today. The empirical approach asserts first that the saving help of this world must come to us in and through the world of daily experience. Then it summons us to find out by such experience how this saving help is actually available, what those attitudes and activities are which will relate us savingly to this world. And here history and psychology, the social sciences and individual experiment, and the rich religious experiences of the past must all be put under tribute.

But it is quite as important to see the meaning of faith for the empirical attitude and method in the field of religion. Faith is man's conviction that he has met the highest, and that in devotion to this and in this alone is to be found both truth and life. The nature of this faith determines the character of the experiment. The highest here demands of man the utmost, and the utmost is the only way to attain the highest. "He that willeth to do shall know." No cautious, tentative attitude will do here. The personal devotion of life is the condition of knowledge. If the Highest be love and righteousness, then His spirit and His power can only be known by those who give themselves to this same life of righteousness and love. In this sphere, only the sharing of life can give the knowledge of life.

And this suggests the significance of tradition for faith and empiricism. Tradition is here used in the simplest and largest meaning as that which is given to the present by the past; it is man's social heritage. The word is in ill repute today in theology because it has meant the unthinking acceptance of inherited systems of doctrine. But that is ruled out not only by the empirical method but by the nature of faith itself. Faith is response to the highest when it wins from us conviction. Faith is not concerned with the systems of the past—each age must work these out for itself. But it is concerned to find the highest. And that which stirs faith and wins it is the highest as it comes in the ideals and insights of the seers and saints and prophets of the past. As with religious faith, so with an empirical theology. It will begin neither with some least theoretical assumption nor yet with an inherited system of ideas. It will take those high ideals and insights which command our conviction, such as Jesus' concept of God and the good life. It will make these the basis of experiment. It will use these for exploration and interpretation. It will consider these in relation to truths gained from other sources, and will question and criticize.

It is clear then that no one term can rightly characterize the theological method. Its inclusive character must find place for the traditional and empirical, for reason and faith.

3. Finally I must describe my own theology as Christian. To describe theology as empirical is to suggest its required method. To speak of a theology of faith is to point out what follows from the nature of religion. These two elements should characterize all theology. But to speak of theology as Christian is to indicate the personal conclusion at which one has arrived. What is meant by this position must be briefly indicated.

Religion roots on the one hand in human need, on the other in man's conviction of a higher world of a spiritual order, which means for most of us the belief in God. Religion is the response to this higher world as it touches our life. So far I have spoken of this world of higher values and final reality in general terms. But the object of religious faith is never an abstract idea of goodness. There is no such thing as religion in general, or faith in goodness in the abstract. Religion lives as faith in a higher world which has come to us in particular historical forms, the gift of tradition. Theology begins with its own historic religious heritage, but it does not necessarily remain there. The Christian religion was my social heritage; it was through its message and in its forms that I found my own way to fellowship with God. But my theology is Christian today because the years of question and observation and reflection, while changing the forms of early belief, have confirmed the central convictions and deepened my appreciation.

In calling my theology Christian I am not committing myself to any given doctrinal system or ecclesiastical authority. Nor am I insisting that there is but one interpretation to be given to Christianity; we are dealing here with an historic *Grösse* that has had a long history and includes many forms. As I see it, its unifying center is not an authoritative set of sacred writings, nor an ecclesiastical institution, nor a set of doctrines. I find its central point of reference and its unifying element in the historic Jesus. The significant fact about Jesus I take to have been a certain quality of spirit expressed in word and faith and life, in which His followers have seen alike the revelation of what God is and of what men should be.

The historical difficulties that confront us here are plain. The portrayal of this spirit is mediated for us through a later generation, whether we find this spirit in the letters of Paul, the synoptic gospels, or the Johannine writings. Yet the New Testament shows us, with all its differences, a unitary and dominant spirit, conceived in like fashion in its essential aspects, a spirit of reverence, of loyalty, of faith, and above all of utter good will. All its writers share in the conviction that in this spirit they see the life of the Eternal, in this life God has spoken to man, and that here is the way which man must take in individual life and in social relations.

Undoubtedly later experiences not only helped to mold the tradition of the life and words of Jesus, but influenced the apprehension and formulation of this ideal. But the decisive matter is not affected by this. For the crucial question is not as to some sole expression in Jesus, but whether this spirit which His followers found in Him is that manifestation of the Eternal in time which Christian faith has taken it to be. If Jesus really expressed that infinite Spirit in His life, then we should expect, as He did, that this Spirit of good will would continue to work creatively in His followers.

It is not then a question of being able to determine the exact words of Jesus' teaching, or even of accepting all the words of that teaching, including its apocalyptic form. It is whether we find here the highest vision of God, the truest way of life, the noblest expression of the human goal, a way of help, or of salvation, whose fruitfulness our experience increasingly confirms.

There are other questions that will arise in connection with the avowal of such a position. How can a theology be called empirical and Christian at the same time? Does not the former mean an open mind and the latter a commitment that shuts out other loyalties? Does not the former stand for a ceaseless search and progressive discovery and the latter for a conclusion in which the mind comes to rest?

Traditional theology certainly excluded the empirical attitude that has here been maintained. We may call its conception of Christianity institutional. It was joined with an extreme doctrine of transcendence. With a varying emphasis upon Scripture, or sum of doctrine, or church, it conceived of Christianity as an objective reality, given over to man by direct deed of God, a divine institution necessarily perfect and established once for all. An unchanged and unchanging theology would here be the ideal. With this there went undoubtedly very often that conception of religion which Dewey has criticized in his *Quest for Certainty*, a religion in which a man may rest from search because he has the truth and from effort because his salvation is in the hands of God.

If I mistake not, this question, already of major interest, is likely to occupy us still more in the future. For that reason I have put the theme in the title of this paper. As children of our age we have caught a spirit which we believe will not pass with this age: the open mind, the search for truth, the conviction that truth must be won by ourselves and cannot simply be handed over, and the realization that the winning depends upon our constant reference to the world of concrete reality and our active experiment in that world.

On the other hand is our conviction as men of religion. As such we believe, not with a knowledge of sense-perception or with the assurance of a logical deduction, but with the deeper certainty of faith, that the world of the spiritual and ideal, the world of values, is real and is supreme and that we may trust in this world. As Christians we believe that this world of higher meaning and power, the world that has its being in God, has come to us in Jesus Christ, that in His spirit we know the Eternal Spirit, and that thus through Him we have found the way of life, alike as the power of life given us in this fellowship and the way of life which waits for our achievement.

Here is no mere search; here is certainty, a certainty so great that it meets the supreme test: men are willing to build their lives upon it, men are willing to face death for it as Jesus did. What is more, men find increasing confirmation of this certainty in the ongoing experiences of life. It is not then a mere matter of traditional theology versus the scientific spirit; it is a question of the nature of religion itself.

As one who would call his theology both empirical and Christian, I can only suggest the considerations which have helped me past what seems to me to be a false antithesis.

There is first of all a false opposition of finality and progress, or, better stated, of achievement and progress, due to a doctrinaire conception of evolution from which we have not yet freed ourselves. What the facts show us is that all along the way definite stages of achievement are reached which in their own proper sphere mark a certain finality. The atom and the living cell mark stages of development which remain the basis for all further progress, in themselves not to be transcended. Man reached his development as a psycho-physical organism probably two score thousand years ago. His further progress had to be in the sphere of the cultural through social heredity. In this cultural sphere there are apprehensions of beauty and ethical insights reached by man long since, which remain a permanent possession. Nor has any progress of the last twenty-five hundred years annulled the prophetic ideal in religion: to do justly, to love kindness, to walk humbly with God. The idea of a ceaseless flux in which all is subject to change is a doctrinaire conception.

It is quite as mistaken to oppose certainty and adventure, to ally the former with "passive acceptance of what is given" alike as to truth and life, and to contrast with it the religion of creative experiment in regard both to the search for truth and the making of a better world. All search and all creative living require some element of certainty. That is not changed by the fact that some men reduce this certainty to a rather meager minimum. Mr. Dewey, for example, believes in "the possibilities of existence," in "a sense of the whole which claims and dignifies the flickering inconsequential acts of separate selves"—a faith whose certainty is quite too much, for example, for a disillusioned Joseph Wood Krutch or for Bertrand Russell in his best rhetorical moments.

Let me illustrate these comments by reference to the Christian religion as interpreted above. The Christian faith is an insight and a certainty. It is the conviction that the power that is back of all is creative and redemptive Good Will as seen most clearly in the Spirit of Jesus, and that this Spirit points out to men the way of life and life's highest good. If this be true, then we have here a new level, not the end of human achievement but that from which such achievement must henceforth move forward. Such a conviction, of course, must be tested out in life, though from its nature it cannot be the subject of demonstration by sense-perception or logical proof. Its service in the interpretation of our total experience, its congruity with truth elsewhere reached, its ministry in the achievement of life, all this will condition its permanent hold on men.

It is clear, however, that this conviction, so far from estopping the human enterprise, is a summons to it. It is a call to thought: to consider the implications of this conviction for our view of man and the world, to study the actual ongoing life of man and nature in order to understand how this creative Good Will works and how man may work with the Eternal. It is a summons to action, to the creation in this world of a humanity in which this Spirit shall rule in order to the achievement of the fullest human life.

Our present world situation would seem to make clear that this way of good will is our only alternative to social chaos. It may be said that this leaves it still undetermined just what this human good is and by just what instruments it is to be achieved. And that is the point of this paragraph: here is no end of the road where we sit content, but a finger that points to a great highway. Only, it is more than a signboard that points men beyond itself. It is the conviction that this way for man is also the way of God, that man moves on with God, that the creative Spirit goes with man and works through man and assures the end even though that end waits man's exploring thought and active effort.

Here then is why I call my theology Christian as well as empirical. It is here that the Eternal has spoken to me and touched my life. It is here that I have found the highest and the most convincing conception of God and of life. But here too I have found not only the possibility but the incitement for thought to move on in exploration and life in creative adventure.

PRINCIPAL PUBLICATIONS

Books:

Der Leibnizsche Substanzbegriff. Halle, Ehrhardt Karras, 1899.
Social Ministry (joint author). New York, Methodist Book Concern, 1911.

A New Testament History. New York, Abingdon Press, 1914. (Second half translated into Burmese.)
A Working Faith. New York, Abingdon Press, 1914.
The Life of Jesus. New York, Abingdon Press, 1917. (Translated into Korean.)
The Teachings of Jesus. New York, Abingdon Press, 1918. (Also published in Spanish, Korean and Hindustani translations.)
Teacher's Manual for the Life of Jesus. New York, Abingdon Press, 1918.
Teacher's Manual for the Teachings of Jesus. New York, Abingdon Press, 1918.
Modern Premillennialism and the Christian Hope. New York, Abingdon Press, 1920.
What Can I Believe? Minneapolis, 1922. Last edition, Chicago, Board of Education, Methodist Episcopal Church, 1933.
The Coming Kingdom. New York, Abingdon Press, 1924.
Week Day Sermons in King's Chapel (contributor). New York, The Macmillan Company, 1925.
The Meaning of God (Emory University, Quillian Lectures). Nashville, Tenn., Cokesbury Press, 1926.
Christianity and Judaism Compare Notes (with S. S. Cohen). New York, The Macmillan Company, 1927.
Christianity Today (editor and joint author). Nashville, Tenn., Cokesbury Press, 1928.
Behaviorism: A Battle Line (contributor). Nashville, Tenn., Cokesbury Press, 1930.

Articles contributed to *Methodist Review, Methodist Quarterly Review, American Journal of Theology, Religious Education, The Journal of Religion, The Christian Century, The Christian Advocate* (New York edition and other *Advocates*), *Union Seminary Review, Epworth Herald, Sunday School Journal,* etc.

THE MORAL WILL AND THE FAITH
THAT SUSTAINS IT

By WILLIAM L. SULLIVAN

(b. November 15, 1872, Braintree, Massachusetts)

Minister of the Germantown (Philadelphia) Unitarian Church

Germantown, Philadelphia, Pennsylvania

THE MORAL WILL AND THE FAITH
THAT SUSTAINS IT

By WILLIAM L. SULLIVAN

I.

WHEN you ask a man what his theology is, you are, I should suppose, more interested in the man than in the theology. What you are seeking is not a pedantic account of the books he has read, the speculations he has worked or trifled with, or the ecclesiastical system to which, as the dreadful word is, he "belongs." Rather your inquiry, so far as it is serious and expectant of a profitable answer, amounts to this, I think: "As you have struggled to know the supreme thing in all existence; as you have eaten the dust of your disillusions; as you have fallen and been trampled on; as you have fought with demons and caught perhaps a glimpse of heavenly presences through the fog in which you have borne life's heavy strife; as you have searched and studied and perhaps prayed; as you have reflected upon the gropings of science and philosophy and the wilderness of history, tell me what you have discovered of magnificence; what has proved a sure support; what radiance still shines despite the dark; what, if anything, as death draws near, sounds to your soul a conquering cry of supreme and final confidence."

That, phrased, I trust, in language not too rhetorical, is what we wish to know when we inquire for a man's statement of his beliefs. A soul is what we want him to reveal, not merely the chambers of an acquisitive mind in which a scholiast stores the miscellaneous cargo of his cognitions and hypotheses. This intellectual ballast we indeed presume him to have accumulated, but his bill of lading in specifications and statistics is not what we hope he will offer for our inspection. Another page altogether of his life's history is what we covet, the page that tells the story of his *Itinerarium mentis in Deum,* his contribution to the vast and glorious book of man's pilgrimage toward the Eternal.

If he will break his silence and tell us that; if, laying aside his protective armor or his artful disguise of *sic et non,* the theologian's or the philosopher's stage-costume in which he practices his imposing virtuosity, he will give us that, then he will speak, faultily no doubt, but as a soul should speak that answers the gravest question that can be put to man.

Such an answer, however, it seems extremely difficult to elicit. The last thing that man learns is himself. He wears a mask until it grows into his face. He parrots and repeats until his automatism is not his second nature but his first. He uses words to conform or to declaim, not to express, his silenced soul. The slave-mind, or at least the indentured mind, is everywhere; it is conspicuous among the learned; it is epidemic in democracies; it rattles its chains among radicals and rebels who protest that the noise is the morning music of independence; it is the chronic state of a multitude of liberals; it is the chief scandal of theologians.

In fact, if a human soul acquainted with the labor of thought and disciplined by the austerity of experience were to address us out of its own depths, and with no calculating eye upon academic, scientific, or theological cautions and conventionalities we should be set a-flutter at the novelty, and should most likely be amused at the candor and shocked at the shaggy strength of its stark veracity. Unfortunately it is often the manifestly foolish who are candid, and they have nothing to say; and nearly as often it is the presumably wise who are not candid, and they have forgotten what utterance should mean.

These, I dare say, are severe words; but a severe and disastrous wrong evokes and justifies them. Let us see how. Augustine established in Western theology the doctrine that babies who die unbaptized go to hell forever; not to the Limbo of "natural but not supernatural felicity" which the compulsions of human decency have finally driven Latin theology to invent as a substitute, but to the hell of fire. Augustine's one concession was that their torment while excruciating was not so awful in anguish as that of the rest of the damned.

For a thousand years Latin Christianity taught this thing, the classic phrasing of it being these words of the Confession of Faith imposed upon the Greek, Michael Palæologus, by Pope Clement IV, in 1267: "*Illorum autem animas qui in mortali peccato vel cum solo originali decedunt mox in infernum descendere, poenis tamen disparibus puniendas.*" For a thousand years religious teachers said to millions of mothers: "Your infants that died before they could possibly be baptized are in hell. They did no wrong but they are for everlasting in the roaring infernal furnaces."

Let us pass over the ghastliness of unredeemable despair that this dogma produced in human hearts and homes. Let us simply consider the grave and reverend lords of sacred learning that repeated it, proved it by texts, and set it up on high as the teaching of Jesus and the will of the loving Father of all men. What shall we say of these custodians of the truths of our blessed salvation, the wise doctors of the queen of the sciences? We had better repress much of what we should like to say, and mention only this, that, if the paradox be permitted, they committed suicide before they committed something like homicide.

They did not express and could not have expressed

their hearts and minds and souls by that appalling savagery of superstition. They extinguished and murdered themselves. They tore themselves loose from all reality. They separated themselves from Christ. They wore the mask of orthodoxy in order to blaspheme Deity. Their implicit purpose was not to illuminate their hour of life by speaking out as grown-up men, but to wreck their essential vocation by making themselves advocates of immorality through servitude to a tradition. They are the worst and most terrible of witnesses to the self-degradation of souls that are called to self-transcendence.

But they are not alone; there are plenty of other witnesses to the same immoral discrowning and dethroning of the spirit's majesty. Today in the Latin rite of baptism the clergyman directly addresses in the second person the devil who inhabits the body of the infant at the font. The devil owns that infant in a deeper sense than its parents own it or than God owns it. God indeed has laid upon its helplessness the burden of His rejection and condemnation. Can any man, if all that makes him man be allowed to assert itself, believe that? If any man heard for the first time of this devil-ownership and devil-possession of babies; if he had caught a rumor of such a dogma from a report of Congo mythology, would he not abhor it and bestir himself to help convert to the Lord of love and the Friend of children a tribe so sunk in darkness?

There is no doubt how these questions should be answered. That horrible aberration no unspoiled human being can endure. But when a human being puts on the mask; when he mutilates himself, when he abdicates selfhood so as to be an echo, an anonymous phantom, an automaton who has obliterated the distinction between belief and make-belief, he can profess anything and consent to anything. When a man lives by words which the lips speak but to which the deep soul gives no resonance he is capable of advocating and apologizing for any enormity and styling it the truth of God.

One illustration more, this time not from the right wing but from the left of the religious Parliament. There has appeared lately in the Unitarian body a party which calls itself humanist. Some of these people are agnostics, others are atheists, but whichever they are they have no use for God; yet because they continue in a church whose historic claim has been not only that it is Christian but that its mission is to recover Christianity in its purest form, they shrink from applying to themselves the term atheist. They have a God, they say. And when we inquire what sort of God, some of them answer: Man is God. One of them lately said that liberalism would not have reached the last logic of its position until it roundly stated that man is God.

Now behind such statements as these there can be absolutely no thought. They are quite insane. They never could have been uttered as the deliberate convictions of a mind able to think and scrupulous in expressing itself as thinking. But just as the Augustinian theologians lapsed from the free mind to the slave mind in order to be not human but orthodox, these humanists have taken the same course in order to be not rational but respectable. They do not put into outer words their inner selves; they annihilate their inner selves and establish artificiality on the ruins.

Such men are like those non-resisters who say in hot perorations that rather than save their mothers from murder by laying ungentle hands on the murderers they would let the crime proceed. Everybody knows that they would do nothing of the kind. No living man would, for it is impossible that such total depravity and utter degeneracy could walk the earth in human form. But in order to be of an intransigent verbalism of logic, and in order that the dike of abstract consistency be not broken by one fatal inch of concession to common sense they let fly out of their mouths this abysmal nonsense. Some of them even pose as martyrs to iron principle and actually contrive to turn the sympathy of frivolous audiences from the mother who is murdered to the self-sacrificing son who lets it be done.

It appears then that it is a hard thing to get at the genuine inside of a man. The sort of answer that one is likely to receive to an inquiry into a man's beliefs is something of this nature: "I will tell you what I hold fast to, but always within the limitations of my subscription to the thirty-nine articles; always subject to my submission to Thomistic theology and Pius X's decree against modernism; always in deference to my status in the radical group of thinkers; always *salva obedientia* to the conventionalities of my academic or professional coterie." Of course, if a man does give utterance to his true self through thirty-nine articles and all those other standards and norms we want him to say so and we shall respect him and thank him for saying so. But if instead of saying what his own true soul is he waits until, *permissu superiorum*, he is informed from outside what it is proper for his soul to be, then we have collapse and decay, and the examples just given show how inveterate and deep-seated the misery is.

In an effort to avert it suppose then we frame our question thus: "What can you not help believing? What would destroy your inner life and make havoc of your whole life if you did not believe it? If you were a poet what is it that you would be under compulsion to sing? If you were a philosopher what is it that you would rejoice to drive home with compelling argument and enlarge to the full sweep of a majestic conception of all human life? If you were a preacher what message would give you no rest until from a burning heart you uttered it? What indeed is it that would make you a miserable man if you were untrue to it, a traitor if you deserted it, a liar if you denied it? What are you inside? When all shams have passed by, when all the applause and hisses have sunk to silence, and when alone with the perfect Truth which is so awful a mystery because perfect and so searing a flame because Truth, you lay down your life for final judgment, what will you cleave to and cling to then?"

These, I believe, are the questions implicitly asked of us here. If so, perhaps silence, awe, a searching of the heart, and a sense of woeful transgressions are the fittest answer to them. But if we are to speak, then on the chance that one's stumbling words may hold up a little candle's light for someone else, let this contributor give such answer as is in his power.

II.

Our editor, scornful of reticence, desires and with some emphasis has expressed the desire, that we should be autobiographical in these confessions. This, I suppose, means that we should not only state our creed, but tell also some of the personal history which has led us to it. If this must be there is nothing to do but accept it, although the editor will understand, I trust, that not without groanings have some of us obeyed him in thus opening to other eyes the chambers of our inner lives. I was, then, reared a Catholic. Through many years I studied and served that system of faith so far as my capacity made it possible. And what that means for any human soul that is in earnest about its earthly course and unearthly destiny it would take too long to say.

Let me only mention one or two of the lasting marks or "signatures," as Jacob Boehme might express it, that are visible in Catholicism and likely to leave their traces upon a man to whom Catholicism has been a long study and an accepted cause. First of all I should put this: Catholicism sets you face to face with a Given. There in front of you is a Reality awful as well as beautiful, austere as well as benignant, commanding as well as appealing, but always utterly actual. Whatever else may be or may not be, God exists and your soul exists. Your soul is to be saved and God alone can save it. There for you is the essential universe. Time and history for you mean the transaction of that august business with the Eternal. And endless life hereafter depends for its felicity or misery on how you have transacted it. A good many churches still teach this, I dare say, and all of them did once.

But the solidity of that Reality, its downright and intractable Givenness, its objective massiveness, its inescapable presence, are presented in Catholicism with an incomparable definiteness and with such a pedagogical apparatus for impressing it on heart, imagination, mind, and will as we can find nowhere else. There is nothing aerial in Catholicism. If you knock your head against it you know that you have hit something, and if you knock your heart against it you know that something has hit you.

Another quality in this great church is what we may call its legality. Not only is there a Real but an organized Real. Catholicism is articulate. It is more than organization, it is organism. It has a voice, and behind the voice a logic of speech. Logic indeed, if not its soul, is the habitation of its soul. To be inaccurate is to be heretical, and to be heretical is most likely to be damned. The law is as indubitable as the Law-giver, the kingdom is as compact and apprehensible as the King. Furnish now this preciseness of system with a majestic length of history throughout which the institution does not sprawl or creep, but marches as with banners; give it a scepter; open the book of its continuous legislation; expand your mind to take in its tradition of immemorial sovereignty; accustom your-

self to the accent of dominion and the port of majesty
—and you will probably, if historical imagination is
not injured by theological prejudice, be deeply moved
by an exactness of order, a positiveness of government,
a magnificence of corporate life quite beyond the reach
of rivalry. The adjective Roman is much more than
a geographical name for the center of the church's unity.
"Roman," in the full spiritual and historic significance
of the term, is the fittest possible word to describe
Catholicism as an institution and a polity.

Lastly, this church, so accomplished in the earthly
art of ruling, is equally resourceful in the heavenly art
of sanctifying. To her spiritually gifted children she
offers a rich cultivation of the devout and mystical life.
If she has a busy Curia officered by astute and clear-
headed statesmen and politicians, she has also in her
varied domain silent cell and quiet sanctuary, where
those who know what Dante calls

> la concreata e perpetua sete
> del deiforme regno,

may slake their thirst in the secret springs of inner and
everlasting life. The church's crown may often oblit-
erate the halo; but at long last it is the halo that is the
truer symbol of her power.

From this it seems to follow that a man who has
ever been seized and penetrated by this tremendous
Catholicism is likely to take from it three lasting dispositions of mind and heart, all three, I believe, in the
highest degree wholesome. First, he will demand a
Given. He will require a Fact. He will be uneasy
before any subjectivism which annihilates or blurs an
objective order and the Principle that animates and
sustains it. He will be quite as unresponsive to any
absolutism or psychologism which reduces his primary
Given, namely his own soul, to the marionette-play of
an all-swallowing Absolute or to the deceptive trickery

of an emotion-focus which is only a queer function of the organism. To him these notions smell of the academic mortuary. They cannot withstand the test of life. They are pompous phantoms from a world of Nowhere. They have no history, and cannot be fitted into history as man has lived it. If ever in the future they do insert themselves into his history I think we may say that his glory will be gone, his wild and perilous vitality paralyzed, his creative power blighted, his renovating joy and mysterious rapture frozen by the pedant's fatal touch. Man's soul is fact confronting kindred Fact. To "reduce" it to something lower is monstrous in logic and destructive to life. No such reduction is possible nor even intelligible.

If a man asserts to me that nitrogen and carbon can in certain conditions work out, let us say, Appel's equations for motion in a dynamic system; if he declares that, given the right conditions again, alcohol, bicarbonate of soda and the enzyme that hydrolizes protein can write the Divine Comedy, I for one do not know what he is talking about, and am quite sure that when he gives his theory a moral value by calling it true he doesn't know either. And if a brother of his comes forward to announce that man's highest spiritual experiences are a mass of irrational wishes when the most manifest fact under our eyes is that they proceed not from a wish but from a commandment, even life's most imperative commandment, for self-fulfilment, the wish being but the fragmentary appearance in one part of man's nature of the essential "drive" of his total nature to transcend the "Here-and-Now," then all that remains to me is to deepen the profound skepticism of academic theories in all fields which a fairly long acquaintance with them has forced upon me. As for the "reduction" of higher to lower, leaving the higher "explained" by the lower, it is to me the most perverse of all ineptitudes, the most empty of all fallacies. It is a feature of that flight from fact, that horror of objectivity, that retreat from history, that itch for a generalization which scorns the particulars within it, that substitution of simplification for simplicity which will furnish to the erudite the best example of romantic "wishing" that they could find.

This soul of mine is here, formed, featured, and indubitable. This universe whose highest is indicated by my deepest—in the name of common sense, by what else can it be indicated?—that too is here, and these massive actualities no fugitive fluttering into any hyperspace where things become words and words become ghosts can ever shake from their solid seat. And this tough practicality alone gives a man a world in which growing learned does not mean growing decrepit, but a world rather in which growing old in mind means growing young in spirit, the only kind of world fit for a militant soul sent forth to a fighting probation.

In the second place there is this consequence of the Catholic impress, that a man wishes his mind to have as determinate a structure as his body. He is meant to have convictions; let him have them. He is meant to say something; let him say it. Even if he is an atheist, let him avow it and not use the word God to designate a memory, a sigh, or a romance. If he says he believes a creed, let him believe it, not deny it on week-days when it is not recited, and affirm it on Sundays because everybody expects him to recite it. Surely amid all our doubt and groping something is, something shines, something intensifies human life. Whatever it is, it belongs to the articulate nature of a mind to utter it, to stand by it, to take joy in defending it. But when a man or a church declares that there is nothing to stand by or stand for; that God-affirming or God-denying makes no difference, and that we should as good democrats be always ready to abide by the majority vote, or as good lackeys hang round a pro-

fessor's back door till he tells us what to believe, since
this is a world anyhow of sweet sentiment alternated
with cunning calculation, and its monarch is a fragrant
"Perhaps"—when this sort of thing grows fashionable,
the first impulse of a man disciplined by Catholicism
is to abhor it. He holds it sound logic to make in-
terrogations preparatory to predications. He inquires
in order to affirm. His mind he will not regard as a
ventilating tube in and out of which opinions carry on
a perpetual transit in a vacuum. He thinks, studies, and
believes in order to be. This is his main business—to
be, and to be by an individual determination of existence. Mere being is donated to him. Kind-of-being
it is his obligation to achieve.

For a moral person existence is and must be a vocation; the *Leben* is merely the raw material of the *Geist*.
As sharp in outline therefore as ever an institution was,
as definite in articulation as ever a system of thought
has been, it is his calling to become. With a disposition to docility he should of course receive the reports
sent in to him from men and books and from past and
present; but upon this whole molten mass of circum-
stance he is to stamp the impress of a personality. The
dilution of a self into a fog of "events," the melting
away of a responsible soul into a "life-stream" or a
"consciousness-stream" or any other aqueous element
of perfectly nonsensical metaphor will not do, will
never do. To be is to be defined. To live is to have
a form. To be and to live as a person is to have the
most luminous definition and most manifest form that
exist.

And finally such a man will find it hard to lose the
sense of the transcendent. The transcendent is not an
objectivity which is big or old or imaginatively terrify-
ing. It is not colossal globes of gas on fire in the sky.
It does not consist in distances measured by light-years
nor of durations calculated by units of ten thousand

centuries. These are impostures when they cast a man down from his true status as a moral being who is to realize himself in quality, to the level of the pictorial imagination which is subject to shivering before quantity, the lowest of the categories.

The transcendent is that in which I lose myself as lesser and find myself as greater. It is that in which spiritual qualities are not adjective but substantive. It is that in which my trust in giving all that I am finds absolute security and the security of an Absolute. It is the discovery that gives rationality to the soul's perpetual search, for mere searching is not rational. It is that which, when reason has decisively seen that we as souls demand more than the contingent, says to us with august voice: "Behold the More-than-contingent!" It is the Given Glory seen in our mortal twilight by one pure ray which floods the whole world with light, the light that no night extinguishes.

If this is unacademic language I suppose I should be sorry, but I am not. My responsibility here is not to perform a dissection. That operation I leave to the cold knives and the cold slabs to be found in every campus. I am trying to tell what one soul lives by and is kept alive by, in the belief that a glimpse of actual life is not irrelevant, however many dissertations we have on what theoretical life may be, should be, or in some realm of possibilities could be. And what I say is that without a transcendent which is kindred and communicant, the contingent world of which I am a part is a scandal to thought, the history of the human spirit is unintelligible, and the validity of reason and the intuitions of souls the most delicate in insight, the most poised in judgment, the most limpid in vision, and the most heroic in will go down together with a crash. If this collapse cannot be, then the transcendent besets us, the great God seeks us, and the darkness in which our grimy hands are groping is being overtaken by the day for the beholding of which our inward eye has been made so pure.

Such are some of the inheritances that one receives from Catholicism. I do not mean that they are exclusive to it; not at all. I only say that they are bestowed and systematically inculcated by it. And having said this gratefully and gladly, as I shall always do, I come to the tragic phase in which by the very logic of the church's teaching certain of her sons and daughters have to stand aside, let the mighty army march by with its proud flags flying and its uncounted voices singing, and take for the rest of their lives the lonely way. What fundamentally happens to such persons is that they are called upon immediately and by individual decision to deal with one of the oldest problems of man, the relation of the one to the many, of the self to an institution, of the unit to its unity. So far as I can, let me set this problem forth.

The very first law on which the church insists is that a man must save his soul. Man has an end and it is not the satisfaction of sentimentality, nor the indulgence of impulse, nor the superior detachment of the esthete or the sage. It is that one day he must lay down the record of his mortal life for the judgment of God most high. That is the climax of existence. The free use of God's gifts constitutes man's ladder of life. After the last rung he steps from use to final responsibility. He must answer for the use. In a merely animal world use would be enough; in a moral world it must undergo accounting, review, and sentence.

It is a tremendous teaching. No length of familiarity with it can diminish its grandeur. No other instruction that a man can receive is fit to stand beside it for power and elevation. There are indeed liberals who fiercely attack it. They say that to be concerned for saving one's soul is selfish, individualistic, anti-humanitarian, anti-social. But I am bound to say that these liberals show themselves as unable to understand anything profoundly human as to believe anything indisputably divine. Because a man has to save his soul, that does not destroy the fact that he must save it in a commonwealth of souls, nor the further fact that his salvation precisely depends on how he has worked with and for these souls.

When we utter the word soul we do not mean an isolated thing all alone in a private boudoir making itself pretty for inspection on judgment-day. That would be absurd, and the religious sense is not absurd. We mean that how I act on other souls I shall answer for to the Lord of souls. We mean that if sympathy is diffused responsibility is concentrated. We mean that action, however far it spreads, comes back with its recorded page, black or white, to the one man who sent it forth, that he must read it to the last syllable in the Presence which there is no deceiving, and must take the station merited by the result. Instead of destroying the social sense I know of nothing that could more heavily charge it with energy, zeal, and love. The social sense is so sacred that its activity is not confined to earth and time; it determines the very judgment of the Eternal.

But if we are to save our souls we are to know God the Moral Infinite whose will is the life of souls. So Catholicism by an incomparable system of public worship and private prayer sends us into the adorable Presence. It urges and presses us to become habituated to the wonder and awe of the All-Holy in His unseen sanctuary. It bids us be as obedient to His known appointment as Jesus was, who in the supreme magnificence of fidelity took the dire cross in order to stand true to the will that must be done. And in the loftier experiences of contemplative prayer it encourages us to lay aside all pictures and imaginative symbols, to suppress all subtle gratifications of merely selfish devotional feeling and, in that great loneliness which yet throngs the world with one Companionship overwhelmingly sufficient, to know God almost face to face, awful, glorious, and absolute; infinite Beauty, Truth, and Right.

Suppose, then, that we try to do this. Suppose that as we do so we learn ever more profoundly that the essentially Catholic habit of adoration must be matched by the essentially spiritual and moral habit of obedience to what we adore and that our adoration is only a formality without it. Then we shall be confronted not with a Categorical Imperative, for that may be an abstraction, and as an abstraction I can find no meaning in it, but with a Will uttering Itself to a soul and waiting for the soul's response. Out of loyalty and love the soul will endeavor to respond, hoping that through a thousand clamors the Voice will grow continually more clear, and seeing as the far goal, pitiably far, the dedicated day when that Will may become its meat and drink. It is to this that Catholic devotion leads the man who has given himself to it. What then must happen when the heavenly Will is found to be in discord with the earthly institution which led him to It? There is the crisis, such a crisis as tears a man's heart and rebuilds his world.

With all its logic Catholicism has no logic for a solution here. No institution has. It can only say: "If you do the will of God you will do my will too." But this is a theorem. It cannot withstand that Given before which all theorems must bend. At last every philosophy or theology must satisfy naked soul. If it does not, it dies. Let me repeat it, the fundamental reason for the departure of a reasonably mature person from a system like Catholicism is not intellectual difficulty taken by itself. A man can easily juggle intellectual difficulties into some play of conformity once he learns that low art. But there is one thing that he cannot do.

He cannot open his inward eye on divine and sovereign Truth and Right and imagine that he can serve this Glory by practicing deceit or approving wrong. To attempt it is such a havoc and horror that men have invented one awful name for it, and that name is hell —the denial in word or act that God is true and righteous.

Without pride, let us hope, without pretense, let us pray, many a man must say that it was not in the haughty library where he read books, nor in the cold study where he inflated his intellect with theories, that he took his first or last step away from his inherited church; it was rather at the altar where he cast himself down before the Holiest and called to remembrance the solitary Christ. Let any voice whatever, though of an angel from heaven as Paul says, speak anything that is unworthy of the Deity that he learned there and it is put upon him and demanded of him to reject it. The institution that cultivated in him the sense of the absolute Will thereby implicitly taught him the pedagogical function of institutions, their provisional place and subordinate authority. The church that bade him save his soul for the eternal Right may not add the proviso that this is to be done by the submission of his soul to a temporal device.

When all the warnings against vagary and the tricks of a rebellious mind have been humbly listened to; when the learned expositions upon the historical and institutional principle as set over against the individualist and anarchic principle have done their utmost in the ablest hands from Augustine to Von Hügel, the stark question is as sharp in outline in the end as it was in the beginning: Will you pretend in order to conform, will you invert the righteous order of your loyalties, will you follow the earthly at the cost of deserting the heavenly within you and above? There is no escaping the conflict; in the nature of things it is irrepressible;

and no apologetic or philosophy of institutions has a solution for it.

The last word of history is soul if the last reality of existence is God. What in particular it was in Catholic orthodoxy that involved a degradation of Deity and a contradiction of His will I shall not state at length. Nothing, I suppose, struck deeper than that millennium of teaching that babies dying unsprinkled were sentenced to hell, and its modern mitigation that they are in enmity to God and destined never to rise to the possession of Him as their Father. Guilt in one not guilty is a notion not merely abhorrent and absurd; it is besides, I deeply believe, most blasphemous, as its corollary is that the Infinite lays a curse and His curse (!) upon the innocent, and His scourge for endless eternity upon those who have been forever helpless.

What in general comes to pass in such an experience of detachment is the substitution of the moral for the dogmatic. I could not but see the havoc produced in men who gave themselves over in unconditioned submission to an earthly corporation, its interests, and its creeds. I saw many a high and glowing mystic emerging from his exaltations of prayer to give approval to the burning of heretics, and the shock of it helped split the ground beneath me; why should it not? I saw the genius of Aquinas and the high ability of an uninterrupted line of theologians perverted from divine light and human sympathy to the contriving of exhaustive proofs that, in the case of a heretic, robbery was virtuous and murder meritorious. I saw pontiffs ordering that children be encouraged to report the secret heresy of their fathers, and so become accomplices in parricide. I read in theological treatises extensive chapters "de Tortura," the infliction of torture upon men and women under suspicion of heresy, and other chapters worse if possible, as for example in Del Rio, on the loathsome lying that was permitted in order to trap a supposed heretic or witch into confession of the charge against him.

These things were and still are for me the darkest and most dreadful mystery in the whole history of evil. For the men concerned in them were religious and Christian teachers. Multitudes through many generations followed them as having by their prayers received divine light, by their high position divine guidance, and by their learning divine wisdom. And then looking from those past ages to the present I saw eminent men repressing all indignation at wholesale murder because their institution approved it, and even venturing an apology for it or putting a fair face upon it as Cardinal Newman and, regrettable as it is to say it, Baron von Hügel are not ashamed to do.

From this the conclusion, harsh I do not doubt but true I am sadly sure, forced itself upon me that there are men more willing to compromise God for the sake of an institution than to censure an institution for the sake of God. The words are painful and I wish that I could forbear writing them, but I cannot, and it would be paltering with things too sacred to be dragged down to the level of our indolent compliances if I tried. If a man gives himself unconditionally to an institution, or assigns to a tradition the authority which only One may possess over us, no learning or culture, no lofty place or distinguished name, and even no practice in mystical exercises can save him from the danger of degrading the moral character in which he should be most like his Maker. Once for all, therefore, I determined to judge all institutions and beliefs by moral law, not moral law by them.

This principle leads one far. It became an impossibility to doctor history and to find in the Bible and in early Christianity what I was supposed to find there. It became intolerable to maintain that certain late dogmas were held in earlier ages when I was certain they were not held then but were repeatedly and without censure denied. It became a burden not to be borne to approve mechanical acquittals of guilt and its consequences as a substitute for inward renovation of the very springs of character. And finally it became disgusting to whisper liberalism in secret to a Freemasonry of Modernists and crypto-heretics who wore their hearts anywhere but on their sleeves and vented their minds anywhere but in public. The furtive had to go; the downright had to come.

And so, to put an end to a narration which it is not pleasant to write, I discovered that the whole orbit of my mind was set in a different space and round another center. Beyond all difficulties in detail there was a fundamental dislocation. I grew to believe that, while man is humbly to learn from history, he is not servilely to be subject to it; that the moral nature is to religion what developed science is to primitive apprehension, the last explication and the highest crown; that the question to be answered in our great judgment will be not what are you inside of, but what is inside of you; and that in trying to follow God's will we may have to let everything contingent and temporal go in the tragedy of moral decision as Christian apocalyptic says they will one day have to go in a catastrophe of physical dissolution.

Institutions I came to regard as I am sure the spiritual eye should regard the body. The body is our indispensable ministrant to life and the means of contact with this scene of our probation. Because it is that, it is priceless. Yet we must every day resist it in order that its ministerial function may not be inflated and aspire to be magisterial. The "sense of body" we have and should have; but if it should fill the mind it certainly will empty the soul. We are, therefore, to look upon our own bodies and the bodies of all other persons as servants of spirit, and until we do we have not emerged from a vain and gross order of thought into the vision which is nobleness and grace and lasting truth.

Spirit is the goal of all. In order to attain it or come somewhere near it we may be called upon not merely to keep the body in its subject place and subject honor, we may also have to yield up its life altogether at the summons of the Higher Will. Not otherwise is it with institutions. The parallel seems to me exact. They too are ministrant and what they minister to is soul.

Soul, the will of God, that is the *Prius,* the fundamental and sovereign mastership, the all-embracing and all-judging reality, the principle which in a spiritual universe assigns a fitting and the only fitting or indeed intelligible function to the contingent. The "sense of history" or the "sense of institutions" is like the "sense of body," good, true, and necessary if in due order. But if the "sense of history" extinguishes moral light and assumes dictatorship of the moral nature it may work as great a havoc as dictatorship of the flesh. The moral universe is wrecked unless, whatever the dangers be that are involved in the principle, soul and character are put absolutely first. And when one reaches this there is a fair likelihood that external infallibilities, whether of books or synods or pontiffs, will disappear.

III.

So at the end of the long journey I have come to this: The first article of my creed is that I am a moral personality under orders.

Never for one moment, even the most skeptical, have the theories that intrinsic moral obligation, to speak truth for example or to follow justice, is not intrinsic at all but a romanticized residuum of my subjection to a herd-convention, or an idiosyncrasy, or a pragmatic calculation for getting on in life smoothly and loftily,

spoken a single intelligible syllable to me. I regard
all that as a monstrous blunder in reading the text of
man's inner life, so monstrous that none but the learned
could commit it. It is to me of an almost theatrical
artificiality.

No man who has ever looked at Right and into Right,
ever understood its absence of argument and the sublimity of its terse imperative, or ever been mature enough
to feel the shame of its reproach for deliberate trans-
gression, can possibly go back to witch-doctors and wig-
wams to account for it. Right is not a trail leading into
the past where men groveled. It is a *via sacra* leading
to a sanctuary where alone souls can worship and be
free. It is not a rudiment, it is a consummation. It is
not a reminiscent left-over of my fears. It is a present
majesty speaking to the most sensitive nerve of my
loyalty and to the most vibrant chord of my love.

I calculate indeed the evidence whether this or that
particular case comes under the dominion of Right, but
I may not calculate whether I am a citizen and servitor
of that dominion. Of this no doubt is possible. Not a
fragment of support either can I find for the notion
that a caucus or popular vote or any equivalent of it
originated and conferred moral sovereignty. The authority of Right is as much above such casual chance as
it is above mechanical necessity. Right is neither neces-
sitarian nor adventitious. It stands in its own sphere, is
unique and irreducible. It belongs to the unshared essence of spirit and constitutes the core of it. The more
nearly I see it approach absoluteness, the less of a herd-
animal and the more of an integral sovereign self I am.

Apart from such a conception there is no rational
ground for authoritatively inserting the ideal into time.
If the ideal is inserted into time it must have mastership
there. It is no longer the ideal if it is only a functional convenience for the comfort or gentility of an
individual or for the will-to-power of a majority. If

it exists at all, it exists by inherent supremacy. It ceases to exist if it is tolerated as a solace for the delicate and the esthetic or is artificially maintained as a convenient instrument of government. Mastership or degradation—that is the law for the ideal.

Once we acknowledge its mastership we put an end to the long torment of debate whether it is "objective." It is a curious and illuminating reflection that modern philosophy which is so frightened of "subjectivism" has produced the most narrowly subjective schemes of thought that have ever been known; and that, professing to follow science into the cosmic order where perception is at home, it so often presents to us a cosmic disorder where the full self, of which perception is only one activity, is forever homeless.

A good deal of philosophy has worked hard to make man a ghost in order to keep him from seeing ghosts. It warns him not to be anthropomorphic, and proceeds to make him egomorphic and at last theriomorphic. It cautions him against admitting feeling into the criteria by which he passes judgment on existence; and then offers him a universe which arouses the utmost intensity of feeling—the feeling of horror, disgust, and despair.

It is indeed a strange region of thought that we are in today, and I should suppose that it will be rated by posterity as one of the flattest and most decisively mediocre that has ever come. We have mutilated man. We have performed the operation of "reduction" upon him. We have made him an animal; made him a focus of sensation; made him a forlorn loon crying amid mad meaninglessness; made him not the proud possessor of high faculties but the unfortunate victim and the shame-faced apologist for them. And then having wrecked the only world that can speak to him, or to which he can speak, we bid him become a fastidious and exquisite Stoic pale with distinguished pessimism, or a thundering actor boisterous with dramatic despair.

And this is the *Zeitgeist* which our decadent day adores. Freidell has given to all this its appropriate, we may almost say its predestined, name—*Schreibtisch-ideologie*—the cosmos of the writing-desk, the sleight-of-hand of the pedant, the polysyllabic suicide-scheme of the scholastic. It cannot be lived. It cannot be deeply and lovingly believed. It can inspire no literature. It can create no vision. It can stimulate no man of will and action. It is the death of both genius and character, and no more serious questions could be asked than whether its appearance does not announce the death of an age.

It can be ended only by putting into the universe a moral as well as a physical teleology. There is a formal and formative principle for souls as well as bodies. There is a coherent world for heart, conscience, and will as well as for gases and corpuscles. There is a law for the spiritual nature as objective as that for the refraction of light or the production of bile. The whole miserable business of "reduction" is a vast sophistry. The universe is graded into uniquenesses which touch as we touch one another's clothing in the street, but are fixed in their inseparable essences as the souls within the garments are fixed in incommunicable loneliness.

The uniqueness of man as a moral person does not mean that, because the physical world will not fit him, therefore there is no world that fits him. That would be an absurdity, though it has become a fashionable absurdity. It means rather that his uniqueness has a kindred uniqueness which does fit him. And the objective actuality of this kindred uniqueness is as drastically demanded by the need for rationality as an external world is demanded for the validity of science, or the legitimacy of inference is demanded for the exercise of thought. A universe rational anywhere is rational everywhere. Therefore if a law for bodies, a law for souls also. What else, then, can we put at the

head of the chapter where the subject is man than this
statement: we are moral personalities under orders?
What in the stable earth is so solid, what in constellate
sky so splendid?

The second article of my simple creed follows from
the first: Life is a sublime peril. If this sounds homiletic,
it is no great matter. I conceive the universe of souls
as fundamentally moral; otherwise it could not be a
universe of souls. And when we formulate this idea
our language is bound to savor of the pulpit. This,
however, does not imply that the idea is commonplace;
it only implies that the pulpit is or ought to be exalted.
But the principle that life is a sublime peril is not meant
to be an exhortation; it is meant to be a canon of interpretation for both private deeds and public history.
It signifies that life is magnificent in its faculties, glorious in its rise, and also appalling in its fall. Its upward
way is luminous but it is straight and narrow. Its true
foundation is a rock that withstands a thousand storms;
but if one builds elsewhere there is only sand to sustain
the structure, and the last phase is the devastating sea,
the leveling winds, the terrible collapse.

How can one escape the truth of this? How can
one not stand in awe before the heap of ruins that
attests it? What is history but a lengthened day of
judgment? States with a world-wide dominion,
churches with continents for jurisdiction, mountains of
money able to purchase everything purchasable have
crashed one after another into the dust. They could
call upon inexhaustible resources, had the wisest of
heads to counsel them, immense armies to protect them,
experience ages old to give them prudence and make
them adepts in sagacity. Yet there they lie dead or
stricken by the score.

However a careful mind may shrink from easy generalization and summary simplification, it should not
shrink from a deduction merely because it is unfash-

ionable, or from an inference merely because the supercilious call it homiletic. I will say then that for my part I see as the chief cause of the monotony of disaster to these consolidations of power the commission of outrage upon the moral order. Everything is curable but that. The displacing of free labor by slaves, the growth of bureaucracy, the depopulation of the countryside, wasteful expenditure, and other such economic and social mistakes any council of wise governors could correct in a generation.

These things are remediable by enactment. But let a Roman Empire degrade a population by the cruelty of its arena and the lust of its stage; let it cover the annihilation of freedom and the destruction of the sense of public duty by the free feeding of the multitude; let a mediæval Papal court degrade religion by abominable traffic and infect character by the hate and savagery of systematic persecution; let arrogant statesmen and political theorists inculcate lying and the spirit of plunder, excusing it by the *raison d'état*, the principle that the righteous will of the Eternal applies only to individuals but that states are officially immoral—let this happen and you have something that is not curable. You have souls poisoned, perverted, destroyed. This disease no man can cure; but there before us is that colossal stupidity of crime repeatedly hurled into fragments as one century succeeds another, to show that the Everlasting still can punish.

Retribution is a correlate of responsibility. A divine Vindicator is inherently implied in moral personality and righteous law. The human process is under not destiny but vocation. Humanity is biological and political only in preparation for becoming in time an organ and revealer of timeless Spirit. The Higher Will and the Eternal Presence enter by right the chambers of state as by right they cross the threshold of the individual soul. And until the energy and resources now spent

upon cunning maneuver and brutal aggression are devoted to utmost equity; until we give civilization a soul;
until we lift political theory and the tradition of states-
manship out of their scandalous indifference to moral
law; until all round we recover from our inveterate
materialism and skepticism, we shall go on in the old
way of disaster as if we were predestined to the dark
crassness of the reprobate mind.

Life is a sublime peril. God is no romantic em-
bellishment. He is not the last and highest "thrill."
He is not stripped of majesty by moral neutrality. He
is not darkened of glory by blindness to wrong. He is
the refuge as well as the foundation of Right. He
is to be won by costly fidelity. He is to be sought and
found in the terror and splendor of Gethsemanes and
Calvaries. He is the Pronouncer of judgment. He is
to be gained by the paradox of love whereby, although
straitened in a very tension of desire for Him, we ask
Him not to let us see Him till we are worthy of the
vision.

The abomination of desolation has come upon us because we think that words like these are high-flown and
impractical. We have never taken seriously a moral
personality, a spiritual universe, a righteous God. These
immense and besetting realities we relegate to rhetoric
and dreams. We leave them to churches, and churches
have left them to oblivion. For this reason more than
for any other, I believe, our philosophy is sterile, our
culture invertebrate, our politics staggering on the rim
of the precipice, our religion without resonance, without
glory, without adoration.

Take seriously the nature of a soul, the vocation of
souls, the Lord of souls, and you have chosen the only
way that I can see out of decadence and its ghastly dangers that now threaten us. Nietzsche himself half-
apprehended this when, sick of flatness and pedantic
routine, he called for the fighter, the conqueror, the

superman. He saw the right goal, but took the wrong road. Character is a conquest and life a glorious battle fought on a stupendous field. But the cause at issue is the Holy Will, and the trophy of the immortal victory is the spread of the Kingdom and the exaltation of the King.

And now for the final article of this short creed of mine. The Captain of the eager host of aspiring souls is Christ. The Christ of the official creeds I find it difficult if not impossible to understand. I fear that Athens and Alexandria, Nicæa and Rome, have overshadowed Nazareth and Capernaum, the sea of Galilee and the hill of Calvary. I am lost in Logos-speculations. I can make nothing of Trinity-Godheads. Those that are not lost in this dark abyss it is superfluous to say that I respect. Envy them, however, I do not, follow them I cannot. But this I trust will not make me unworthy of some place in the following of the Master and Lord who is to me as none other ever can be, the Way, the Truth, the Life. Let me say a few words on the leadership personal to me and, by right universal to mankind, which I confess in Christ.

I cannot bind myself to the letter of the Gospel-biographies. The first reason is that the Gospels are fragments. The second is that they are interpretations as well as descriptions, justifiable and inevitable interpretations indeed, but giving me the interpreter not Christ. And the third reason is that if the Lord's first followers misunderstood him in His lifetime, as there is no doubt they did, they very likely failed in understanding Him after His death. It devolves upon us, therefore, to be interpreters ourselves, and from the priceless data that the four biographies give us, to reconstruct the mind and heart and soul of the Son of Man. There is danger in the procedure obviously, but the danger becomes less as we carry forward toward substantial certainty our analysis of the documents. At all events this task of reconstruction is imperative; we cannot escape it, and beyond a doubt we shall be rewarded for having tried it.

Jesus then to me stands forth as a man of will. In the swiftness of His decision, in the finality of His resolution, in the uncompromising sharpness of His demands, in the challenging and stinging hyperbole with which He tried to arouse the indolent, the dull, and the conventional, we see a man sure of himself, sure of His universe, sure of His God. Be defined! do something! do something utterly real and radically true! that was what he asked. Play-acting—*i. e.*, hypocrisy—mumbling by rote, posturing by precept, He could not endure. To the utmost be true, He said. He was no adept in speculation, no artist in theory-making, no deviser of ritual, no contriver of catechisms. Commit yourself! get the "once for all" quality in your heart and will! strike the plow in the furrow and look back no more! Thus He flung forth the electric energy of His soul. Thus forever He set religion beyond the power of decadence, for decadence there cannot be where there are a dedicated will, a soul conscious of its call, a heart quickened by the living loyalty of a supreme and pure attachment.

In the next place Jesus involves the temporal in the eternal without compromising the eternal by the temporal. He demanded nothing that time can change. He made essential only what is everlasting. He commanded no form of words which the progress of the ages leaves unintelligible. He required no assent to dubious history or insecure tradition. He gave to the imperishable lift of man's spirit the indestructible Reality which has lifted it. The will of God as hunger and thirst and food and drink, the love of the Perfect through pain and darkness and the bearing of a cross as our one solution and fulfilment; the supremacy of the soul above institutional coercions, above synagogues which will cast us out, above governors and kings who will summon us for sentence and penalty; the lonely way with one Presence to suffice us, though high voices of church and state cry out that we have a devil and belong to Beelzebub—this is His deathless gospel, the creation of a new type of mind in us, the guarantee of a new age for the world.

Liberty, but humbly and completely consecrated to a resplendent obedience; the denial of the apparent world and then the reabsorbing of it by the soul which after illumination affirms the world in a higher category of providential purpose; the leaving nothing that is human to insignificance, since everything in man has its part in the besetting solicitude of Him who marks a sparrow's fall; the service of the least by the greatest; the watchful eye for unobtrusive good; the courageous voice against accepted wrong—these are, I think, correct readings of the teaching of that luminous soul whom it should be life's chief study to understand.

Let His spirit touch us; let the great solitariness of His loving heart move us; let us but rise up to follow when He calls; let us put Him to the test of practice, and such power comes upon us as nothing else is able to bestow. He is the center of God's providence for man. In His life and death the mystery of our existence passes over into the mystery of God's existence, a mystery not in the sense of a bewilderment but as the unfolding of consummations beyond our capacity to comprehend but felt for and sought for by our capacity to aspire, to trust, and to adore. As manifestly as we are sent here to carry on a spiritual strife toward immortal issues, so manifestly was Jesus of Nazareth sent here to be the leader of mankind in the transfiguration of the world.

And so I end. What I have had to say can be briefly put. I am a responsible soul. I live in a universe that is under the law of souls. There can be no such universe without one Sovereign Spirit and His sovereign purpose for it. There can be no such vocation for man without peril. Institutions are ministerial not final. Liberty is made perfect when it discovers a sacred cause to which to dedicate itself. Earthly occasions are to be molded into the likeness of spirit even as our bodies are to be refined into some suggestive resemblance of the souls that use them. God's will permits no exceptions to its dominion. History is a chapter in the existence of Spirit, and Judgment is the affirmation of that Spirit's supremacy. And Christ is the shower of the way through probation and endurance to the fulfilment whereof the very threshold is dark from excess of light.

That this is not orthodoxy I know. That some will call it not even Christian I surmise. But I must refuse to add to it words learned by rote, words that do not wake that secret and deep chord within us which gives the response of our whole nature to the touch of Truth. Such profession of faith as it is at all events, it absolutely commands and owns me; it makes the world fit for reason, and life significant for will; it gives to history a meaning higher and at the same time simpler than any other that I know; it affirms liberty but keeps the independent soul within sight of the uplifted cross, the symbol of the obedience which liberty must always be prepared to pledge; and it provides the only foundation that I can discover for making man integral with a universal principle and purpose. For one human being at least it is a creed that exalts life and speaks the promise of life immortal.

PRINCIPAL PUBLICATIONS

Books:

Letters to His Holiness. Open Court Publishing Co., 1911.
The Priest. Sherman, French Co. (now the Beacon Press), 1912.
From the Gospel to the Creeds. Beacon Press, 1919.

Articles:
> "Our Spiritual Destitution." *The Atlantic Monthly*, Vol.
> 143, pp. 373-382, March, 1929.
> "The Anti-Religious Front." *The Atlantic Monthly*, Vol.
> 145, pp. 96-104, January, 1930.
> Also, articles in the field of theological and related studies
> in various professional periodicals; and, recently, a con-
> siderable amount of reviews of theological and philo-
> sophical books for the Sunday Book-Section of the New
> York *Herald Tribune*.

THE RELIGIOUS EDUCATION OF A PROTESTANT

By LUTHER ALLAN WEIGLE

(b. September 11, 1880, Littlestown, Pennsylvania)

Dean of The Divinity School and Sterling Professor of Religious Education, Yale University

New Haven, Connecticut

THE RELIGIOUS EDUCATION OF A
PROTESTANT

By LUTHER ALLAN WEIGLE

WHEN, at the age of thirty-five, I resigned the John Chandler Williams professorship of Philosophy in Carleton College to accept appointment to the newly established Horace Bushnell professorship of Christian Nurture in the Divinity School of Yale University, I made it my first business to read Bushnell's book on *Christian Nurture,* with which I had been acquainted only at second-hand, principally through the references made to it by Professor George A. Coe. I confess that I took it up with some misgiving, wondering whether it contained old ideas and outworn forms of thought which might tend to limit the freedom of the incumbent of the new chair.

I found just the opposite. Old though the book was, the vitality and vigor of Bushnell's thought proved to be emancipating. I read and reread *Christian Nurture* and subsequently edited it for appearance in a new edition, with interest and enthusiasm. And I wrote a long letter to my father about it, with all the zest of one who has made a discovery, outlining to him its main positions, and telling him of my happiness to find so free a charter for the new work which I was undertaking.

My father replied that he agreed with all that I had written about Bushnell's book, which he had known and prized ever since his own days as a theological student. In proof of this he sent me his copy, bought and first read in 1876, bearing evidences of much use, and with

margins well marked and annotated at most of the
points which I had so eagerly commended to him. Then
I made a real discovery—that Bushnell was but describing what I had seen and known and shared throughout the whole of my life, that the spirit of my father
and mother was akin to his, and that I was myself a
child of Christian nurture.

My father was a minister, and my mother—I now
know—an ideal minister's wife. My early education
in religion was through the influences and associations,
the habits and conditionings, of life in the home of a
Christian minister who sincerely believed in his work
and thoroughly enjoyed it. Religion was a naturally
accepted base-line for all of our life and thought.
There was nothing strained or morbid or professional
about it. My childhood was thoroughly happy and
normal—at least it seemed so then, whenever I stopped
to think about it, which I very seldom did; and it seems
so now, as I look back upon it.

As a family, we shared in a number of religious observances. We gave thanks to God as we gathered for
our meals; we engaged in a brief service of family worship after breakfast each morning; we read the Bible
and books of Bible stories, and memorized great passages of Scripture which father selected for us; we
studied Luther's Small Catechism and the Sunday
school lessons; we went together to public worship in
the church, to prayer meetings and Sunday school, to
missionary societies and the Band of Hope. Some of
these observances were required of us children, and
some were not; but none of them bore upon us with the
weight of compulsion. They so obviously meant a
great deal to father and mother that we were glad to
share in them. We had ample time and freedom for
other things also—for reading and work and play. And
I now see that deeper than any or all of these observances was the spirit of love and good fellowship that so

constantly lighted our life together—a spirit which likewise was accepted by us as a matter of course. If we thought about it at all, which I cannot remember that we did, I am sure that we had difficulty to distinguish between the love of God and the love of father and mother—a predicament which is not undesirable for youngsters, and which does not worry them in the least.

The church which my father served for the nine years which carried me from the age of six to that of fifteen had a large membership—about eleven hundred—and fostered a wide range of activities, from oyster suppers and dramatic entertainments to cottage prayer meetings and revivals. I attended most of these. There were no motion pictures in those days, dancing and cards were frowned on, and my parents were rightfully dubious about the few shows and plays that came to our local theatre; so that in all honesty it must be admitted that the church was one of my best available sources of entertainment.

It was a Lutheran church, belonging to the least conservative of the Lutheran bodies, the General Synod; and it was different from most Lutheran churches in an evangelistic temper which inclined it toward "new measures," revivals, and "protracted meetings." My father would not employ an itinerant revivalist; he believed that each minister should be an evangelist in his own pulpit and to his own people. Among my most vivid memories stand out the "protracted meetings" which I attended in the large lecture-room of the church, when for six to eight weeks between the first of January and Easter, my father would preach on every week-night except Saturday, as well as twice on Sunday, extending to sinners the invitation of the gospel and calling upon them to repent and be converted. Folk did repent and were converted under his preaching; each year, after a suitable period of instruction, many such were received into the membership of the church.

One year, as people began to stand and ask for the prayers of the church, and to come forward to the seats which had taken the place of the older "mourners' bench," I wanted to join them. When I told my father of my desire, he replied that I need not wait until the invitation would be given in the public meeting that evening, but that I could come to God at once, in the privacy of his study, and that he would be glad right then to talk with me about any of my questions or problems, and to pray with me. I accepted his invitation; and he turned what was at first, I fear, mere suggestibility into a genuine religious experience.

My father was an effective teacher. In accordance with the time-honored custom of the Lutheran churches, he conducted classes in preparation for church membership, one of which, for children ten to fourteen years of age, met on Saturday afternoon from October to Easter, and the other, for young people and adults, met on Friday evening for the same term. The work of these classes was based on Luther's Small Catechism, but it was far from the meager, formal memorization which many associate with the idea of catechization. In a simple, vivid, interesting way it covered the main points of Christian belief and practice. I had four years of this work, two in each class. In my last year, when I was a sophomore in high school, I outlined its content; and I was surprised to find, when I reached the theological seminary six years later, that this was a fairly good outline of the elementary principles of systematic theology. If any reader is disposed to comment that this only proves that my father taught theology to his people, I answer that in my judgment that is what every minister ought to do, that classes such as my father conducted would benefit every church, and that the systematic theology taught in our seminaries ought to be vital enough in content to be adaptable to such use.

In another class for young people and adults, meeting on Wednesday evening after the weekly prayer meeting, my father conducted systematic Bible study, of the sort made popular by Dwight L. Moody in the eighteen-eighties. I joined this class also, and greatly enjoyed it. I learned more from these classes taught by my father than from all my years as a pupil in the Sunday school.

My mother recently gave me a scrap-book in which she had treasured newspaper clippings of family interest. In it I found a group of reports of sermons preached by my father forty years ago, with a short clipping which acknowledges my services as reporter. The latter recalls "the thrill that comes once in a lifetime." Here it is, under date of July 4, 1892: "For the report of a number of sermons recently preached by Rev. Mr. Weigle, of the First Lutheran Church, *The Times* is under obligations to that gentleman's little son, Luther Weigle, who, although but 11 years of age, handles the pen with a vigor and discrimination which would be creditable to one of more mature years."

I have quoted that because it indicates how intimately my father let me be associated with his work. I was always free to browse in his library, and of course to go to him for counsel and source-materials when I had to write an essay or prepare for a debate. Better yet, as I became able to do it, he let me begin to work with him. He bought me a typewriter, and I often typed for him the manuscript or outline of one of his sermons for the coming Sunday. Here again there was no compulsion; he did not exploit me, and I am sure that he could have preached quite as well from his own notes as from my typescript. But I liked the work, and it became a sort of informal apprenticeship in theology and homiletics which contributed to my education.

Let no one think that this was undue domination of my mind. It was simply that my father shared with me, in the measure of my boyish capacity, his interests, his convictions, and his work. There was remarkable freedom in our relations. He let me enter with him into the realm where reality and truth lay for him, then encouraged me to do my own thinking and to make my own decisions. What better thing could a parent do? It is a decadent generation that cherishes no beliefs and holds no convictions which it cares to transmit to its children, and fondly imagines that they will achieve freedom if they are let alone to discover everything for themselves and to do as they please, without information, guidance, or discipline.

Two of my father's sayings, in this connection, have stayed in my memory, and grow more meaningful as the years pass and my own sons and daughters are growing into manhood and womanhood. One of these sayings dates back to my early childhood. When I would say, as children will, "Daddy, when I grow up I want to be just like you," he would laughingly answer, "Then I'll be ashamed of you, because you must stand on my shoulders." The other was but a few years before his death in 1923. In the course of social conversation my father and I expressed differing judgments on some point, whether of politics or theology, and a member of the group who possessed more initiative than tact called his attention to this divergence of view—"Why, Dr. Weigle, your son does not believe as you do." He answered, "My son believes as I think I would believe if I faced his problems and had his work."

Horace Bushnell had a great phrase to describe the goal of parental instruction and discipline—"the emancipation of the child." My father's dealing with me was in the spirit of that phrase. Evidence of this is afforded by the fact that ultimately I made important decisions which were not in line with his desires—I chose college teaching as my vocation rather than the preaching ministry; my work took me away from the Lutheran into the fellowship of the Congregational churches; and finally I felt obliged to decline a position which had always been his dearest ambition for me. Yet we had no word of dissension over these decisions; and he never made me feel that my choice of another path was an act of disloyalty to him.

One decision I made, as a freshman in college, which was an act of disloyalty. I became a member, secretly, of an organization which my father had forbidden me to join, in spite of the fact that he was providing for the full expense of my education and that even the dues which I paid to this organization were part of his bounty. For four years throughout my college course and for one year more in theological seminary, I kept up this deception. Then came an evening in the summer vacation, when, as I was preaching to an audience of young people in a distant town, I sharply realized my unworthiness to preach to others while my own life cherished this lie. I wrote a long letter to my father, confessed what I had done, told him how sorry I was, asked his forgiveness, and promised to repay what I had so spent. In answer I received a telegram: "It is all right. I forgive you. I knew it two days after you did it." Then I could look back and could see how, on various occasions throughout those five years, he had made some approach that afforded me the chance to tell him what he already knew. Though I failed him, he waited and loved me anyhow. He did not fail me, did not give me up.

I count that one of my life's crucial experiences. Shame for my misdeed and relief at my father's forgiveness gave way to a flash of illumination and were transcended in the wonder and joy of a new insight. That insight was not only into unsuspected depths in

my father's character; it was a new vision of the fatherhood of God.   My father's love and patience and
understanding became to me a revelation of the love
and patience and understanding of God.   I had found
the gospel.   I had a message to preach, a faith to live
by.   What I had before heard about God I now saw
and understood for myself.   I could say with Job: "I
had heard of thee by the hearing of the ear; but now
mine eye seeth thee."

Some years later, I read Royce's discussion of atonement, in *The Problem of Christianity*.   Atonement
takes place, he says, when an act of wrong becomes the
occasion for another act of such creative, redemptive
quality that the final result is better than it would have
been if the wrong act had not been done.   In just that
sense, my father made atonement for the wrong that
I had done to him.   His deed was such that all was
better in the end.   My deception was not blurred over
or blotted out; it remained wrong.   But he met it
with a love so resourceful as to transmute its consequences to good.

I came to see that God does likewise with human
sin.   He makes even the wrath of men to praise Him,
not because He crushes it with power, but because He
overcomes it with love.   That is the meaning of the
divine atonement in Jesus Christ.   I saw why Martin
Luther so prized John 3:16, the verse which he said
contains the gospel in miniature: "God so loved the
world, that he gave his only begotten Son, that whoso-
ever believeth on him should not perish, but have
eternal life."   I was helped, too, by the writings of
two men who were not of Lutheran but of Calvinistic
heritage.   President Charles Cuthbert Hall's little book
on *The Gospel of the Divine Sacrifice* came into my
hands, as it happened, within a day or two after I had
received my father's message, and it gave me an illuminating statement of principle: "The atonement not

the cause of God's love, but God's love the cause of the atonement." I was profoundly stirred by Professor A. B. Bruce's definition of the Kingdom of God: "The reign of divine love exercised by God in His grace over human hearts believing in His love and constrained thereby to yield Him grateful affection and devoted service."

In one of the essays of *The Will to Believe*, William James pictures the relation of man to God in a striking figure. Man may be like a novice at chess playing against an expert. The novice is eager and confident; he may by chance make some good moves; he will surely make poor ones. The expert does not know what moves the novice will make, but he does not need to know. He understands how to meet every possible move, and the issue of the game is certain. The expert will win.

This is an exceedingly suggestive analogy. But it is in one respect misleading. In the chess game one player must lose. If the expert wins, the novice loses; if the novice wins, the expert loses. It is not so in the game of life. God is not our opponent; He is no enemy to be outplayed or outwitted. Life is a game where both players win or both lose. If we win, God wins; if we lose, He suffers defeat. We must play with Him, not against Him.

James's analogy would be closer to the truth if it were stated in terms of the pupil-teacher relation, or the relation of son to father. The teacher does not know what mistakes his pupil will make, but he knows how to meet and correct them. The father does not know what ambitions his son will conceive, what good sense or what folly will possess him; but, if he be as wise as fathers ought to be, he will meet whatever happens in such ways as to further the son's development into free, right-minded, and responsible manhood. Here is not opposition, but community of interest. If the pupil wins, the teacher wins; if the pupil fails, the teacher loses. If the son wins, the father wins; if the son is defeated in the game of life, the father is defeated, too. So it is with God, if God is what Jesus revealed Him to be—our Father.

At Gettysburg College I was most stimulated by the work in logic, by a rigorous course in Noah Porter's *Elements of Intellectual Science*, and by four years' study of Greek under Professor Oscar G. Klinger. After three years of training in Greek in the secondary school, I was prepared to enjoy Greek literature, and found in Klinger a most interesting teacher. Best of all, he introduced me to Greek philosophy. We did not get into it very deeply, but his lectures and my reading of a text-book in the history of Greek philosophy gave me an elementary knowledge of its main currents; we translated several of Plato's dialogues, and browsed about in Burnet's *Early Greek Philosophers*. An incidental result was that I became absorbingly interested in the writings of Walter Pater, especially his *Plato and Platonism*, *Marius the Epicurean*, and the *Essay on Style*.

The only course in biology that I took in college was one on human physiology; but I was brought into contact with the theory of evolution by the work in geology. Again aided and abetted by Professor Klinger, I did a good deal of reading on this subject in senior year, being especially concerned with its implications for ethics and theism. Among the first books, outside of text-books, that I bought for my personal library were some that I read then—Spencer's *First Principles*, Huxley's *Evolution and Ethics*, John Fiske's *Destiny of Man, Idea of God*, and *Through Nature to God*.

I spent most of the summer vacation following graduation from college in writing out my reaction to these volumes, under the modest title, "Some Notes on the

Genesis of Sin." I submitted it for publication to *The Independent*, but it never appeared in print, and when, after the lapse of some months, I wrote to inquire, the editor answered that he had seen no such manuscript. So perished my first serious literary effort. I knew by that time, however, that it was no loss to the world, for I had been doing more reading and had found more light in Henry Drummond's *The Ascent of Man*, George Harris's *Moral Evolution*, and E. Griffith-Jones's *The Ascent Through Christ*. I entered the theological seminary with my ideas fairly well straightened out on that issue; I was convinced that one could accept the scientific principle of evolution and yet hold to the Christian conception of God and the Christian view of human life.

For two years I was a student in the Lutheran Theological Seminary at Gettysburg, where I was most helped by President Valentine in systematic theology and Dr. Edmund J. Wolf in New Testament and church history. We got practically nothing of the modern critical method as applied to the Old Testament; Dr. Wolf, though generally conservative in his conclusions, gave us a fair idea of the methods of historical and literary criticism as applied to the New Testament.

As for many beginners in theological study, my central problem was that of the value of the Biblical studies. It did not shape itself, however, as it does for some today, into a doubt of the value of history in general; the most radical of us in the first years of the twentieth century were too conservative to think of that. My question was rather about the meaning and method of revelation and inspiration. In what sense is the Bible the Word of God? My teachers at the Seminary afforded excellent guidance at this point, for they took the christocentric view of the Scriptures which was characteristic of Luther, disavowed mechanical theories of inspiration, and taught that the divine revelation is progressive, not because God holds back truth, but because it is relative to occasions and suited to the capacity of man the recipient.

I was greatly helped by a little book of President William DeWitt Hyde, entitled *God's Education of Man*. As a student at Yale, I read Bruce's *The Chief End of Revelation* and Ladd's massive *Doctrine of Sacred Scripture*, with the result that, when William Newton Clarke's *Sixty Years with the Bible* appeared some dozen years later, I found that it had no particular message for me—I had long since made the adjustments he described, or had never needed to make them.

The study of the Bible has always interested me, and much of my reading is in Biblical history and theology. For several years, I taught a course to seniors at Carleton on the philosophy of the Christian religion, for which we used as common reading the admirable volume by Professor A. B. Bruce entitled *Apologetics, or Christianity Defensively Stated*. It is now forty years old, and its philosophical section is out of date, but its sections dealing with Biblical history and literature seem to me to be yet worth reading.

In the second year at the Seminary my interest centered about the problems of the person and work of Jesus Christ. I read a great deal, and in more substantial books. Among those that helped me most were two that are now almost if not quite forgotten, D. W. Simon's *Reconciliation by Incarnation* and Thomas Adamson's *Studies of the Mind in Christ*, and two that were widely influential, Principal Fairbairn's *The Place of Christ in Modern Theology* and D. W. Forrest's *The Christ of History and of Experience*. It is a subject that has never been far from my thought, and to list the books that have contributed to my thinking upon it throughout the years would make this essay unduly bibliographical. I mention just a few of

the most stimulating—Harnack's *What Is Christianity,*
Forrest's *The Authority of Christ,* Mackintosh's *The
Doctrine of the Person of Jesus Christ,* Rashdall's *The
Idea of Atonement in Christian Theology;* and I cannot forbear a word of grateful acknowledgment of the
admirable recent book by Professor John Baillie on
The Place of Jesus Christ in Modern Christianity and
the trenchant study of *The Mind of Christ in Paul* by
my colleague, Professor Frank C. Porter.

For a period of several months during my first year
at the Seminary, Professor Klinger was ill, and the
authorities of the College asked me to teach some of his
classes in Greek. I lay awake most of the night before
meeting my first class. I had never taught, and these
students had been sophomores when I was a senior.
I had visions of their trying me out by some of the
ways of annoying a teacher which I knew so well. But
they treated me fairly, and I so enjoyed the experience
of teaching that I began to think that it might be my
vocation.

In the following year I gave half-time to teaching in the academy associated with the college, and
then my mind was made up. I wanted to teach, and
must go on for graduate study. Should it be in Greek?
I debated that, but finally decided for philosophy and
for Yale. My decision had been helped by counseling
with Professor Klinger, who wanted me to study with
Professor George T. Ladd, and who gave me eight
volumes of Ladd's works as a parting gift.

The decision to prepare for teaching did not involve
forsaking my ambition to become a Lutheran minister.
College teaching was a well-recognized form of ministerial service, and many members of college faculties
preached more or less regularly. I supplied Messiah
Church, Harrisburg, during the summer before I entered the Yale Graduate School; and I was licensed to
preach by the East Pennsylvania Synod. In the **sum-**

324 CONTEMPORARY AMERICAN THEOLOGY

mer of 1903, after a year at Yale, I served as missionary pastor of the newly organized church at Mount
Union, Pennsylvania; and in September, having been
called to the pastorate of the First Lutheran Church of
Bridgeport, Connecticut, I presented myself for ordination at the meeting of the Allegheny Synod. One of
my former teachers at Gettysburg objected strenuously.
He based his objection not on any lack of preparation
or any defect in doctrine, though he felt that my views
were a bit too synergistic, and he had heard me deliver
a sermon in which I used an illustration drawn from
William James's classic chapter on "Habit" which
seemed to him materialistic. He objected solely on
the ground that I ought not to be given permanent
standing as a Lutheran minister until I had completed
my course at Yale and the Synod could see how I
turned out.

Fortunately, my father was present, having come to
see me ordained. He was not then a member of the
Allegheny Synod, but he had belonged to it for nine
years, and had been its president. He was given the
privilege of the floor; and at the end of his plea for his
son there was only one vote against my ordination—
that of the professor who had raised the objection. It
chanced that he had been scheduled to deliver the ordination sermon, which he now refused to do. The officers of the Synod thereupon asked my father to take
his place; he accepted the invitation, and I had the joy
of being ordained with the laying on of his hands.

For the second of my three years as a student at Yale,
I held the pastorate of the Bridgeport Church, spending half of the week in Bridgeport and half in New
Haven. I then resigned this church in order that it
might have the service of a full-time minister.

The years at Yale were enriching. I reveled in the
resources of the University Library, and even enjoyed
writing papers for seminars. I read Aristotle's *Meta-*

physics in the Greek with Dr. Stearns, and Schopenhauer's *Die Welt als Wille und Vorstellung* in the German with Dr. Montgomery; I studied the history of philosophy under Professor Duncan, and ethics under Professor Sneath; and I had courses and seminars in psychology, epistemology, metaphysics, Kant's *Critiques,* and the philosophy of religion with Professor Ladd. I was appointed assistant in the Psychological Laboratory, then under the direction of Professor Charles H. Judd; and my work with him in experimental psychology afforded a training in the principles and methods of the natural sciences which I much needed, and for which I have never ceased to be grateful.

In his *Pragmatism* William James remarked that the theistic philosophers like Ladd and Bowne must feel themselves rather tightly squeezed between the absolute idealists on the one side and the radical empiricists on the other. If Ladd ever felt so constricted, he gave no evidence of it. His teaching was not querulous, apologetic, or merely defensive. In football parlance, he chose to carry the ball himself, rather than to use his energies in stopping his opponents. A truer figure would be to say that he steadily advanced, like a well-equipped army through territory lending itself to slow but inevitable conquest, through the areas of psychological investigation and philosophical reflection which he had set himself to traverse in the comprehensive series of books which began with his *Elements of Physiological Psychology* in 1889 and concluded with the two-volume *Philosophy of Religion* in 1905. Undergraduates could not understand him, and scoffed at his definition of psychology as the science of "states of consciousness *as such*"; but we graduate students found him a stimulating teacher and gained profound respect for his prodigious learning.

During the period of my work under his direction,

Professor Ladd was engaged upon the writing of his *Philosophy of Religion*. We usually found him so occupied, when any of us would knock upon the door of his office in Lawrence Hall. He sat as he wrote in an ample cane-seated rocking-chair, one arm of which was enlarged to make a fairly good substitute for a desk. His detractors used to comment blithely that his books read as though they were composed in a rocking-chair —a remark which we who were his friends would indignantly reject as slanderous and as evidence merely of their inability to understand him.

I had two courses with Ladd in the philosophy of religion, and was a member of two seminars which he conducted in connection with these courses. One year he devoted to a general treatment of the subject, starting out with the data of what we would now call the history of religion and the study of comparative religion; the second year dealt with the philosophy of the Christian religion. I read Jastrow, Menzies, Tiele, Max Müller, Tyler, D'Alviella, Jevons, Reville, J. G. Frazer, Hatch's *Influence of Greek Ideas and Usages upon the Christian Church*, and A. D. White's *History of the Warfare of Science with Theology*—to name at random authors and titles of descriptive and historical works which come immediately to my memory; and on the philosophical side John and Edward Caird, A. C. Fraser, Flint, Bowne, Pfleiderer, Sabatier, Guyau's *Irreligion of the Future*, Balfour's *Defence of Philosophic Doubt* and *Foundations of Belief*, Orr's *Christian View of God and the World*, and Martineau's *Study of Religion*. I profited greatly by the study incident to the writing of major papers for the seminars, especially one on the problem of evil and another on the meaning of revelation and inspiration.

The best work that I did with Ladd was in the study of Immanuel Kant. In a comparatively small seminar group, we devoted one year to the *Critique of Pure*

Reason, and the next year to the *Critique of Practical Reason* and the *Critique of Judgment.* I became so interested in Kant that I chose to write my dissertation upon some aspect of his philosophy; and I was directed by Professor Ladd to the fact that the full significance had not yet been explored of Benno Erdmann's discovery that the antinomy of reason rather than the issue between rationalism and empiricism was the real clue to the development of Kant's thought, and the motive which led him to the principle of Criticism.

I sent to Germany for a copy of Erdmann's *Reflexionen Kants zur Kritik der reinen Vernunft* and other necessary materials, and went to work, with the result that, after the usual despair and travail of soul, I finally completed a dissertation entitled *An Historical and Critical Study of Kant's Antinomy of Pure Reason.* It was one of the dissertations of that year which received a subvention from the University to help defray the cost of publication; but publication was not then required, and I felt that I wanted to work it over again before putting it into print. Then I began to teach— it is a not uncommon story—and got so occupied with my work that the revision was never completed. If anyone wishes to consult my doctoral dissertation— which no one has ever wished to do, so far as I know— he must ask to see the typewritten copy in the Yale Library.

I have never regretted devoting so much time to the study of Kant. I often suspect, when I read some glib reference to him, that the writer has not read the *Critiques* for himself and is merely turning over the common stock-in-trade of the text-books. Kant's philosophy is not negative, but positive, in intent. Faith was for him no last resort, no after-thought; the *Critique of Pure Reason* was meant to be followed by the *Critique of Practical Reason.* Grant, as we must, that one hundred and fifty years of science, discovery, and invention have expanded the empirical content of knowledge far beyond anything that Kant could dream, and that even mathematics is no longer as rigidly *a priori* as it was for him; it yet remains true that no reasoning that is based upon facts only can reach incontrovertible conclusions upon the one side or the other of the great issues concerning the ultimate character of reality; it remains true that philosophy must take account of man's moral nature, of human obligation, ideals, and values; it remains true that, with respect to God, freedom, and immortality, our minds are not coerced but that reasonably valid convictions are inevitably based in part upon the choice of attitude, conscious or unconscious, toward moral obligation which Kant calls faith. My colleague, Professor Macintosh, is far from a Kantian—and I personally believe that his realism is a truer account of knowledge than Kant's phenomenalism—yet the "moral optimism" which Macintosh so consistently upholds is akin to Kant's principle of faith.

The study of Kant's antinomies led me to certain articles in the *Revue de Metaphysique et de Morale,* and these in turn to Henri Poincaré's *La Science et L'Hypothèse.* Discussions on almost daily walks with John W. Withers, now Dean of the School of Education of New York University, who was writing a dissertation on the philosophical implications of the non-Euclidean geometries, helped me to get the point of Poincaré's discussion and to see how the work of Lobachevski and Riemann was undermining the rigid certainty of the mechanistic science of the nineteenth century. Though we did not know it at the time, we were looking from afar at the early stages of the movement which was destined to issue in the new physics and Einstein's theory of relativity.

I was not interested in mathematical physics, however, but in religion. And convictions which had begun to shape themselves in my mind as a result of the studies which I have described were sharply clarified when I read William James's *The Will to Believe.* The first five of these essays—particularly the first, which gives the title to the volume, and the fifth, on "The Dilemma of Determinism"—impressed me greatly. The title is easily parodied, and much fun has been made of the wistful *wish* to believe or of the stout-hearted, determined man who clenches his fists, gets red in the face, grits his teeth, and mutters, "I *will* believe." But criticism based upon such misconceptions of James's essay is as cheap as it is easy, and does not affect the central truth of his discussion of the logic of faith. James was about as different from Kant as another philosopher could be. He was a radical empiricist, to whom Kant's rationalistic habits of thought and architectonic ways were anathema, and for whom the categorical imperative was simply a moral demand; yet the two men are not far apart in the place they give to faith.

There were things to be said on the other side, of course. I think I gave due consideration to them. While I worked on Kant I was also reading Guyau and especially Schopenhauer, whose pessimism is the antithesis of Kant's faith. James's essay sent me to Huxley, who coined the term "agnosticism" so that he too could have a name, and whose spirit of open-minded sincerity in the search for truth commanded my unqualified admiration; and to W. K. Clifford, whose "Ethics of Belief" is a clear, over-confident statement of positivism. Clifford's article was first published in the *Contemporary Review* for January, 1877; and I found in the number of that magazine for the following June a reply bearing the same title, by Professor Henry Wace, which is so pointed and convincing that it ought to be reprinted and made generally accessible. Wace's discussion of the conditions of faith remarkably anticipates some of the conditions propounded in James's essay. "The object in moral matters," he says,

"is to act, not only to act rightly, but to act promptly
. . . while the object in matters of science is to know,
and to know accurately, and for that purpose to reserve
a decision for as long a time as may be necessary." Clifford's "universal duty of questioning" would make the
practical business of living impossible, for society can
only exist upon a basis of mutual truth and faith. "Life
was not made for men of science, but for men of action;
and no man of action is good for anything if he cannot
sometimes form a belief on insufficient evidence, and
take a leap in the dark."

The general problem of the relations of knowledge
and faith and the concomitant problems of the mutual
relations of science, morality, and religion, have been
so central in my thinking, and so foremost in the intellectual life of the twentieth century, that I am in
danger here again of lapsing into bibliography. I mention merely a few recent books that I have read with
profit: D. M. Baillie's *Faith in God and Its Christian
Consummation*, B. H. Streeter's *Reality* and *Adventure*,
the essays edited by Joseph Needham under the title
Science, Religion and Reality, and William Adams
Brown's *Pathways to Certainty*. I have been stimulated by the writings of A. N. Whitehead and by those
of Henry N. Wieman; and I owe more to William
Ernest Hocking than to any other of my contemporaries.

From about 1907 to 1910, in company with the
general run of mankind, I had an attack of pragmatism.
I read James, Peirce, Schiller, and Dewey assiduously,
and expounded the movement before various groups
of folk who were curious about it, just as groups have
since been curious about Coué's practice of auto-suggestion, Watson's behaviorism, or Freud's psycho-
analysis. But I never quite succumbed to pragmatism,
and in due time recovered, the principal remedies being
my robust philosophical constitution, the writings of

Josiah Royce, and the pointed little book by James B. Pratt entitled *What Is Pragmatism?*

John Dewey has survived the passing of the vogue of pragmatism, and is now our most widely known philosopher. I have been most helped by his *Democracy and Education* and by the *Ethics* which he wrote in collaboration with Professor Tufts, which I used as a text-book with eight successive senior classes at Carleton. The "instrumentalism" in accordance with which he proposes that philosophy be reconstructed leaves me cold. Within my experience, notable extensions of the principles of scientific method to new fields have been made; and each such achievement is cause for rejoicing. We need all of the knowledge we can get; and we should hold our religious beliefs as well as our scientific hypotheses subject to revision in the light of further experience. But Dewey abolishes the "dualism" between science and morality and achieves the triumph of "instrumentalism" only by an undue simplification of the problems involved in a theory of values and by arbitrarily ushering metaphysics and religion out of court. In his autobiographical account of his transition "From Absolutism to Experimentalism," he associates his discarding of religious faith with personal experiences, and gives as reason for his failure to discuss the problems of religion a fundamental conviction that the religious tendencies of men will always adapt themselves to any required intellectual change.

Whenever, on the last page or two of one of his books, Dewey hesitatingly refers to religion, he describes it as a sense of the possibilities of existence and devotion to the cause of these possibilities. One of his most sympathetic interpreters, Professor Wieman, has thus phrased it: "Religion consists in giving supreme devotion to the highest possibilities of value which the existing world can yield without knowing specifically what these possibilities are." Rather abstract and vague, yet a robust, adventurous, youthful sort of religion. We need its spirit.

I venture to think that such a religion involves more than human self-confidence, however; more than the belief that the future holds possibilities of value as yet unimagined. It involves a certain confidence in the structure of the universe itself, a certain metaphysical faith—a faith that this is the kind of universe in which values are bred, which yields to honest effort, a universe in which values can be gained and kept, advances made and held. Just as science is possible only because, beneath all changes, it holds fast to the principle that nature is consistent and understandable, religion affirms that, beneath all mutations of human life and fluctuations of opinion, the universe is dependable. Meaning and value are there to be discovered; they are not merely self-confident, man-made projections of human desire.

From 1905 to 1916 I was professor of philosophy in Carleton College, and for five years of this period Dean of the college. I found Carleton an institution of about three hundred students, based upon the best New England tradition, and I shared in the early stages of the remarkable development which it has experienced under the administration of Donald J. Cowling, who became its president in 1909. I taught psychology, using Angell's text-book and Seashore's manual of experiments, until the growth of the work led to the employment of a second teacher, to whom I surrendered this course. I started a department of education, which in due time was also handed over to someone else. I helped to train and place about four hundred graduates of Carleton as high school teachers; and in 1913 I was president of the Minnesota Educational Association.

My main interest, however, was the teaching of philosophy; and, to my joy, nearly every student who did not drop by the wayside in freshman or sophomore year, elected one or more courses in my department. The history of philosophy was my chief course, as I have always felt that this constitutes the best introduction to philosophy. Most students elected it, and throughout the year they read Rogers's *Student's History of Philosophy*, some of the more important sources such as Descartes's *Meditations* and Berkeley's *Principles* in the convenient Open Court editions, William DeWitt Hyde's *From Epicurus to Christ* (republished as *Five Great Philosophies of Life*), Royce's *Spirit of Modern Philosophy*, James's *Pragmatism* and *Will to Believe*. In ethics, as I have said, I used Dewey and Tufts and with this Royce's *Philosophy of Loyalty*, a really great little book which ought to be read more than it now is. In logic we studied Hibben; and in the philosophy of religion the students read the interesting combination of James's *Varieties of Religious Experience* and Royce's *Religious Aspect of Philosophy*. Text-books and readings changed from time to time, of course; but the list I have given is of the books which lasted longest, and may serve to characterize the occupation of my mind in eleven happy years of teaching philosophy at Carleton.

In 1909 I was asked by the Lutheran Board of Publication to write for them a text-book for the training of Sunday school teachers. The work took all of the time I could spare from my classes for two years, and in 1911 the book was published with the title *The Pupil and the Teacher*. It chanced to be one of the first text-books of a new type, and began at once to sell widely, then later was incorporated into the first syndicated series of teacher-training text-books issued in accordance with principles agreed upon by the Sunday School Council of Evangelical Denominations and the International Sunday School Association, which were soon to unite as the International Council of Religious Education.

The reading of this book by my former teacher, Professor Sneath, led to my call in 1916 to become Horace Bushnell Professor of Christian Nurture in the Yale Divinity School.   In 1924 this chair was assigned to my newly appointed colleague, Robert Seneca Smith, and I was made Sterling Professor of Religious Education.   In 1928 I was elected Dean of the Divinity School, succeeding Dean Charles R. Brown.

The years have brought increased responsibilities and multiplied contacts, and have opened to me many opportunities for cooperative and interdenominational service.   I have been since 1914 a member of the International Sunday School Lesson Committee, and have served on many committees of the International Council of Religious Education, of whose Educational Commission I am now chairman.   Since 1917 I have been a director of the Congregational Education Society and the Congregational Publishing Society, and have been for some years chairman of the Administrative Committee of the two societies.   I became in 1924 chairman of the Commission on Christian Education of the Federal Council of the Churches of Christ in America, and in 1928 was made chairman of the Administrative Committee of the Federal Council.

Since 1928 I have been chairman of the Executive Committee of the World's Sunday School Association. An unforgetable and enriching experience was my sharing in the meeting of the International Missionary Council at Jerusalem for the two weeks prior to Easter, 1928.   In 1929 I was elected chairman of the American Standard Bible Committee, a committee of fifteen scholars to which are given the custody and control of the text of the American Standard Edition of the Revised Bible.   This Committee is undertaking a thorough revision of the American Standard Version, which it will not release for publication before 1941, and I count my participation in this important work one of my major tasks for the next ten years.

I have been honored by four theological seminaries with appointment to endowed lectureships, and I have fulfilled the duties of these appointments, except for my obligation, in one case, to publish the lectures. I have written several books, but what I hope will be my *magnum opus*, based on the lectures just mentioned, is unfinished, and I shall not find time to complete it until I can take a sabbatical furlough. My primary interest, which is also my greatest enjoyment, remains what it always has been—the work of teaching. And I feel a certain justifiable pride in the students who have here come under my instruction—more than eight hundred ministers scattered through all the major Protestant denominations, and sixty recipients of the higher graduate degrees, most of whom are professors of religious education in colleges and seminaries, while others hold high administrative posts with the International Council or related organizations.

I kept my connection with the General Synod of the Lutheran Church until 1916, though there was no English Lutheran church for me to join in Northfield, Minnesota, where Carleton College is located. I came to feel that it was wrong to remain without a local church membership, and my wife and I joined the Congregational church with which the college was associated. When we went to New Haven, I had gotten so occupied with various aspects of the work of the Congregational churches that it seemed wisest to retain that relationship, and I transferred my ministerial standing to the New Haven West Association of Congregational Churches and Ministers. This transfer involved no change in my theological views. I am glad that the freedom of the Congregational fellowship can embrace a Lutheran in theology.

Not that I care for party names. My years of teaching men who come from twenty to twenty-five denominations have made me tolerant of their differences of creed and polity, and sensible of the common faith that undergirds them all. Our agreements are far more important than our differences. To be a Christian is the great thing and the hard thing.

Yet I have used a party name in the title of this autobiographical confession—"The Religious Education of a Protestant." That means not simply that I reject the dogma of papal infallibility, the doctrine of transubstantiation, and the system of sacramental penance. It means positively that I conceive and hold my Christian faith in the spirit of the Protestant Reformation. I sought to describe that spirit in an address before the students of the Yale Divinity School at the formal opening of the last academic year. Let me conclude this personal confession by setting down here some of the things I then said.

Protestantism is democracy in religion. That does not mean that God is elected by popular vote, or His Kingdom liable to fickle revolution. It does not mean that all men are equally qualified to understand and declare His will. It does mean that Protestantism recognizes the right of every man to stand on his own feet before God, to obey his own conscience and to determine his own beliefs, in the light of what he deems to be the will of God. It affirms the right of individual judgment and the universal priesthood of believers. It believes that God is accessible to every soul that seeks Him, without the intermediation of ecclesiastical officialdom. It conceives the Church as the congregation of believers; and assumes that, when men gather in groups to worship God or organize themselves for His service, the laws of social psychology operate in these as in all other human relationships.

Protestantism is concerned with our common life. It conceives religion not in terms of monastic cells, celibate vows, and withdrawal from the affairs of this world with a view to the accumulation of merit in the next; but in terms of the fresh air, the wholesome affections, the common duties, and the homely responsibilities of this present world. Salvation, for the Protestant, is living in the power of the grace of God. Such salvation is possible here and now; one need not die to gain it. It lifts one out of meanness and pettiness, out of bondage by lust and fettering by habit, to the levels of high affection and generous deed. For Luther such salvation came as a joyous vision of the fatherly love of God; for Calvin it was submission to His kingly decrees; but for both men the old distinction between the sacred and the secular began to vanish. The will of God may be done on earth as in heaven. All life is sacred; every good calling is a divine vocation. All that humanism stands for, in positive affirmation and achievement, is normal to Protestantism.

Protestantism trusts the human mind. It believes in the competence of man to apprehend God, to respond to Him with faith, and to gain new insights and increase of power by the experimental method of basing activity upon such knowledge as we have and such faith as we dare venture. Grant, as we must, that the being of God lies beyond the power of our finite minds fully to grasp, comprehend, and formulate; grant, too, that these minds of ours are too commonly blinded by sin, biased by complexes, prejudiced by the traditions of yesterday, and cramped by the social pressures of today —yet these minds are the only minds we have. If we cannot trust them, we can trust nothing. Protestantism is realistic in its view of the human mind, and awake to its failures and follies; yet it refuses to fall into skepticism or agnosticism. It insists that such minds can cope with problems of value as well as with matters of fact; that they can seek and find God as well as probe the laws of nature. Man's fallibility does not shut him out from saving faith in the infallible God or from growth in knowledge of God and of His will.

Protestantism believes in the divine initiative. Its God is not dead, but living; not absent, but here; not in passive hiding, waiting to be discovered, but active, disclosing Himself in every impulse toward goodness, beauty, and truth. Granting that all human analogies are but symbols of the exhaustless being of God, Protestantism yet affirms that the least inadequate symbols, the forms of thought and speech that most nearly approximate what we know and may believe about God, are drawn from the relations that ideally hold between parent and child. God is no mere king, or judge, or exacting creditor; He is a Father, loving, gracious, merciful, and infinitely patient.

Protestantism finds its most definite assurance of the divine fatherhood in the life and teaching, the death and resurrection, of Him who most completely fulfilled his sonship to God—Jesus Christ. It is not merely as an ethical teacher, or even as example of what human life may be, that Jesus Christ is the central figure in human history. It is because He is more than an historical figure. It is because He affords us a glimpse of ultimate Reality, because we see in Him the character and disposition of God dwelling among men, because God was in Christ reconciling the world unto Himself. That vision of God in Christ is the gospel of Protestantism; its evidence is the power that it has exerted throughout the centuries, and that it now has, to awaken conscience, to inspire love and trust, and to save men from folly and wrong. When we affirm belief in the living, eternal Christ, we declare our conviction that the character and disposition of God thus glimpsed is consistently true and forever dependable.

Protestantism is more than an organization. It is a spirit; a way of thinking and living. To realize this

gospel in my own life and to equip young men to be
its effective ministers is my vocation.

PRINCIPAL PUBLICATIONS

Books:

> *The Pupil and The Teacher.* Philadelphia, Lutheran Pub-
> lication Society, 1911 and 1916.
>
> Editor, *Horace Bushnell's Christian Nurture.* New York,
> Chas. Scribners' Sons, 1916.
>
> *Training the Devotional Life* (with H. H. Tweedy). New
> York, Geo. H. Doran Co., 1919.
>
> *Talks to Sunday School Teachers.* New York, Geo. H.
> Doran Co., 1920.
>
> *Training Children in the Christian Family.* Boston and
> Chicago, The Pilgrim Press, 1921.
>
> *American Idealism* (Vol. X in *The Pageant of America*
> series). New Haven, Yale University Press, 1928.
>
> *Religious Education* (with J. H. Oldham, Vol. II of *The
> Report of the Jerusalem Meeting of the International
> Missionary Council*). New York, published by the
> Council, 1928.

Other Publications:

> "The Educational Service of the Christian Churches in the
> Twentieth Century" in *Education for Christian Service.*
> (A Volume in Commemoration of the One Hundredth
> Anniversary of The Divinity School of Yale University).
> New Haven, Yale University Press, 1922.
>
> Chapters I and II of *The Teaching Work of the Church.*
> New York, Association Press, 1923.
>
> "The Report on American Education for the Universal
> Christian Conference on Life and Work" at Stockholm,
> 1925.
>
> Chapter on "Education" in *Christianity and Social Adven-
> turing,* edited by Jerome Davis. New York, The Cen-
> tury Co., 1927.
>
> "Religious and Secular Education," published by the Ameri-
> can Tract Society, 1927.

"What Is a Christian College?"   An address delivered on
the inauguration of Edmund Soper as President of Ohio
Wesleyan University, 1929.

Articles and Lectureships:

"Repentance" (Article Twelve of the Augsburg Confes-
sion).   The Holman Lecture on the Augsburg Confes-
sion, Gettysburg Theological Seminary, 1921.
"The Biblical Argument for Graded Lessons" in *The
Church School,* 4:52-54 (November, 1922).
"What Makes Education Religious," in *Religious Education,*
18:90-92 (April, 1923).
"The Christian Ideal of Family Life as Expounded in
Horace Bushnell's 'Christian Nurture,'" in *Religious
Education,* 19:47-57 (February, 1924).
"The Principles of Christian Education." The Sprunt Lec-
tures, Union Theological Seminary, Richmond, Virginia,
1925.   The Avera Lecture, Duke University, 1926.
"The Psychology of Religion." The Duncan Lecture, The
Presbyterian Theological Seminary, Louisville, Kentucky,
1926.
"What Is Religious Education?" in *International Journal
of Religious Education,* 2:24 (June, 1926).
"The Place of Religion in the Education of Children," in
International Journal of Religious Education, 3:14 (Octo-
ber, 1926).
"The Relation of the Current Movements in Psychology
to the Psychology of Religion." The Norton Lectures,
The Southern Baptist Theological Seminary, Louisville,
1928.
"The Relation of Church and State in Elementary Educa-
tion," in *International Journal of Religious Education,*
5:12-14 (November, 1928).
"What Is It to Be a Christian?"   *Yale Divinity News,*
November, 1928.
"Where Is Authority?"   *Yale Divinity News,* November,
1929.
"The New Paganism and the Coming Revival."   *Yale
Divinity News,* November, 1930.
"Can Protestantism Endure?"   *Yale Divinity News,* Janu-
ary, 1932.

THE RECOVERY OF THE RELIGIOUS SENTIMENT

By WILLIAM KELLEY WRIGHT

(b. April 18, 1877, Canton, Illinois)

Professor of Philosophy in Dartmouth College

Hanover, New Hampshire

THE RECOVERY OF THE RELIGIOUS SENTIMENT

By WILLIAM KELLEY WRIGHT

THOSE who have now reached middle life have observed a marked decline in religious interests and activities. Fewer persons attend church services and engage in private devotions at home. The fundamental drive toward such practices is the religious sentiment. In the past, the churches affirmed doctrines that have ceased to be convincing to thoughtful people today. Acceptance of these doctrines was supposed to be indispensable to induce a person to engage in religious worship or to enable him to acquire a religious sentiment. These doctrines were, and still frequently are, emphasized in sermons, prayers, and hymns. Persons not accepting them, but supposing them to be essential to religion, gradually abandon public and private worship. Hence the present indifference to religion.

There are reasons for affirming that the minimum of belief necessary logically to justify religious worship is much less than has been supposed. It is to be hoped, as a result of wide interest now shown in the scientific and philosophical study of religion, that it will presently become clear, both precisely what this minimum is, and also that it is probably true. Once this occurs, the churches will learn to emphasize this minimum in their services and to eliminate intellectually dubious superfluities. A general revival of interest in the churches will ensue, and will be accompanied by a recovery of the religious sentiment by individuals. It will be the purpose of this paper to elaborate this thesis,

343

and to disclose what personal experiences and philosophical reasoning have led me to it.

Half a century ago, in those small towns in the
Middle West where New England traditions of a still
earlier period persisted, it was customary for the whole
family to attend the Sunday school, the Sunday morning and evening church services and the wid-week
prayer meeting. My father and my mother belonged
to different churches (Congregational and Presbyterian)
and I went alternately with the one and with the other.
As I grew up, I could see no great difference in the
worship or in the doctrines preached, and I could not
understand why, in one small community, there should
be two struggling churches so nearly alike. I felt entirely at home in each, completely in sympathy with
the ministers and with the people.

In our home (as doubtless in most others) family
prayers were offered every morning and evening. In
these I participated. The Bible was reverently accepted
as the Word of God. My mother used to read a chapter every day in her private devotions, and when I had
learned to read I followed her example. In this manner I read the entire Bible through three times during
childhood and early adolescence. God we loved and
trusted. Our religion was one of love rather than fear;
although, to be sure, my father often used to pray that
in the future life we might be a completely reunited
family.

My father was reputed to be unusually gifted in
prayer. His prayers at home and in the church prayer
meeting were earnest and sincere, eloquent but free
from anything at all bordering on the hysterical or the
mystical. They expressed his wisdom and good judgment, and his appreciation of spiritual values. From
observation of my father I learned that the essence of
religion is prayer, and that prayers for spiritual values
are efficacious. This lesson, strengthened in later years

by reading Auguste Sabatier, has led me to believe that the problems of the philosophy of religion largely center about the nature of prayer as a psychological process, the values which it is able to conserve, and the truth of the beliefs which the practice of prayer assumes.

When I was twelve, my maternal grandmother suggested that I "make a profession of faith" and join the church in company with some older boys and girls who had decided to do so, as the result of a series of "protracted meetings." I gladly assented, perhaps with a little pride that I was regarded as competent to take such a step two or three years younger than was customary. As I recall the incident now, I have no doubt of the genuineness of this religious experience from a psychological standpoint. It was a genuine religious awakening, not a pseudo-conversion.

As I now review my memories of childhood, I believe that I was brought up in the right way, religiously, for those times. It was normal for children to observe the religious worship of their elders, and to participate in it as well as they could. Although they understood but little when small, they formed habits through imitation and suggestion. Among many the religious sentiment became a deep-seated although largely subconscious constituent of their personalities, which later matured and came to self-consciousness during early adolescence through a process of gradual awakening or, in some temperaments, of conversion. Under present conditions, which allow little opportunity for a religious sentiment to incubate in childhood, no very profound religious awakening during adolescence can ordinarily be expected. There cannot be an awakening if there is nothing to awaken.

My intellectual beliefs gradually changed from fundamentalism in childhood and youth to liberal philosophical theism a decade later, without emotional disturbance. Although disposed to worry about most affairs, I have never lost a minute's sleep over religious difficulties. The importance of creeds had never been impressed upon me as a child. In my teens I was introduced to conceptions of evolution and higher criticism, guardedly at Lake Forest Academy, and frankly and unreservedly at Amherst College by scholars who were deeply religious, like Tyler and Genung. Thus my difficulties from a religious standpoint had been anticipated and solved before I had even become aware of them. As an illustration, I was introduced to the writings of John Fiske before I read Darwin, Spencer and Huxley. While I greatly admired the latter three from my first acquaintance with them, it seemed to me that Fiske had solved whatever religious difficulties their conceptions of evolution might suggest. By the time that Fiske ceased to be my supreme authority for a religious interpretation of evolution, Darwin, Spencer and Huxley had already been placed in a subordinate position in comparison with more recent authorities.

The latter two years of my college course were taken at the University of Chicago. There, partly at the University religious services, and partly at places of worship in the city which I visited, I heard many Protestant, Catholic and Jewish divines, as well as Dr. Salter at the Society for Ethical Culture. The chief impression that these preachers made upon me was how much they had in common. All wished their listeners to have about the same ideals in life, and to seek to attain them in what seemed to me essentially the same way, except for unimportant differences in theological verbiage. While a child, I had seen no serious differences between the churches of my father and my mother. Now, I could see no difference of real consequence between the various congregations in Chicago. I agreed with Pope that one may equally well address God as "Jehovah, Jove and Lord," and that

For modes of faith let graceless zealots fight;
His can't be wrong whose life is in the right.

With the superficiality of an undergraduate, I failed
to observe that each religious sect appreciates and con-
serves values with a different emphasis, and that each
has its own peculiar merits and faults. Nevertheless,
I still believe that the more important values are conserved in some measure by all of the great historic religions. Features peculiar to any sect, or even to any
religion, are likely to be of subordinate importance. Of
all religions, Christianity, interpreted liberally, is best
suited to the needs of the ordinary American who is not
a Jew. It emphasizes what is of most moral worth,
and conflicts least with scientific knowledge. The
finality of the Christian religion is not something that
can be proved *a priori*. Christianity will continue to
prevail, if, in the future even more than in the past, its
supporters modify it continually, keeping it ever
adapted to human needs in environments of constantly
changing moral demands and scientific knowledge.

After having completed my graduate work, and
taught philosophy for three years, I went to the University of Wisconsin in 1909, where one of my courses
was in the philosophy of religion. At this state university, my students were of all religious persuasions—
most, to be sure, Protestants, but there were numerous
Catholics and Jews. So I explained to my classes that
it would be improper to favor any particular confession in a course in which all were represented. Topics
must be chosen that would raise no issues between the
various Christian denominations, or between Christianity and Judaism. This enabled me to avoid discussion of invidious controversial subjects like the Virgin
Birth, the resurrection, and miracles in general, and to
concentrate on topics of major philosophical importance.

Kant had taught me that the main problems of religion with which a philosopher should concern himself are God, freedom and immortality; but I thought that the metaphysical consideration of such questions ought to be prefaced by a psychological study of religious experience, both from the point of view of the history of religions and from that of the study of individual cases.   James's *Varieties of Religious Experience*, Ames's *Psychology of Religious Experience*, Starbuck's *Psychology of Religion*, Irving King's *Development of Religion*, Coe's *Spiritual Life*, Cutten's *Psychological Phenomena of Christianity*, and the studies by Hall, Leuba and Pratt then available, were among the books that interested me most from the psychological side. While I respected Tylor, Höffding, Frazer and Wundt as brilliant interpreters of the preceding generation, they seemed to have little to say upon the topics that most interested me that had not been improved upon by more recent investigators.   This is also the reason why I have not cited them more frequently in my published writings.   On the metaphysical side, I began with Kant and Auguste Sabatier, and became considerably influenced by Hobhouse's *Development and Purpose,* when it appeared, as well as by the works of Bergson, when my attention was called to them through reading James's *Pluralistic Universe* shortly after its publication.

The class in the philosophy of religion kept asking for a precise definition of religion.   I could find none that seemed to me satisfactory.   Most definitions were idealistic and normative, not descriptive and factual. They stated what their authors conceived that religion ought to be—something edifying of course, but not at all true of most religions during most of their history as practiced by most of their adherents.   Often authors put into their definitions what was actually true of the particular sects in which they had happened to be brought up, but not true of religions generally. I could find no definition that seemed to have been formulated by a writer who kept in mind distinctions between facts and ideals, or between differentiæ, properties and accidents.

A working definition of religion should, I thought, be free from such logical inadequacies. From it ought naturally to develop the relationships between religion, magic, animism, morals, art and science. It ought to form a basis for comparing the historic religions in some fruitful way. The definition had best be descriptive of the subjective attitude of worshipers, and not the evaluation of twentieth century philosophers and theologians. The definition once agreed upon, sociological interpretations of the function of religion in human activities and metaphysical doctrines regarding the independent reality of the objects of religious faith could be considered in logical order. Conclusions on these latter points would not be begged in advance, since the initial definition would merely be one of subjective attitudes, and would have been reached inductively.

After three years' discussion with succeeding classes, the definition finally arrived at was expounded and defended in a paper read to a joint meeting of the Western Philosophical and Psychological Associations as well as to friends at Indiana University where I was then teaching for a short time. Profiting by the criticisms received, the paper in revised form under the title "A Psychological Definition of Religion" was published in the *American Journal of Theology* in July, 1912. The same definition was employed in my *Student's Philosophy of Religion* ten years later. It is as follows: "Religion is the endeavor to secure the conservation of socially recognized values, through specific actions that are believed to evoke some agency different from the ordinary ego of the individual, or from other merely human beings, and that imply a feeling of dependence upon this agency." I have always been painfully aware of the ponderousness of this definition. I can understand why authors, in order to advance a definition that can be easily quoted and remembered, especially if it contains some striking phrase, have become oblivious to the claims of strict accuracy.

This definition insists, with Leuba, that religion always implies the invocation of a higher power. It also calls attention, with Ames and King, to the function which the religious act endeavors to accomplish, and to the social status of religion in the community. I have always found the definition of religion pedagogically useful. When a class comes to understand, as they quickly do, the significance of each term in the definition, they have made a good beginning toward a comprehension of the fundamental character of religion from a psychological standpoint. And this has been done, as they realize, without prejudgment on the moral value or metaphysical truth of religious beliefs—questions to be considered later in the course and on which they expect to differ somewhat with one another and with their instructor.

I found it possible to simplify this definition a few years ago in the discussion of a specific problem, the relation between morality and religion. A religion is "the attempt of a group to secure the conservation and enhancement of some of its socially approved values, through the invocation of a superhuman agency that is not purely mechanical, but in some sense is spiritual." [1]

I am still disposed to defend these definitions. A definition of religion is justifiable, provided it logically circumscribes a coherent group of phenomena which can conveniently be studied together scientifically and interpreted philosophically. This, I think, has been

---

[1] *Essays in Philosophy* (ed. by Smith and Wright), p. 70.

true of these definitions up to the present time. Will it continue to be true of them in the future?

The rise of humanism raises the issue whether a society which offers a service in which there is no prayer, no sacrifice, no invocation of a non-human agency, should be called religious rather than purely ethical. Furthermore, there is the striking fact that the communistic movement in Russia has many of the features that in the past have been characteristic of religions. Is it a religious movement? If, without invocation of the supernatural, humanism and communism are found to present most of the phenomena of the historic religions, it will become convenient to include them within the conception of religion, and my definitions will have to be abandoned. If, on the contrary, the absence of worship shall prove to be attended by more differences than resemblances to the historic religions, then these movements will not be classified as religious, and my definitions will remain defensible, for a while longer.

At Cornell University, where I was an instructor from 1913 to 1916, one of my courses was devoted to the evolution of religions and another to the philosophy of religion. There colleagues and students—perhaps as a result of a tradition established by Andrew D. White—attached more importance to the study of religion from a speculative standpoint than had been the case at Wisconsin. I developed two sets of lectures which I later rewrote and published in 1922 as *A Student's Philosophy of Religion.*[2]

Part I of this book corresponds to my lectures in the evolution of religions at Cornell, and is built around the definition of religion to which reference has been

---

[2] Besides the authorities already mentioned, I had now become influenced by Rashdall, Marett, Durkheim, Lévy-Bruhl, Royce, Bosanquet and Pringle-Pattison in different ways. A pupil of the pupils of Dewey, my views may owe more to him than I realize. Professors Tufts· and Creighton have influenced me greatly.

made. Each religion discussed shows a different way in which the attempt to secure the conservation of values has been made. With the exception of Brahmanism and Buddhism, chosen to afford a contrast for pedagogical reasons, the chapters are intended to give a notion of the evolution of primitive religion, followed by the evolution of religion in the Occident. This is to enable the student to understand the religious situation in his own time and country today. Mohammedanism, Confucianism, Zoroastrianism and other important Oriental religions were omitted as irrelevant to this purpose.

The second part of *A Student's Philosophy of Religion* deals with the religious sentiment. Other features of this have been treated in two papers, "Instinct and Sentiment in Religion" and "Certain Aspects of the Religious Sentiment." The term "sentiment" is an old one in psychology, going back at least to Adam Smith, and is a more satisfactory designation for a normal organization of impulses and emotions about a cognitive object than "complex," which is currently used most often with reference to morbid states.

A sentiment is not a mere emotion; it is an enduring organization of impulses and emotions about some object of attention and interest. A man's ruling sentiments are the firmest, most enduring and most influential constituents in his character. This conception of the sentiment I owe, with only very slight modifications, to William McDougall (*Social Psychology*, 1908), whose version is in turn a simplified but substantially improved modification, as I think, of the interpretation developed by Alexander F. Shand (now best stated in his *Foundations of Character*). I have endeavored to show that the religious attitude is a sentiment and not an instinct or an ordinary habit or emotion, how this sentiment develops, what are its specific constituents, and under what conditions it becomes the virtue of reverence. I believe that my conception is functional rather than structural, although, of course, any enduring disposition must have a structural basis.

Acceptance of my conception of the religious sentiment does not necessarily commit anyone to McDougall's doctrine of instincts.[3] I, indeed accept the latter, and think that his interpretation of instincts in his *Social Psychology*, subsequently revised and improved upon in his *Outline of Psychology*, and *The Energies of Men* (London, 1932) is most valuable. But since there has been so much controversy about instincts, I have pointed out in my *General Introduction to Ethics* that all that the conception of the sentiment necessarily implies is that a group of deep-seated impulses have been organized about some object. These primary impulses, instead of being regarded as instincts, may, if one prefers to follow Watson (under whom I studied as a graduate student and whose behaviorism I have always liked in some ways) be viewed as "conditioned reflexes" acquired during infancy and early childhood.

At any rate, among persons who acquire a religious sentiment, the impulses and emotions in later childhood become integrated into a system directed toward God and perhaps toward some subordinate objects (in the case of Christians, Christ; and for Catholics, the Blessed Virgin Mary and other saints). This sentiment varies in strength among individuals. Among the deeply religious it is the ruling sentiment in their characters. Among many it is moderately strong, but does not dominate their lives in every way. Some people (perhaps the majority of those who grow up in a period of religious depression like the present) do not acquire the

---

[3] Conferences with McDougall at Oxford in 1912 made clear to me that the really important conception in his psychology for the student of religion and ethics is not his doctrine of instincts, but his doctrine of sentiments, and it has always seemed to me regrettable that the importance of the latter has not been generally appreciated, controversy having centered chiefly about the instincts.

sentiment at all; which does not necessarily prevent them from being persons of the highest moral character, a notable instance being John Stuart Mill. The religious sentiment may be a virtue, or indeed the synthesis of all the virtues in a truly good man. On the other hand, it may be a terrible vice, as in a bigot, a fanatic, or a superstitious man. In its distorted forms it may, I suppose, either be a cause or an effect of insanity.

No religious experience or sentiment can serve as a certification of the truth of the beliefs attached to it, nor as a moral justification of the values which it affirms. The amount of truth contained in religious beliefs is a question that usually must be referred to metaphysics. The existence of God and personal immortality, for instance, in the present state of human knowledge are metaphysical questions. If, indeed, a religious belief asserts the truth of some historic event, this is a question for an historian; but if the alleged historic event is a miracle, the historian cannot dispense with philosophy in deciding whether miracles are possible or probable. In all cases the truth of religious beliefs cannot be determined without the aid of investigators in fields other than religion itself. Nor can moral questions be decided upon religious grounds alone. A comparative study of values, with a view to determine their relative importance in life together with the conditions and the manner of their pursuit by human beings, comes either under ethics, esthetics, or value philosophy in general, depending upon the problem under consideration. Religion, therefore, must be evaluated by philosophy, both as to its truth and as to its worth.

On the side of worth, the function of religion can be stated quite simply. Religion is a means, an instrument, for the gaining of ends, the ends themselves being the values of life, chiefly ethical and esthetic. Religion certainly *ought* to enjoin what is moral and to forbid what is immoral. What should be our attitude on any of the moral questions of the day—war, prohibition, divorce, birth control, capitalism, and the rest? We cannot decide what today is good and right upon the basis of what Scriptures and church fathers have said in bygone ages. We cannot go to religion to find out what is right and wrong. For this we must go to ethics or to the social sciences. But when we have learned from these what is right we may have recourse to religion for reinforcement of our spiritual strength. The follower of Jesus and the servant of Moses may feel added consecration to their tasks from the thought that if they could listen to Jesus and Moses speaking today, they would hear them enjoining as duties the recommendations of the social investigators of our own time. Religion is a means for the conservation of values rather than for the ascertainment of values; its function is not to provide light so much as to produce warmth and fervor, consecration and devotion.

In consequence of holding this position on the relation between religion and morality, my views have sometimes been criticized as "too pragmatic," "too instrumental," or "too ethical." Possibly in my work in the philosophy of religion I may have inclined too much at times toward pragmatism and instrumentalism, although I think that I have always been a realist in my view of the nature of truth. But is it possible for anyone to be "too ethical" in his view of religion?

Now as to the truth of religion. In the manner in which I subscribe to it, religion chiefly affirms four articles of belief. These constitute my *Credo* at present. If one is to seek the conservation of socially recognized values through God, if one is to develop and retain a religious sentiment in which one's primary impulses are integrated in the service of God, one must believe that God is objective, that in some realistic sense God actually exists. Accordingly the *first* article in my religious platform is, *I believe in God*. Furthermore, if one is to engage in religious activity, one must believe that man may commune with God, and that God comes to his assistance through what theologians might call grace. Accordingly my *second* article is, *I believe in prayer*. *Thirdly, I believe in the freedom of the will, in the sense of moral responsibility*. None of the determinist or indeterminist theories appears to me wholly satisfactory, but the fact of moral responsibility seems as sure as anything outside of mathematics and formal logic, more certain than anything in physics, or than my other three articles of faith. *Fourthly, I believe in a future life, which in some sense is personal*.

It will be convenient to discuss these four articles of belief in a different order. Let us consider the third article first.

The moral responsibility of a sane adult under ordinary circumstances appears so obvious that it is hard to see how anyone has ever doubted it. I wonder if anyone ever has been able to do so consistently in an argument. Let us note what it would really mean to deny all moral responsibility and to assume mechanistic determinism. If in all of our actions we were mechanically determined, that is, determined in the same manner as a stone when it rolls down hill, no one would ever be praiseworthy or blameworthy for anything that he ever did. No person could ever reasonably commend or condemn himself or anyone else. The saints, apostles, prophets and martyrs would merit no praise or veneration. Liars, thieves, adulterers and murderers would deserve no censure. No action could be either morally right or wrong. You and I could never intelligently feel responsible for any thought, word or deed; it would never be true that we have ever done what we ought not to have done, or left undone what we ought to have done; nor could we ever rationally rejoice because we have kept in check some evil inclination, overcome some defect of temper, acted prudently in some crisis, or responded generously to an opportunity to be of service to others.

It shows a proper scientific spirit for psychologists to try to explain human behavior causally and for sociologists to endeavor to state social processes in terms of law. One can sympathize with the attempts of criminologists to prevent mentally sick persons from being sent to prisons rather than to places where they can be treated and in many cases cured. But, when anyone goes so far as to deny that there is such a thing as moral responsibility, he is asserting a crude metaphysic which is as contradictory to the most obvious facts of everyday experience as it is incompatible with every respectable system of philosophy.

Since, then, there is moral responsibility, and we can seek good and avoid evil if we choose, can feel sin and after repentance can again gain peace with ourselves and with the world, does it follow that we can look to God for assistance in our moral difficulties? This leads us to the second article of my religious platform. That prayer as a matter of fact actually is efficacious is the testimony of religious experience in the literature of nearly all religions. Very primitive religions in which prayer has not yet emerged as a specific act, and Hinayana Buddhism, in which meditation serves as a substitute, are almost the only exceptions. The efficacy of prayers of praise, communion, and petition for spiritual benefits to the individual worshiper or group of worshipers and those with whom they are in contact, is well established on psychological grounds. Prayer of this description calls for no interference with the accepted laws of nature. It assumes no questionable hypothesis such as telepathy. The great bulk of hymns and prayers in the ordinary Christian or Jewish manual of worship come under this head. Prayers for rain and dry weather and the like are few.

The fact of the efficacy of prayer (within the scope mentioned) is insufficient to establish the existence of God, the first article of my faith. So far as psychology alone is concerned, the efficacy of prayer might be wholly a matter of auto-suggestion. In fact, to explain prayer in terms of subconscious psychical and neural processes seems the proper attitude for a psychologist to take. God is not a suitable hypothesis for any science to assume. He no more belongs in the psychology of religion than in astronomy, physics, geology, biology, economics or historiography. Yet no scientific explanation makes the presence of God impossible, whether in prayer and other forms of religious experience, in the motions of the stars, the hardening of the earth's crust, the emergence of life and its development in various genera and species, or in the course of human events from primitive times to the twentieth century. The presence of God in religious experience can never receive either confirmation or refutation by appeal to any science taken by itself.[4]

The situation is different, however, when a synthesis of scientific points of view is attempted by philosophy. When I say, by philosophy, I do not mean exclusively by men who hold academic chairs in departments of philosophy. Substantial contributions to contemporary philosophy are being made by men of science who naturally are best acquainted with the work done in their own fields. Anyone, for instance, whose examination of data in one or more sciences raises the question whether the facts indicate a world of pure mechanism or a world of partial purposiveness, is in some degree a philosopher. Such a question is not a scientific question; it is a philosophical question.

---

[4] The proper relationship between philosophy and one particular science in the interpretation of religion I have endeavored to state in a paper entitled "The Relation of the Philosophy of Religion to the Psychology of Religion."

All attempts to establish the existence of God by some kind of deductive or *a priori* argument or dialectical device have proved futile. The ontological, cosmological and teleological arguments of the eighteenth and preceding centuries were demolished by Hume and Kant. Kant's own arguments based on moral obligation, the idealistic arguments advanced by his German successors in the early nineteenth century, and epistemological arguments of every kind imply assumptions that the man of the twentieth century is usually unwilling to concede. If there were any facile way to prove the existence of God it would have been found long ago, and no intelligent person would doubt it today. If, on the other hand, there were any facile way to disprove the existence of God, it would have been advanced long ago, and there would be as few intelligent people today who believe in Him as there are who believe in astrology or fortune-telling or witches.

The best that can be done at present, as it seems to me, is to review the data made available by the sciences, reinterpret them from a philosophical point of view, and inquire whether they indicate or suggest the presence of God. Such a review, made from the standpoint of emergent evolution, shows a teleological trend in terrestrial evolution, first of the earth's crust, next of organic life, and finally of human society. This teleological trend, to be sure, has not always been successful. It seems to have operated under tremendous difficulties. The course that it has followed is more suggestive of the *élan vital* of Bergson than the God of Thomas Aquinas or John Calvin. If this trend had been more successful—if it had not merely been a trend—there could not have been so much evil and frustration in the world. John Stuart Mill's posthumous *Three Essays on Religion* are conclusive on this point. None the less, that there has been a teleological trend seems unmistakable. And where there are evidences of teleology it seems most reasonable to assume a Purposer.[5] By a Purposer is meant a Being who consciously forms plans for the future which He endeavors to carry out; in this sense, as well as in others, God is personal.

It cannot be insisted upon too much that, in the present stage of human knowledge, no philosophical presentation of the case for the existence of God can appear at all plausible unless it seriously takes into account the cosmological picture presented by the natural sciences. Only through a favorable interpretation of this picture can be found one absolutely indispensable link in the argument for God.[6] Once, however, it is seen that considerations of terrestrial evolution (geological, biological, social) favor the hypothesis of a purposing God, it is possible to make deductions from this hypothesis that can be verified, and so greatly strengthen the probability of the hypothesis itself. For on the hypothesis that God has been endeavoring to carry out purposes in terrestrial evolution, we should expect Him to have revealed Himself to mankind as rapidly as they have been capable of receiving such revelations. The gradual evolution of the idea of God as disclosed by comparative religion, and the testimony of countless individuals to their personal experience of the presence of God are empirical evidence for the truth of this hypothesis. The contradictions between the reports of

---

[5] This form of argument was advanced in Part III of *A Student's Philosophy of Religion,* and has since been developed in subsequent papers, most recently in one entitled "God and Emergent Evolution."

[6] It is amazing to find theologians still imagining that they can dispense with this link in the argument, and establish the existence of God by the testimony of religious experience, the sense of duty, the consciousness of values, and the like. Such considerations as these furnish corroborative evidence, once the cosmological picture can be shown to be favorable. But if it were unfavorable, God might be a product of human imagination, duty the subjective emotion resulting from social pressure, and values the hypostatization of human desires.

worshipers in the different religions and stages of culture is no greater than might be expected. What is remarkable is the large amount of agreement in such
experiences, as is brought out, for instance, by William
James in his *Varieties of Religious Experience,* and by
Evelyn Underhill in her *Mysticism.*

The chief difficulty which leads thinking people today to reject the conception of God is, I think, that to
them, as a result of childhood training, it necessarily
implies a Being that is literally infinite and absolute
in His wisdom, power and goodness. The facts of
everyday experience and science seem to them to belie
the existence of such an infinite Being. So they conclude that there cannot be any God at all. It cannot
be sufficiently emphasized that the choice is not limited
to the two possible alternatives of an infinite God and
no God at all. There remains the possibility of a
finite God.

This hypothesis of a finite God is the one to which
the empirical evidence points. There is a teleological
pattern in evolution, but it is an imperfect pattern.
That suggests the presence of a God whose purposes
are being carried out slowly, with frequent interrup-
tions, and who probably has been forced at times to
modify His plans. Biological evolution, for instance,
does not seem by any means to have been aimless, and
yet it has not been the completely logical unfolding of
a perfect plan. Think on the one hand of the remarkable progress from the amœba to man; that surely is
a purposive plan. Think, on the other hand, of the
many blind alleys which have blocked countless forms
of plant and animal life, and think of the many faults
and imperfections in the body and mind of man.

Only the hypothesis of a finite God meets all of the
evidence—a God like that of John Stuart Mill and
William James, a God in time, with an environment
like ourselves, and who, like us but of course on an

immeasurably vaster scale, is gradually gaining control of His environment and becoming increasingly able to carry out His purposes. Though finite, this God is a greater God than the one of whom orthodox theology dreamed when it supposed that His chief achievement had been to create our little heaven and earth some six thousand years ago. This finite God has already been operative in the evolution of the earth for billions of years. If we accept the judgment of Sir James Jeans that human life on the earth will probably endure for another trillion (million million) years,[7] God will be carrying out plans upon the earth at least that much longer.

Such a God, who has brought us into existence, and led us on to the civilization that we have already achieved, is a God whom we can surely love and trust. Only very little children fancy their fathers to be infinite; but, as they grow older, reasonable children continue to love and trust fathers who deserve it. God is incalculably wiser, stronger and more loving than any human parent. He can and will help us in more ways than any human being. He needs our cooperation, just as human parents need the help of their children. If children help their parents, the latter can better provide for them, and assist them to grow up into lives of greater usefulness for themselves, for their parents and for society. So it is with us in relation to our Heavenly Father. Whatever His designs upon the earth may be—and no believer in a finite God professes to be able to guess as much about them as the orthodox theologians used to declare about the eternal decrees and purposes of their infinite God—these purposes include the realization of higher values by human beings. So if we constantly endeavor, with His help, to realize such

---

[7] Sir James Jeans, *The Universe Around Us,* pp. 324-331.

values, we shall be cooperating with Him and helping Him to make the earth a success.[8]

I find it hard to understand the man who exclaims that for him a finite God would be no God at all! I feel like retorting that only a finite God, one who is anthropomorphic enough to have plans which He is seeking to carry out in the future, and to love human beings whom He expects to assist Him in carrying out these plans which include their good—only such a God seems to me a God at all! A despot who wilfully created a universe in which he foresaw that the bulk of mankind would suffer everlasting torment, such as traditional theology has sometimes conceived—such a God to me would simply be unbelievable! Nor would the neo-Hegelian Absolute, as interpreted by Bradley and Bosanquet, for instance, which lacks personality and transcends moral distinctions, be more satisfactory.[9] If the only choice were between an infinite God (responsible for creating a world full of evil or else oblivious to evil), on the one hand, and no God at all on the other, atheism would be the preferable alternative.

However, this is beside the point. The nature of God is not a question that can be decided in accordance with our feelings or even with our moral convictions. The question is, What kind of God probably exists, in the light of the evidence? It is a question of facts, not of values. And the facts display a preponderance of evidence in favor of an existent but imperfectly realized teleology, and therefore, of a finite God.

From a practical standpoint it might be observed that the plain man who has not had the opportunity to study

---

[8] Tennant's *Philosophical Theology*, Brightman's *Problem of God* and Tsanoff's *Nature of Evil* are to be commended on problems regarding the nature of God in connection with the problem of evil.

[9] *Cf.* D. C. Macintosh, *The Reasonableness of Christianity* and the *Pilgrimage of Faith* on the unsatisfactoriness of Neo-Hegelianism from a religious standpoint.

science and philosophy cannot be led to believe in God by arguments based upon twentieth century cosmology. The only way to convince him of God is by appeals to his own religious experience and to the observation of others, couched in language that he can understand. There is a measure of truth in this, of course. But it is not the whole truth. If the plain man were convinced that the great majority of thoughtful people who have investigated the subject were agreed upon the existence of the kind of God which he is exhorted by the churches to accept, he would readily give his assent. Appeals to religious experience would then be effective in his case as today in fact they often are not.

The masses of people today accept the Copernican astronomy and believe that the earth is round and moves about the sun. They laugh at anyone who thinks the contrary, although not one person in a thousand understands the evidence. It is safe to predict that in another generation belief in the animal ancestry of man will be as nearly universal. In the long run the plain man is certain to find out the general drift of expert opinion on any subject, and to accept it, even without understanding the reasons. The masses of people today are skeptical and indifferent about religion to a large extent, because such is the case with the intelligentsia. Once the scientists and philosophers are agreed on any propositions regarding the existence and nature of God, it will only be a comparatively short time before these propositions become generally accepted by the public.

Now for my fourth article of faith. Consciousness as we know it is the function of a bodily organism. If we infer that God exists because evolution reveals a teleological tendency, and the latter implies a purposing Mind, the conclusion follows that the earth, or the whole universe, or a considerable part of one or of the other, somehow functions as an organism whose Mind is God. In our present lives, our bodily organisms are parts of the organism of God, and probably rather important parts, analogous to ganglion cells or something of the kind. Our cognitive, affective and conative processes contribute in some way to the conscious experience of God. Yet, on this hypothesis, God has His own Personality, His own Consciousness, that includes and transcends ours, and yet in a sense is His own, is individual. And we have our own personalities and consciousnesses that are individual and distinct; we also have free wills, so that we can cooperate with Him or refuse to do so, as we choose.

When a man dies, his bodily organism ceases to exist. Yet, as I believe, his conscious personality endures as part of the divine Mind. I have sometimes tried to use an analogy to make the hypothesis clearer. The separate cells in our brains may be attended by consciousnesses of a lower order than our own. Our minds, then, are functions of these cells and consciousnesses in their integrated activity. The cells in our brains continually wear out and are replaced. Yet our conscious life continues, and today each of us remembers what he said and did ten years ago, although his conscious life then was a function of brain cells now no longer in existence. The conscious life of the brain cells that perished ten years ago is living today. So our conscious life may persist in the Mind of God after our bodily organisms have passed away. The analogy is imperfect, of course, and may suggest pantheistic conclusions which I do not mean to imply. So I do not wish to press it further.

Is it indeed possible to escape a pantheism in which after death the personality of the individual human being would simply be submerged in the consciousness of God? I cannot claim to have solved the problem. I am looking for more light. At least I can argue in this way. God, if He loves us as much as I think that He does, and if He is as powerful as I suppose Him to be, must have found some way to conserve as distinct personalities the conscious beings whom He loves. God would be a lonely Being if He alone endured. His life is richer and fuller if He lives in a society with lesser personalities who also endure. Men, after the experience of one bodily life in which they have learned to appreciate and conserve values, ought to be competent to make further contributions to the progress of the universe. Their extinction would be a loss to God. From the standpoint of the conservation and enhancement of values, the world is a more successful enterprise if human minds are immortal than it could be if they were not.

If any men have future lives, it seems to me that this must be true of all. There is so much that is bad in the very best of men—as recent biographers are making us painfully aware—and so much that is attractive in even the worst of men that it is hard to advance any moral argument for conditional immortality. And there certainly are no obvious differences between the bodily organisms and minds of men to suggest that some minds survive bodily death while others do not. Parents love bad children not less than good ones; they seek to save those who are lost. Can God do less?

However, there must be some distinction between the immediate future of a good man and of a bad man. Perhaps the analogy of a graded school may be suggestive. Rarely if ever is a pupil's work so bad that he needs to be placed in a lower grade than the one he has failed to pass at the end of the year. But very retarded pupils need to repeat a grade. Less backward pupils sometimes have to pass into an "opportunity room" where they can advance as rapidly as they are capable, and if industrious enough they may ultimately catch up with their classes again. Unusually good pupils are given special privileges as honor students, or are permitted to skip a grade. So perhaps in a future life. No man probably lives so badly that for his own good he needs further demotion than to have to lead another life over again under conditions generally similar to those we know on earth. Even on a retributory theory of punishment, that surely would be as much of a hell as the worst of sinners deserves! And the retributory theory is generally discredited in ethics today. It is hard to see how any but a reformatory theory of punishment can have a place in God's relation to sinners in a future life. Promotions to higher states of existence are based on capacities for service of a higher order proved by accomplishments already made.

The final goal for all, though reached more rapidly by some than by others, will be the life of the Blessed, a life of constant, intimate and loving communion with other colleagues who have also reached this goal, and with God. God, and those who now comprise the company of the Blessed, aware of all the good that has been achieved, are working unceasingly for the straightening out of the now imperfect teleological pattern. They know all truth that has yet been discovered, enjoy all beauty that has yet been achieved, share all goodness that has yet been realized, and press forward united in love and understanding to further achievements that will benefit all conscious beings.

Today we are passing through a period of religious depression not less severe than the concomitant moral and economic depression. Few are interested in religion to the extent that our fathers were. Such conditions have sometimes previously occurred after great wars. For instance, the generation following the American Revolution was indifferent to religion. On the other hand, the generation following the American Civil War, while it underwent severe moral and economic depression, retained its religious fervor comparatively unimpaired. In both cases economic exhaustion, moral disillusionment and apathy followed the enthusiastic idealism and self-sacrifice of a war.

Why was there religious depression in the one case and not in the other? The answer may be that in the post-revolutionary period a theology was still preached in the churches that repelled the scientific, philosophical and humanistic spirit of the times, and alienated the intelligentsia, whom the masses followed out of the churches. Later on, after a more liberal movement in theology had considerably mollified the teaching of even the orthodox churches, the intellectuals again were brought into a more sympathetic attitude toward religion, the masses again followed, and a recovery of religious interest was effected, and continued until after the close of the century. No general discontent with religion was felt by intellectuals at the time of the Civil War, so that the religious interest after the war remained undisturbed by the economic and moral slump of the Reconstruction period.

How soon religious recovery will come in the twentieth century it is impossible to predict. One encouraging indication is that there is a very great deal of discussion now going on regarding the relations between science, philosophy and religion. A multitude of books and journal articles on such subjects appear every month, mostly of a popular but often of a scholarly character. So much attention is being given to the subject that if it is possible to arrive at conclusions that can claim a decided preponderance of probability in their favor, the fact will become widely known, and the conclusions generally accepted.

If my thinking on religion has been anything like right, these conclusions will affirm that probably a finite God exists, in a realistic sense, who loves us and who comes to our assistance when we pray to Him. He will help us to make the most of our lives, for which we are morally responsible, both before and after death. If such conclusions ever become generally accepted, religion will possess sufficient sanctions, so that people will be interested in its practice.   If, further, the churches prove to be wise enough to put the emphasis in discourse and ritual upon the few conclusions which philosophers and scientists shall have come to accept, and to eliminate, or at least decidedly subordinate, everything in church services that now antagonizes intellectuals, the intelligentsia will resume church attendance. The masses will presently follow their example. Family worship will again be observed in homes. The religious sentiment will take root and develop among children as it used to do fifty years ago. After a generation of children with vital religious sentiments has reached manhood, there will be a new age of faith. Recovery of the religious sentiment will be complete.

If, indeed, recovery is the right word to use. For it will be a period of progress, not one of reaction, as I believe. The majority of mankind, for instance, will never again bow down to the infinite and absolute God of previous ages. Doctrines and forms of worship in both Christian and Jewish communions will be so unlike those of the nineteenth, and still more, of every preceding century, as almost to be unrecognizable. Values, as men will acknowledge and seek to realize them, will be in sharp contrast to those of the past. Yet all of this will be a recovery of the religious sentiment, if by the latter we mean the integration of human desires directed toward God as the object of adoration and service, in the endeavor to conserve those values believed to be the highest.

PRINCIPAL PUBLICATIONS

Books:

A Student's Philosophy of Religion. New York, The Macmillan Company, 1922.

General Introduction to Ethics. New York, The Macmillan Company, 1929.

Co-author:

"The Relation Between Morality and Religion," in *Essays in Philosophy,* by Seventeen Doctors of Philosophy of the University of Chicago. Edited by T. V. Smith and W. K. Wright, Chicago, Open Court Publishing Co., 1929, pp. 61-82.

"God and Emergent Evolution," in *Religious Realism.* Edited by D. C. Macintosh, New York, The Macmillan Company, 1931, pp. 431-475.

Articles:

"A Psychological Definition of Religion." *American Journal of Theology,* 1912, pp. 385-409.

"Instinct and Sentiment in Religion." *Philosophical Review,* 1916, pp. 28-44.

"The Relation of the Psychology of Religion to the Philosophy of Religion." *Philosophical Review,* 1918, pp. 134-149.

"On Certain Aspects of the Religious Sentiment." *Journal of Religion,* 1924, pp. 449-463.

"A Realistic View of Theism." *Crozer Quarterly,* 1930, pp. 5-23.

INDEX

Adamson, T., 322.
Addams, Jane, 5, 82.
Adler, F., 70.
Alexander, S., 41.
American Standard Bible Committee, 334, 335.
Ames, E. S., 1 ff., 348, 350.
Anderson, M. B., 246.
Angell, J. R., 332.
Apostolic succession, 153.
Aquinas, Thomas, 49, 282, 294, 359.
Aristotle, 43, 216, 217, 220, 324.
Arnold, Matthew, 35, 36, 211, 223.
Art and religion, v. religion.
Atonement, 108, 183, 318, 319.
Augustine, St., 54, 58, 253, 279, 281, 293.

Bach, S., 234.
Bacon, B. W., 108.
Baeck, Leo, 206.
Baillie, D. M., 330.
Baillie, J., 33 ff., 323.
Balfour, A., 326.
Baptism, infant, 279, 280.
Barthianism, 52, 53, 254.
Beethoven, 234.
Bergson, H., 38, 115-117, 348, 359.
Berkeley, G., 333.
Bible, the, xvi, xvii, 76, 137 ff., 144 ff., 165, 166, 169, 170, 173, 174, 187, 188, 197, 198, 201 ff., 210, 217, 219-223, 224 ff., 304, 321, 322, 344, 355; v. Theology, Biblical; Criticism; New Testament; Old Testament.
Boehme, J., 283.
Bosanquet, B., 38-40, 50, 351, 363.
Bowne, B. P., 325, 326.
Bradley, F. H., 37, 363.

Brandes, G., 120.
Briggs, C. A., 69, 70, 79.
Brightman, E. S., 363.
Brontës, the, 35.
Brown, C. R., 334.
Brown, F., 69.
Brown, W. A., 63 ff., 330.
Browning, R., 20, 246, 250.
Bruce, A. B., 319, 322.
Burnet, J., 320.
Burton, E. D., 166.
Bushnell, H., 105, 311, 312, 316, 334.
Butler, N. M., 70.

Caird, E., 326.
Caird, J., 326.
Calvin, J., and Calvinism, 229, 253, 337, 359; 36, 54, 76, 77, 105, 137, 138.
Campbell, A., 1, 4.
Carleton College, 311, 332, 333.
Carlyle, T., 35, 36, 106.
Catholicism, Roman, 80, 95-97, 153, 188, 263, 279, 280, 282 ff., 290 ff., 302; Greek, 95.
Channing, W. E., 105.
Chicago School of Philosophy, 4.
Christianity, nature of, 16, 27, 75 ff., 87 ff., 91, 93, 94, 110-112, 114, 124, 126, 139, 144 ff., 150-152, 154, 158 ff., 167-168, 171 ff., 179, 180, 182, 184, 206-208, 227 ff., 230 ff., 236-240, 247, 248, 267-271, 281, 304 ff.; function of, 12, 15, 81 ff., 115, 145; and the social order, 115, 129, 158 ff., 164, 169, 177 ff., 226 ff., 251 ff.; v. New Testament, two religions in; re-

371

and the social order, 81 ff., 152;
religion and institutionalism, ix,
xv, 87, 171, 208, 269, 284 ff., 293,
296, 307; religion and the sciences, ix, xix, xx, 16, 17, 50, 68
ff., 78, 81, 126, 140 ff., 165, 173,
175, 181, 259, 262, 321, 347, 358;
contemporary religious thought,
viii ff.; religious epistemology,
120 ff., 128; religion and empiricism, 262 ff.; religious realism, 118 ff., 128; religion and
poetic imagination, 148 ff., 211 ff.,
216 ff., 232 ff.; religion and con-
servatism, xvi, 148, 155, 174, 202
ff.; religion and liberalism, xvi,
53, 98, 139 ff., 148, 154, 155, 174,
202 ff., 229, 282, 347; religious
depression, 343 ff., 353 ff., 367,
368; v. Theology; Psychology of
Religion; Social Gospel; Ritschlianism; Mysticism; Christianity.
Revelation, 148 ff., 257, 258, 322.
Reville, 326.
Revivalism, 313 ff.
Riehl, A., 247.
Riemann, 328.
Ritschl, A., and Ritschlianism, 47,
51, 52, 54, 87, 89-91, 109-112, 114,
115, 179, 180, 212, 229, 247-249.
Rivers, 4.
Rogers, A. K., 333.
Roman Catholicism, v. Catholicism,
Roman.
Rousseau, J. J., 58.
Royce, J., 3, 113, 318, 331, 333, 351.
Ruskin, 35.
Russell, 209.
Russell, B., 143, 271.

Sabatier, A., 94, 326, 345, 348.
Sacraments, 158 ff., 253.
Saintsbury, G., 36.
Salter, 346.
Salvation, 152, 158 ff., 228, 253,
254, 258, 265, 337.
Schaff, P., 69, 71.

Schiller, F. C. S., 330.
Schleiermacher, F. E. D., 46, 47,
49, 51, 52, 54, 75, 87, 111, 112,
114, 229, 248.
Schopenhauer, A., 3, 209, 325, 329.
Schürer, E., 209.
Schweitzer, A., 141.
Sciences, scientific methology, ix,
xviii, xix, xx, 17, 148; v. Re-
ligion and the sciences; Theol-
ogy, empirical, and the sciences.
Scott, H., 209.
Seashore, E., 332.
Shand, A. F., 352.
Shedd, W. G. T., 69, 77.
Simon, D. W., 322.
Small, A. W., 167.
Smith, A., 352.
Smith, H. B., 77.
Smith, H. P., 202.
Smith, R., 5, 202.
Smith, R. S., 334.
Smythe, N., 3.
Sneath, E. H., 325, 334.
Social Gospel, the, 12, 66, 82 ff.,
84, 141 ff., 151 ff., 175, 176, 250,
251.
Socialism, 141, 142.
Socrates, 107.
Spencer, 320, 346.
Spencer and Gillen, 4.
Sperry, W., 21.
Spinoza, 49, 247.
Starbuck, E. D., 4, 348.
Stearns, 325.
Stein, L., 247.
Stevens, G. B., 246.
Streeter, B. H., 330.
Strong, J., 251.
Sullivan, W. L., 277 ff.
Sumner, W. G., 3, 69.

Tennant, F. R., 363.
Tennyson, A., 35.
Thackeray, 35.
Theism, 118, 127, 128, 137, 180, 184,
191, 254, 260, 261, 356, 361 ff.;
v. God; Theology.